Out of One,
Many Africas

Reconstructing the Study and
Meaning of Africa

Edited by
William G. Martin
and Michael O. West

University of Illinois Press
Urbana and Chicago

© 1999 by the Board of Trustees of the University of Illinois
Manufactured in the United States of America
1 2 3 4 5 C P 6 5 4 3 2
♾ This book is printed on acid-free paper.

Library of Congress Cataloging-in-Publication Data
Out of one, many Africas : reconstructing the study and
meaning of Africa / edited by William G. Martin and
Michael O. West.
p.   cm.
Includes bibliographical references (p.   ) and index.
ISBN 978-0-252-02471-9 (alk. paper)
ISBN 978-0-252-06780-8(pbk. : alk. paper)
1. Africa—Study and teaching (Higher)—United States.
2. Africa—Study and teaching (Higher).
3. Africa—Historiography.
4. Historiography—United States.
I. Martin, William G., 1952–   .
II. West, Michael O. (Michael Oliver).
DT19.9.U5O98   1999
960'.0071073—ddc21   98-58006
CIP

To African youth, at home and abroad,
for their inspiration,
their perseverance in the face of miseducation,
and the optimism they bring to our futures

Contents

Acknowledgments

This volume results from the confluence of unusual forces and friendships. Formally, it constitutes in part the proceedings of an annual symposium of the Center for African Studies at the University of Illinois, for it contains some of the papers presented there. This particular event, held in April 1994, constituted something of a coming-of-age bash, marking as it did the twenty-first in a series of such meetings.

This volume is also an expression of several forces pressing against Africa-related scholarship and pedagogy as they have been dominantly constructed in the United States and elsewhere in the North for the past two generations. In planning the conference and in preparing this volume, we sought to engage the issue of reconstructing the study and meaning of Africa during what we saw as the beginning of the end of the hegemonic approach to the study of Africa and African peoples everywhere. Toward this end, we attempted to bring together an irregular set of scholars, drawing from white Africanist, continental African, pan-African, and diasporan studies traditions. And although we might like to claim foreknowledge of subsequent debates on the future of area and African studies, the theme of the conference was actually determined by earlier, more immediate and consistent forces—namely, student dissatisfaction with the teaching of Africa, whether expressed in our classrooms, in demonstrations on our campuses, or in broader youth culture.

It was against this backdrop, then, that we set out to organize the symposium that led to this edited volume. Nonetheless, although the gathering together of scholars is a favorite academic pastime, conferences, unlike much of what they sometimes yield, are not cheap. In the academic enterprise, filthy lucre rules the roost: scholars might propose, but it is usually the funders who dispose. We must therefore thank the institution—the University of Illinois—

and its component units for making the conference possible. An incomplete list of institutional underwriters includes the two key sponsors of the symposium, the Afro-American Studies and Research Program and the Center for African Studies, along with International Programs and Studies; the College of Liberal Arts and Sciences; the Departments of English, History, and Sociology; and the Illinois Consortium for International Studies Programs. Individually we wish to thank Don Crummey, Eren Giray, Gladys Robinson, and Sue Swisher, all of the Center for African Studies, as well as Delores Hill, Gina Manning, Monica Shoemaker, and Eva Ridenour, of the Sociology Department, for their assistance in organizing and running the conference.

We owe a tremendous debt of gratitude to the many friends and colleagues who have supported us and this project in ways too numerous and varied to mention here. We are especially grateful to Alice Deck, a coorganizer of the symposium, and to Ibrahim Abdullah, Merle Bowen, Farida Cassimjee, Patricia Clark, Al Kagan, David Johnson, Julius Nyang'oro, Mwenda Ntarangwi, and Gloria Waite. As fellow writers will appreciate, we also benefited greatly from the incisive comments and suggestions of reviewers for the press—later revealed to be Gerald Horne and David Wiley. Our task as project organizers has been ably facilitated by Karen Hewitt and the fine staff at the University of Illinois Press.

Last, but by no means least, we gratefully and seriously acknowledge the contribution of the many students, past and present, who have sustained our efforts and renewed our strength in ways they may not even have imagined. We are confident that these young people, regardless of their cultural, ethnic, or racial background, will heartily endorse our dedication of this volume to African youth globally.

Introduction: The Rival Africas and Paradigms of Africanists and Africans at Home and Abroad

Michael O. West and William G. Martin

For students and scholars of Africa, the 1990s have proven to be a puzzling, even startling, decade. Quite unexpectedly Africa emerged as a major refrain within U.S. culture: symbols of Africa reverberated through popular music, film, video, and advertising, while op-ed pages carried heated exchanges over Africa's place in the nation's cultural heritage. Meanwhile the once buoyant centers for the study of Africa have witnessed a steady erosion in institutional support and intellectual legitimacy, both within and outside the academy—a crisis of purpose that has resulted in unease, bewilderment, and excitement. The result has been an often acrimonious debate over the future among students of Africa.

For many senior scholars, the winds of change herald the decline, if not the passing, of a noble two-generation-old effort to construct a body of knowledge about Africa and to interpret the continent for various audiences in the United States, notably the university community, policymakers, and the media. Some younger Africanists, too, view with dismay the declining value of their expected inheritance, material as well as intellectual. Other students of Africa, far from bemoaning a world turning upside down, embrace the new challenges as an opportunity to reconstruct the study, meaning, and definition of Africa and Africans. There is, however, a common thread running through these diverse responses to the crisis in African studies: all agree that a rising tide of discontent has decentered and destabilized the conceptions, institutions, and communities dedicated to the study of Africa.

At the heart of the crisis stand the hitherto sturdy pillars of African studies in the United States—the Africanist enterprise—namely, the paradigms, programs, and international networks that arose and flourished after World War II but have now fallen on increasingly hard times. Nonetheless, however hegemonic the Africanist enterprise may have become over the past two generations, the story of the study of Africa can hardly be confined to a single epistemic approach. As even leading Africanists concede, new initiatives emanating from within and outside the academy have encroached on their terrain, posing the threat that central components of African studies might be siphoned off by competing programs. Even worse for Africanists, many such initiatives are already taking institutional form, potentially paving the way for alternative locations in the study of Africa.

This volume of essays seeks to unearth and explore this tumultuous state of affairs. It stems from a conference organized by the editors at the University of Illinois, Urbana-Champaign, in 1994.[1] We were (and still are) concerned with broadening the discussion of the study of Africa beyond a hitherto dominant European and North American focus, moving out from the Africanist heartland and encompassing much broader intellectual and institutional settings, including the new agendas of competing disciplines, university administrators, and public and private funding agencies. Transcending Africanist conceptions of the study of Africa entails, in the first instance, incorporating excluded voices and agendas, such as those inspired by feminist, indigenous, and cultural studies scholarship.

Toward these ends we brought together scholars and perspectives grounded in three quite different locations or paradigms: the European–North American Africanist establishment, the continental African school, and an admittedly more amorphous group linked by transnational visions grounded variously in diasporan, pan-African, or Afrocentrist imperatives. The juxtaposition of scholarship based in such disparate locations and perspectives provides novel results, as evidenced by the Illinois conference, which featured frank, lively, and sometimes volatile engagements across competing paradigms and epistemic approaches (see Johnson 1994). Our aim here, as at the conference, is not merely to chart rival positions or to admit new outlooks and discordant voices to the pantheon of African studies (which we are eminently unqualified to do, both objectively and subjectively). The purpose of the undertaking, rather, is to advance a dialogue aimed at transforming the study of Africa—a project that we take to be crucial to ensuring the future of the field. Accordingly, the objective of this introduction is twofold: to chart, in broad outline, the contours of the present predicament and to place the volume's individual contributions in the larger context of a three-paradigms argument.

Fears of the Ghetto: Africanist Dilemmas after the Wars

Despite its dominance in the more confined context of the study of Africa, the Africanist enterprise, together with the programs it spawned, has rarely figured prominently on the national academic scene. From the formation of the field after World War II down to the present juncture, the Africanist enterprise has grown and prospered in the shadow of far broader and more powerful constituencies, academic programs, and federal educational priorities. It therefore came as a surprise when, in March 1995, the *Chronicle of Higher Education*—a weekly organ read by university deans, presidents, and chancellors, among others—devoted its prized "Point of View" page, perhaps the most prominent forum in American academia, to an essay entitled "Ghettoizing African History."

Fears of marginalization have long constituted an undercurrent among Africanists. When the architects of African studies were building programs after World War II, concerns of becoming an isolated program or "ghetto" within the academy were expressed, both privately and publicly (Herskovits 1958:11; Vansina 1994:101–3). Now, four decades later and in a very different, post–cold war climate, the ghettoization argument had made a comeback, but this time the rhetoric was more unctuous, provocative, and racialized. Standing at the head of the redux was no less a personage than Philip D. Curtin, who brought to the task impeccable credentials: a founding father of the Africanist enterprise and widely cited historian of the Atlantic slave trade, he was also a past president of both the African Studies Association (ASA) and the American Historical Association.

Significantly, distress with inadequate support for and appreciation of African studies, a perennial gripe among Africanists, was not what lent Curtin's opinion piece its allure and potency. Indeed, the two most often cited forces pressing against area and African studies—the emergence in the 1980s of alternative global studies programs and the "rising tide of cultural pluralism"—were cast as positive and complementary developments. The attraction of Curtin's claims rested, rather, on his assertion that African history and by extension African studies were becoming "ghettoized" as not only marginal but black enclaves through "the use of racial criteria in filling faculty posts." This trend, Curtin lamented, was due to a widespread practice by university administrators of acceding to "demands from African-American students that courses in African history be tailored to meet the concerns of contemporary African Americans" and that such courses "be taught by African Americans or, when not many African-American candidates are available, by Africans, with whom students want to feel a common heritage." Such practices, Curtin alleged, were leading to an exclusion of "able" white scholars, declining academic standards, and "ghettoization" of African history through "intellectual apartheid" (Curtin 1995:A44).

In a blistering response fifty black historians of Africa attacked Curtin's assertions, designating them a "cruel inversion of reality." Curtin's "racial criteria" were a reality, the historians retorted, but they had been deployed to exclude black scholars from employment, major professorships, editorial posts on leading journals and book series, and the directorships of key programs in African history and African studies (Atkins et al. 1995).[2] Indeed, as one of Curtin's own former students demonstrated during the course of the "ghettoization" debate, Ph.D. production and employment data provide little evidence to support the claim—vividly dramatized in the illustration accompanying Curtin's op-ed piece—that white Africanists were being swamped by a black peril (Spear 1995).

The exchanges quickly spread, rippling outward to the larger African studies community in the United States and overseas: the board of directors of the ASA formally dissociated itself from Curtin's essay, and an affiliated body organized a well-attended plenary session at the ASA's annual meeting where Curtin and his critics and supporters squared off. On the other side of the Atlantic, major African research institutes such as the Council for the Development of Economic and Social Research in Africa (CODESRIA) in Dakar and the Southern Africa Political Economy Trust (SAPES) in Harare circulated and reprinted the exchanges in their official organs.[3]

The Lonely Africanist

In addition to casting light on the racial hierarchy and sentiments that pervade African studies in the United States, the entire Curtin debate showed the extent to which Africanists' anxieties are indeed rooted in the realities of an uncertain future. The sources of these anxieties, however, are to be found not in an irrupting horde of Kente-clothed black scholars but rather in the abandonment of the field by powerful supporters as the academy proceeds to restructure bureaucratically and the federal government and private foundations establish new priorities. Outside the ivory tower and the halls of power, meanwhile, Africanists have shown a decided inability to relate to new constituencies interested in the study and cultures of Africa and Africans at home and abroad.

Indeed, as our chapter in this volume points out, fundamental cracks have appeared in the structures that have supported African studies over the last two generations. Most prominent is the ebbing of federal and foundation support, weakening the central pillars of the major programs and centers. This may have been a debatable proposition in the late 1980s, but by the mid-1990s the actions of the Republican Congress had shaken the Africanist establishment, for Title VI funding, USIA and USAID funding, and the Fulbright-Hays program, among others, were threatened by the budget-cutting ax. Without such support, many if not all of the overseas research, language, outreach, and faculty and student exchange programs would end.

Although most of these programs have survived federal budget cutting, the downward spiral of federal support for area and especially African studies can no longer be denied. The bold plans hatched in the 1980s for a stronger, more centralized federal commitment to area and African studies are only wistful memories in the late 1990s. The fate of the one successful initiative from this period, the National Security Education Program (NSEP), reveals all too well the forces at play. As discussed in Horace Campbell's chapter, NSEP was originally promoted as part of the post–cold war peace dividend, infusing funds from and management by the Department of Defense. Since its inception, however, NSEP has been attacked by budget cutters while conservatives have sought to reestablish the original requirement that all student-fellows work for military and intelligence agencies. As even NSEP supporters acknowledged, the latter requirement would have created an untenable program (Rubin 1996). It remains to be seen whether a slightly modified requirement, allowing student grant holders to work for any federal agency concerned with national security interests, will revive the program (see Association of Concerned African Scholars 1997).

Lending emphasis to such trends are parallel developments within private foundations, nonprofit educational institutions, and state and university administrations. The Social Science Research Council (SSRC), which has played a pivotal role in organizing support for area studies programs for almost two generations, recently jettisoned an area structure for its funding and research efforts despite vociferous protests by area studies scholars. The SSRC's actions are, moreover, driven in large part by a similar movement away from funding area studies research by the SSRC's own supporters, notably large private foundations such as Mellon, Ford, and Rockefeller (see, e.g., Williams 1994; Heilbrunn 1996). Downsizing by university administrations reveals similar trends. Lacking departmental status and competing with the core disciplines, African and other area studies units have become key targets as restructuring and new budgetary and management principles are applied. There is, in short, little sign that state or nongovernmental sources will make up for a shortfall in federal funding, as they did in the 1970s and 1980s; indeed, continuing budget cuts are likely to be imposed by university administrations.

African and other area studies programs are not, of course, the only units facing such pressures from above, as accounts from ethnic, cultural, and women's studies attest. Nor do federal, private, or university policymakers have a clear, unambiguous set of priorities suited to a post–cold war world order. By comparison to many other interdisciplinary programs, however, the African studies establishment has few defenders within the academy and even fewer relationships with those pursuing new funding priorities and agendas, whether within or outside the academy.

This fact is starkly evident in the steady erosion of U.S. interest in Africa during the post–cold war period, whether one examines military and security interests, state-corporate attention, or levels of trade and investment. The stripping away of Africa-related funding and postings in the State and Defense Departments, which began in the 1980s (see Chege 1992; Michaels 1993) and continues to the present, is only one sign of Africa's virtual absence in the discussions of central U.S. governmental and commercial bodies as they revise their agendas to meet the demands of a post–cold war world marked by new and uncertain rivalries. In ways quite unintended by its original formulators, the phrase "Africa for the Africans" now serves as a rationalization for the abandonment of the African continent by policymakers and those, including many academicians, who take their cue from them.

Shifting national political and economic priorities are, furthermore, slowly but surely working their way through the academy, undermining and recasting longstanding agendas and institutions. As we show in chapter 4, the place of African studies in the academy was cemented as part of the expansion of U.S. hegemony during the cold war, with the study of Africa becoming part and parcel of the core disciplines' developmentalist project, promoting models of state and economic development for the poor states and peoples of Africa.

Expectations of either economic or political development for Africa have now disappeared. Instead Africa has become an allegory for a chaotic and anarchic world that the United States can no longer understand, much less control (see, e.g., Kaplan 1994). Developmentalist projects, to the extent that they still resonate within the academy or the state, have been localized in the newly defined world areas of the Pacific Rim and Northeast Asia; in a world where even industrialization has been devalued, no one speaks any longer of even the most basic industrial development in Africa (with the sole exception of South Africa, which is rarely seen as part of Africa). Indeed, Africa-related policy and aid have largely been reduced to economic stabilization imposed by structural adjustment programs, supplemented by charity and relief efforts. Moreover, aid to Africa is increasingly being channeled through nongovernmental organizations (NGOs), the United Nations, or international financial agencies (the International Monetary Fund [IMF] and World Bank)—institutions that have few ties to, or need for, the African studies establishment.

The demise of Africa on the national political agenda has accordingly affected a broader group. As Africa has "fallen off the policy map," those working for institutions directly engaged with Africa-related aid, development, national security, and exchange programs have sought to create a "new constituency" for the continent. The most prominent effort is the forthcoming three-year-long National Summit on Africa, created by C. Payne Lucas of Africare in 1995 with major foundation support (reportedly $1 million in the first year alone). Whether and to what extent such efforts can revive flagging interest in Africa on the part of government policymakers and the wider public remains to be seen (we have argued this is unlikely; see West and Martin 1997, 1998; Martin 1998).

Indeed, Africanists and Africa policymakers face a common difficulty—namely, the emergence of new national policy and educational agendas that, although directed to the world beyond the borders of Europe and North America, appear to leave little room for things African. The most prominent of these is associated with the study of "globalization." As U.S. economic prominence waned in the 1970s, national policymakers focused their attention on the educational system's contribution to enhancing the United States' capacity to compete in a hostile world market. By the mid-1990s notions of "globalization" had led to new theoretical, curricular, and institutional initiatives in the professions, the core disciplines, interdisciplinary programs in information and high-technology studies, and even cultural studies.

The implications of globalization for African and area studies have been contradictory. On the one hand, globalization has redirected attention to the world beyond the borders of North America, a positive development. On the other hand, benefits have largely flowed to those programs and scholars with ties to areas of the world that pose economic problems or opportunities for the United States—and Africa clearly is not a member of this select group. In addition, globalization calls for a cross-cutting of world areas rather than the narrow, intensive focus on a particular region or continent common to area and African studies. To the limited extent that deans, provosts, and chancellors have implemented "global studies" initiatives, they have invested not in area studies units, which are now seen as "enclaves of overspecialization," but rather in global studies programs more attuned to corporate and national strategic priorities.

Concurrent developments within African studies have unwittingly operated to reinforce these trends. Most prominent is the burgeoning literature charting the West's construction or "invention" of Africa as an imagined Other, whereby the "Africa" of classical and modern writers becomes but a mirror of its creators in the West (e.g., Mudimbe 1988; Miller 1985, 1990). Based on the pioneering work of Edward Said on orientalism (1978), this line of research has the unintended effect of undermining Africanists and African studies from within, as the field becomes depicted as an insular, introverted community whose research tells us more about the West than about Africa. The comparison with the studies of orientalism is instructive, for like orientalists, Africanists cannot abandon their subject, Africa, without also abandoning their enterprise altogether.

Developments in cultural studies, pivoted as they are on a postmodern perspective, have had a similar effect for quite different reasons: by asserting the primacy of a postpositivist method and local voices, postmodernists have removed cultural and African studies ever further from the policy world of the state, educational administrators, and the "scientific" core disciplines. The result has been the field's growing separation from its core creators and funders. Even if Africanists of the postmodernist variety shift their cultural gaze from the continent to the United States, the application of their skills and perspectives will likely find little appreciation or reward: studies of tribalism and witchcraft at home, for example, are unlikely to resonate with those who control resources and set agendas in the disciplines, the academy, and the country.

Not out of African Studies: The African Cultural Renaissance

Set against the many and varied trends of the past decade is a more surprising and potentially rewarding development for those interested in the study of Africa—namely, a burgeoning demand for ethnic, racial, and Africa-related courses, curricula, and faculty. In all these categories, however, Africanists are conspicuous by their absence. The reasons are not difficult to discern: as the Curtin-inspired debate illustrates and many of our contributors show, members of the predominantly white Africanist establishment have long sought to separate sub-Saharan Africa, the object of their study and research agendas, from the African diaspora and issues of race.

One result of this sundering of African studies from the extracontinental African world is the inability of Africanists to engage with, much less inform, what might be called a fourth wave of black nationalism in the United States (see West forthcoming), marked by the burgeoning presence of black artists in literature, music, and film who often express a relation to the ancestral continent. From an academic standpoint, these trends are best reflected in cultural studies, where the output of black writers has spawned new literatures ranging across discussions of race, the meaning of the African heritage, and most notably, a resurgent black feminist thrust. For more popular and younger audiences, the world of music, in all its aural, visual, and performative expressions, has been especially important. Born from the intermingling of Caribbean and mainland North American musical traditions, by the late 1980s rap and hip-hop—as exemplified by the lyrics of groups such as Public Enemy, the Poor Righteous Teachers, X-Clan, and Arrested Development, to name just a few—became suffused with images of African redemption. As even Michael Jackson intoned: "Do you remember [the glories of the ancient Nile]?"

This is, moreover, a phenomenon that not only recalls Africa but addresses Africans worldwide, breaching continental boundaries. As any visitor to major African cities knows, contemporary African American cultural forms are quite visible and influential, especially among youth. Given Africanists' and African scholars' rigid separation of the study of continental Africa and the United States, these relations have rarely been perceived, much less examined. Thus despite inventive academic studies of rap music (e.g., Kelley 1994), we have no equivalent, for example, to Paul Gilroy's (1993) treatment of the transnational call of black British music; even more distant is the study of the cross-fertilization of African musical imagination between North America and continental Africa. What Africanists miss, however, may be discerned in popular magazines and even newspapers in both the United States and Africa (see, e.g., Chideya 1997; Mabaso 1997): a rising cultural renaissance, particularly among youth, moving back and forth across the "black Atlantic."

The world of film, dominated as it is by corporate Hollywood, has been far less open and inventive, yet even here Africa has appeared in new configurations. Well-received but independently produced films such as *Sankofa* and *Mississippi Masala* easily transgress continental boundaries of racial identity and oppression, but even the major studios have boosted their portrayal of Africa and African youth, albeit in more stereotypical ways, from the naive and patriarchal prince of Eddie Murphy in *Coming to America* through the more common depiction of rampaging Afrocentric students in *Higher Learning* to Steven Spielberg's *Amistad,* where even former U.S. presidents can be heroes amid slavery. Caught in this maelstrom, contemporary black artists and actors, following a long tradition dating back at least to the Harlem Renaissance, routinely express a yearning for African sensibilities, often in new magazines targeted at both black and nonblack audiences— hence Wesley Snipes's interview in Quincy Jones's *Vibe* magazine (Oct. 1993, p. 47), where the film star's Afrocentric musings are set against an image of his naked torso adorned with an "African" cross.

The captains of industry, commerce, and advertising have also attempted to capitalize on hip-hop culture by launching lines of clothing based on fanciful African-style patterns and colors. Although the commodification of the continent and its cultural heritage has a long history in the West, the current manipulation of Africa through a hybrid of classic pejorative stereotypes, newly romanticized images, and widely admired black personages operates through a novel amalgam. Take, for example, the 1996 commercial featuring National Basketball Association star Charles Barkley: standing inside a glorious Egyptian temple, Barkley is dressed in colonial kit as he exhorts us, in an affected upper-class English accent, to be "more civilized" by using Gillette's *colorless* "clear gel" Right Guard deodorant, which leaves no *white* powder residue.

The subordination of an enchanted Nile to the cleaner, more civilized Anglo-Saxon world is clearly a domesticated framing of the most important public debate over Africa in the United States, the battle by black activists to insert a positive African heritage into the nation's educational and cultural institutions. Writing in such publications as *Newsweek,* the *New York Times,* the *National Review,* and the *Chronicle of Higher Education,* champions of the status quo have launched a fierce counteroffensive against those demanding that the nation and its institutions of higher learning rid themselves of Eurocentrism, white domination, and curricula stipulating assimilation into a mythical Western consensus. This intellectual drama has also played itself out in more sustained forms, as in Martin Bernal's magnum opus, *Black Athena* (1987, 1991), whose attempt to demonstrate African contributions to ancient Greek culture (a thesis by no means original with Bernal, who draws on the work of various black scholars) has been disdainfully rejected by critics such as Mary Lefkowitz, author of the opprobrious response *Not out of Africa* (1996).

Significantly, Africanists have mostly watched the Afrocentrist-Eurocentrist debate from the sidelines, both on and off campus. Indeed, it seems clear that most Africanists perceive these developments as a threat to their four-decade-long mission to produce purer and more objective knowledge on sub-Saharan Africa. As even Curtin noted, however, increasing numbers of students—now predominantly black but also white, Latino/a, and Asian—are insisting on African materials that speak to Africa's historical and contemporary relationships with Europe and North America. Such demands offer significant opportunities for the expansion of African courses, curricula, and faculty. Nonetheless, committed as they are to the separation of the African diaspora and touchy about the predominantly white character of their enterprise, especially at the highest levels, Africanists have utterly failed to understand these concerns, let alone address them.

Africanist Reactions in the United States and Europe

As the various cultural and intellectual manifestations suggest, the challenges facing Africanists extend far beyond fiscal pressures. Even setting aside as improbable an engagement with insurgent black scholars and students, by the mid-1990s Africanists could no longer wish away the implications of radical transitions in national educational as well as cultural and foreign policy priorities. Some university administrators put it bluntly. A newly appointed dean sympathetic to international studies told the advisory committee of one Title VI (federally funded) African studies center, "In five years you will not exist in your present form; state, university, and federal funding will be gone."

Such statements are alarmist, but the problem of Africanist disengagement is real. As we show in chapter 4, few U.S. Africanists in the 1980s and early 1990s have attempted to assess the need to reshape the field in the light of contemporary realities. Two mid-1990s collections did address the wider issues associated with the reorganization of academic and intellectual agendas. One is a truncated collection on the future of African studies in the Winter–Spring 1995 issue of *ISSUE,* the public opinion journal of the African Studies Association, whereas the other is a report by Jane Guyer (Guyer, Virmani, and Kemp 1996), director of the Program in African Studies at Northwestern University. Neither work originated as an effort of leading Africanists or the ASA: the first resulted from an independent initiative by the editors of this volume, and the Guyer report was commissioned and its publication subsidized by the Ford Foundation.[4]

Guyer's report comprehensively documents Africanists' difficulties: the loss of support for language training and overseas field research; the growing separation of Africanists from continental African scholars, the policy-making community in Washington, NGOs, and other international agencies; the dominance of disciplinary agendas in selecting, training, and promoting graduate students and young scholars; and the uncertainties surrounding programs dependent on federal funding. Guyer nevertheless remains confident in the stability of African studies and the ability of Africanists to address institutional and intellectual shifts in the larger academic and policy worlds. The emergence of new global, diasporan, or cultural agendas is noted, but they are cast as complementary rather than competitive. If, Guyer argues, "in the new thinking about internationalization, Africa is *already* marginal," this is hardly a new phenomenon: "Africa has always been, in fact, a 'special case'" (Guyer, Virmani, and Kemp 1996:83). Solace about the future is thus rooted in a rich Africanist legacy. Guyer continues:

> Research on Africa, by African scholars as well as ourselves, is not just a geographical stake in an "area studies" world; it is a contribution to the understanding of global phenomena and common human experience that has made African cultures and societies "special cases." . . . The leadership has begun to turn over, and now includes more African-Americans, women, and younger men who are ready to recognize the need for change and embrace it. These people will carry on for many more years, because they are clearly valued in their universities which have—on the whole and surprisingly—protected African Studies from the rounds of initial cuts. (Guyer, Virmani, and Kemp 1996:84)

Such conclusions undoubtedly represent the collective wisdom of leading Africanists—as was evident in the deliberations of those attending the Ford Foundation workshop organized around the Guyer report. Similar views can be found in commentaries by Africanists in *ISSUE,* where, for example, former ASA president Edward Alpers (1995) applauds the greater diversity in paradigms and personnel and Jane Parpart (1995) charts the promise of postmodern and cultural studies. As we note in chapter 4, most of the contributions to a 1997 collection on the future of African and area studies organized by Angelique Haugerud for *Africa Today* (44, nos. 2, 3) covered similar ground, with Africanists largely defending their field in reference to the core disciplines and new global initiatives. The notable exceptions were Robert Bates's defection to the "scientific" core disciplines (1997) and Christopher Lowe's attack on global studies (1997a).

As Guyer concedes, however, these discussions—much less their conclusions—are not shared by those calling for a radical reshaping of the Africanist enterprise, as can be seen in many of the essays in this volume and in our own contributions to the *ISSUE* collection (Martin and West 1995), which formed our opening address at the Illinois conference, and to the *Africa Today* collection (West and Martin 1997; see the criticism by Lowe [1997b] and our response [West and Martin 1998]). Equally radical visions of the future are offered by those who foresee the end of traditional area and disciplinary constructions. Thus Immanuel Wallerstein—past president of the ASA, current president of the International Sociological Association, and the well-known founder of the world-systems school—asserted in his contribution to the *ISSUE* collection:

> It is by no means sure that the African Studies Association (or any other area studies associations) will still exist as we come into the twenty-first century; or if they do exist, that they will be more than dusty relics. . . . The world university structures are about to enter a period of intellectual turmoil and restructuring at least as great as that which occurred in the nineteenth century. . . . The future of African studies is scarcely something that will be decided autonomously or in isolation from the more general restructuring of knowledge production. (1995:22–23)

To explore such a vision would carry us far afield indeed. If the origins and framework of the Africanist enterprise are any guide, however, radical transformations in the study of Africa may indeed be upon us, though to highlight such potentials would require moving beyond the shores of the United States to the larger Anglo-European academic world. As Catherine Coquery-Vidrovitch's chapter on African studies in France shows, uncertainty and consternation regarding the future are hardly confined to U.S. Africanists. Central facets of her story will be familiar to North American scholars: the initial centrality of anthropology and its separation from other disciplines, the present-day marginalization of African and development studies in the academy, and the challenges presented by the collapse of conceptions based on "modern" France and "traditional" Africa.

Yet stark contrasts also exist, most notably in the relationship Coquery-Vidrovitch charts between continental African and French-based scholars. In this regard she raises the prospect of a new era, one where the recognition of globally imbricated cultures dissolves old dichotomies and where an initially much sharper, antagonistic division between continental African and French scholars gives way to more equitable intellectual encounters. In large part this openness is traced to the emergence of a new, postnationalist gen-

eration of African scholars trained in Africa and operating with the assur-
ance that comes from the existence of indigenous institutions and training.
Coquery-Vidrovitch's conclusion might startle U.S. colleagues. Unlike the
United States, where both African studies and the greater society often strike
visitors as embroiled in racism, France, she argues, has witnessed developments in the study of Africa that hold forth the possibility of accepting shared
cultural and intellectual endeavors across black/white, African/Africanist
divides.

It would be difficult to imagine such a future for British Africanists, a group
with whom U.S. scholars have always had much stronger ties. As Christopher
Fyfe's chapter notes, the emergence of African studies in Britain, as in France,
took place as colonialism gave way to ties with independent states—but in
Britain, in contrast to France, historians dominated the field far more than did
anthropologists (see also Kirk-Greene 1995). Indeed, Fyfe demonstrates a different evolution of the field after the 1960s boom. Whereas successive French
governments and particularly presidents cultivated a strong, continuing relationship with the former colonies and their dictators, in Britain decolonization led directly to an era of "British disinvolvement." The 1980s and the
Thatcher years—marked as they were by support for white settlers, disdain
for black Africa, and an onslaught on the autonomy and funding of British
universities—were nothing less than devastating. In five quick years the proportion of the British Social Science Research Council budget dedicated to
Africa fell from 2.3 to 0.8 percent, while universities on their own transferred
"resources from area studies where African history most often found its most
congenial allies back into core disciplines where Africanists tended to be
peripheralized" (McCracken 1993:242). By the end of the decade the number
of teaching Africanists had fallen by 16 percent; 40 percent of British Africanist
historians had not visited the continent since 1983, and even the flagship British
journals (e.g., the *Journal of African History* and the *Journal of Southern African Studies*) were publishing articles written far more often by North American authors than by British ones (McCracken 1993:242–43).

As British Africanists faced the 1990s, they foresaw a bleak future indeed.
A. G. Hopkins, left bereft of a single first-year Ph.D. student in African economic history at Birmingham, could conclude only that "the subject is dy-
ing because its practitioners are fading away" (1987:100). Hodder-Williams's
conclusions were equally blunt: "Policy-makers in this country are content
to see the virtual demise of the study and teaching of Africa" (1986:604), leading to the "nightmare prospect that by the year 2000 the study of Africa in
British universities would be in the hands of some elderly professors, a handful of middle-level academics thinly spread across the country, and . . . perhaps, if positive action is taken soon, some young scholars, the postgradu-
ates of the 1990s" (Hodder-Williams in Twaddle 1986:444).

Few U.S. Africanists have yet imagined such possibilities, despite all the warning signs of declining interest and investment in Africa on the part of public officials and university administrators. As the analyses by Coquery-Vidrovitch, Fyfe, Guyer, and others stress, the United States remains firmly tied to Africa by a factor missing in Europe: a large population of African descent that has kept Africa on the public agenda, even in the most difficult of times. The present era, as we argued previously, is no exception.

The great difficulty, of course, is that the African renaissance in North America's black communities is pitted against a predominantly white and male Africanist establishment. As the Curtin exchanges indicate, moreover, a vast gulf separates African American and continental African discourses and interests from those of Africanists. It is hardly surprising, therefore, that the current grassroots surge in the reconsideration of the meaning of Africa has originated at a now tertiary level, far outside the major programs associated with African studies.

Interestingly, a similar situation exists in England, where Africanists have been far more blunt and open than their North American colleagues. As Twaddle reported on a 1986 conference on the state of African studies, "changes in consciousness, sense of identity, and aspirations of what could loosely be called the 'black community in Britain' [have] over the years resulted in important innovations in teaching at school but not university level" (Twaddle 1986:442–43). John McCracken's more recent comments are even more direct, recounting "the mutual incomprehension that still exists between the predominantly British African historians on the one hand and the community of Afro-Caribbean intellectuals on the other" (1993:251). Thus, McCracken continues, "today we are faced with what at times seems the almost impossible dilemma of indicating role models capable of inspiring a wider audience on the one hand while avoiding the production of Africanist Heritage pap on the other" (1993:252).

Similar sentiments, such as barely veiled disdain for Afrocentric and pan-African perspectives, are not hard to find among U.S. Africanists—as the Curtin exchanges again illustrate. Celebrations of "diversity" in African studies notwithstanding, there is little evidence that the resurgent black interest in Africa can be engaged by Africanists. Indeed, an examination of the origins of the study of Africa *outside* the Africanist establishment indicates both a different history of the field and the foundations of alternative, non-Africanist futures for the study of Africa.

Continental and Transcontinental Traditions

Besides the Africanist perspective, two other intellectual traditions or paradigms in the study of Africa can be identified: these we will designate as "continental" and "transcontinental." The continental tradition is so called for two reasons: it was founded in Africa, and its exponents insist on studying the continent as a whole, north as well as south of the Sahara.[5] This contrasts to the Africanist school, which besides being non-African in origin historically has staked out sub-Saharan or "tropical" Africa as its intellectual turf, leaving North Africa to the orientalists or Middle Eastern area scholars.

The third intellectual approach to the study of Africa—the transcontinental one—is the oldest. It has its antecedents in nineteenth-century attempts to construct an intellectual defense of the African past, a project that was centered in the black Atlantic world and spearheaded by Africans of the diaspora. We designate this tradition "transcontinental" because its exponents approach the study of Africa cross-continentally, in contrast to the typical area studies divisions on which both the Africanist and continental schools are premised. As in the case of the continental paradigm, so too with the transcontinental one: an identifiable group of scholars with similar worldviews, publishing outlets, and informal and formal networks exists quite separately from the Africanist enterprise.

The Continental Tradition

The continental tradition is largely a reaction to the intellectual hegemony of the Africanist enterprise and the hubris and racial arrogance of Africanist scholars. Today the leading centers for the production, organization, and dissemination of continentalist scholarship are a number of research institutions that have emerged over the past quarter-century, the most noted of which are the Dakar-based Council for the Development of Economic and Social Research in Africa and the Harare-based Southern Africa Regional Institute for Policy Studies (SARIPS/SAPES). These organizations are complemented by many smaller and newer research centers, such as the Centre for Basic Research in Kampala, as well as Africa-wide professional bodies such as the African Association of Political Science (AAPS) and more insurgent groups such as the Association of African Women for Research and Development (AAWORD).

The ascendance of research institutions as centers of continental and regional networks parallels the deteriorating conditions of academic life and research at universities and university-based research centers across the continent (for the moment, at least, the exceptions to this rule are to be found mainly in southern Africa). Zenebeworke Tadesse's contribution charts this history, from the blossoming of subregional universities in the late colonial period, through the vast expansion of national universities in the wake of independence, to the increasingly bleak conditions that emerged in the 1970s. This process accelerated in the 1980s as salaries and research funds fell dramatically, university libraries stopped buying books and journals, facilities fell into disrepair, and key staff fled to much better paying posts in southern Africa and, for senior faculty, Europe and North America. State repression and disinvestment have been central to the disintegration of African universities, processes that began in the 1970s and deepened in the 1980s as IMF-mandated structural adjustment programs, with their deep cuts in educational and social expenditures, were imposed on numerous African states.

As Tadesse notes, more is known about the changing material conditions faced by African scholars than about trends in the institutionalized production of social science knowledge on the continent. As she further suggests, however, several key themes may be distinguished: the replacement of *subregional* with *national* university structures as decolonization proceeded, the early postindependence modeling of African universities on European ones (replete with institutes for development studies and even African studies), and the increasing assertion of state control over academic and university freedom and autonomy. Indeed, the establishment of research institutions outside the gates of the university has been a response to these factors, as leading scholars have sought both independence from state control and a larger regional if not continental role.

Cutting across these periods, however, is the constant theme of African scholars' and universities' relationship with their much more powerful colleagues situated in Europe and North America. As we note in chapter 4, as early as the mid-1960s Africanists in the United States were debating how to counter increasing resistance on the part of Africans to northern scholars' use of the continent as a field laboratory. Writing from the African side, Tadesse demonstrates how this development represented a blossoming of a continental intellectual tradition. Spurred by the indigenization of staff, new academic traditions, most notably in historical studies, emerged in Nigeria, Tanzania, and Senegal, among other places. Such an outpouring of scholarship produced not just the major books of the 1960s and 1970s but also a plethora of essays in new journals, often linked to regional or continental professional associations. This was, in many ways, an ironic outcome for U.S. Africanists: having defined a new "Africa" separate from the United States, they could only acquiesce as African scholars proceeded along similar lines.

The contribution by Mahmood Mamdani—formerly executive director of the Centre for Basic Research in Kampala and now director of the Centre for African Studies at the University of Cape Town—illustrates well key themes in current African scholarship: the promotion of indigenous paradigms and intellectual networks, a rejection of Africanist generalizations, and an immersion in the concrete problems and conditions of the continent. Few subjects could illustrate this better than the one Mamdani tackles: understanding the phenomena associated with the resurgence of civil society, ethnicity, and democratization. In so proceeding, he restates the critique of

Africanist scholarship he made in public exchanges in the wake of a conference on governance in Africa organized by the Carter Center at Emory University (Mamdani 1990), namely, that Africanist models not only ignore African scholarship and realities but are irrelevant to local issues of social justice
and transformation.[6] Instead of invoking Western models of the past or
present—which have shifted from abstract models of nation and state building in the footsteps of the West to conceptions that pit civil society and the
free market against corrupt African governments—Mamdani tackles the civil
society–state relation within the historical formation of the legal, social, and
political order.

As Mamdani shows, this entails more than a confrontation with the construction of a bifurcated, racial colonial order; it also includes the deracialization of the state, without a parallel deracialization of civil society, in the
postindependence period. The legacy for the present, under conditions of
structural adjustment, is charted through the fractured and fragmented rural and urban movements that mirror the state they confront. By stressing local
social and political configurations as they have been interwoven with repressive forces overseas, Mamdani illustrates trends in the work of scholars associated with the new African research institutions, an agenda that calls for more
indigenous theoretical formulations as well as intensive local research.

As an archetype of the continental school, Mamdani's contribution reveals
both this tradition's passionate vibrancy and its contradictory future. On the
one hand, the movement toward indigenous perspectives not only has been
a pioneering intellectual force but also has contributed notably to the reconstruction of "civil society," which accelerated with the waning of the cold war,
minority rule, and dictatorial and developmentalist African states. On the
other hand, it has been difficult to sustain the independence from repressive
states and Africanists that continental scholars have sought given that these
forces continue to control intellectual resources and power. As Tạdesse poses
the conundrum in chapter 6: "Are such independent research centers likely
to grow in number and forge a culture of critical inquiry and a cumulative
knowledge base? How autonomous—that is, nondonor driven—are they
likely to remain?"

As the curious phenomenon of overseas evaluations of African research
centers reveals (de Vylder and Ornäs 1991; Sawyer and Hyden 1993)—can one
imagine Africanist centers being judged by scholars flown in from Africa?—
research institutions such as CODESRIA and SAPES have been sustained
primarily by foreign donors, with Scandinavian funding (the Swedish International Development Agency [SIDA], Norwegian Agency for Development
[NORAD], Swedish Agency for Research Cooperation with Developing
Countries [SAREC], and Danish International Development Agency
[DANIDA]) providing core, open-ended support.[7] Whether and to what

extent such funding can be ensured remains an open question in view of trends in European and North American private and public funding. Official development assistance is falling rapidly from all sources, plunging 48 percent in 1996 alone (Katsouris 1997:1). Assistance from Scandinavia, and even Japan, which has often been touted as the new giant in African aid (Seddon and Sato 1997), also seems likely to decline sharply, following the U.S. pattern of new foreign policy priorities and reduced aid budgets (see, e.g., Sanger 1997). Moreover, as African commentators noted even earlier (e.g., Ake 1994; Gadir 1994), even if such funds continue to flow, to what specific institutions and agendas might they be tied?

An equally difficult dilemma is posed by the long-term production of new generations of scholars, which only universities can do. The research institutions, particularly CODESRIA, were the handiwork of African scholars who belonged to what Thandika Mkandawire (1995), past executive secretary of CODESRIA, has called the "first generation" of African academicians. This generation is composed of individuals who received their education overseas and returned home during the euphoric 1950s and 1960s to staff the new universities and train a second generation, the members of which usually went overseas for graduate education and, in Mkandawire's assessment, generally did not return home. As political and fiscal pressures mounted in the 1970s and especially in the 1980s, African academicians began to move outside the state structures that had supported the postindependence university boom but had now begun to abandon if not repress academic institutions outright. It is these scholars, working under increasingly harsh conditions, who have sought to reconstitute—in the "private sector" and on a broader continental and regional scale—the initiatives begun by their forebears in the now-faltering national universities.

Such networks have provided key support for the present, third, generation of scholars, who received both their undergraduate and graduate education at African universities and now live with the bleak conditions of university employment and research. Compared to the second generation, much less the first, younger scholars have little access to current scholarship and even fewer ties to external research and funders, hence their avid pursuit of regional and continental research networks. Nevertheless, even the best-funded regional research institutions cannot replace the facilities and scholarly communities provided by healthy universities, a particularly serious issue for the production of the next generation of scholars.

As already noted, Africanists have been forced to confront similar long-term issues. Their responses, defenses of African (and area) studies by virtue of their past contributions to the core disciplines and universal knowledge, have been far less innovative than African scholars' pursuit of new institutional and intellectual endeavors that cut across old boundaries of nation and discipline. Although the varied responses undoubtedly reflect divergent locations in global educational networks, it is somewhat surprising that Africanists and continentalists have not forged a more common response to the marginalization of continental Africa and the promotion of free market and global perspectives by common funders—developments that continental scholars have argued are part of a worldwide backlash against independent scholarship and academic freedom (see Diouf and Mamdani 1994).

Indeed, as the chapter by Mamdani illustrates and as other continental African commentaries on the future of scientific knowledge production have argued (e.g., CODESRIA 1996; Taiwo n.d.; Hountondji 1995), the pursuit of a purely self-enclosed indigenous tradition is an illusory task in the face of the increasingly transcontinental production of knowledge and scholarship. Mkandawire, for instance, notes that the productivity of the first and second generations of African scholars blossomed in part as a result of engagement with international scholarship, an opportunity now being foreclosed. Yet there has been no real effort to communicate across the continental-Africanist divide so as to forge a common approach to the globalization challenge. Of course, the enduring obstacle to such collaboration is the legacy of entrenched inequality between the two groups, as well as continental scholars' long tradition of pursuing an independent path, even under harsh conditions. Although Africanists might well celebrate the appointment of a few continental Africans as directors of major centers—as has occurred in the last five years, often where students and scholars have rallied to end white dominance of African studies—there are still few sign of any serious rapprochement between the two schools.

The Transcontinental Tradition: Rise, Demise—and Renaissance?

The issue of rapprochement with the Africanist enterprise is even more remote for the transcontinental paradigm. Rooted in the early development of pan-Africanism, this school and its practitioners have always been excluded from the funding sources, research institutions, and university posts dominated by Africanists.

In its original form, the transcontinental school was the outcome of a project aimed at "vindicating" Africa and Africans, at home and abroad, and was perhaps the most notable intellectual achievement of nineteenth-century pan-Africanism. The primary goal of the vindicationists was to valorize the African past, to construct a historiography to refute white supremacist notions that Africa and Africans had played no part in the development of world cultures and civilizations. Accordingly, various individuals—publicists, memorialists, and other writers—set out to demonstrate, largely through historical research, that Africans had been at the forefront of the early development of governmental institutions, monotheistic religions, science, technology, and the other accouterments deemed to be evidence of high culture. The implication, if not the outright assertion, was that continental Africans and their descendants in the diaspora, once freed from the shackles of slavery, colonialism, racism, and oppression, could and would rise again to greatness.

Vindicationism, like most of the earliest pan-African initiatives, was centered in the Anglophone black Atlantic world, though it was never confined there (see, e.g., Gregoire 1957). The majority of the vindicationist writers had little formal training in the emerging academic discipline of history, and their sources consisted mainly of texts from sacred and profane literature, to use the contemporary language. Chief among these were the Bible, notably the King James Version, which is also the authorized pan-African version; the works of various Greco-Roman writers; and more contemporary European historical accounts that supported their arguments (Shepperson 1974). The products of this research often included the word *vindication* in their titles, hence the vindicationist tradition, as it has been christened by St. Clair Drake (1987). Although spearheaded by blacks, the vindicationist project also included significant white contributions.

There had always been a certain amount of national and transnational coordination and cooperation in the production and dissemination of vindicationist literature, but it was only in the closing years of the nineteenth century that a successful attempt was made to institutionalize the tradition. This happened in the United States, where in 1897 the American Negro Academy, apparently the first black research institute, was founded. Despite its name—over which there was disagreement among the founders, with some preferring "African" to "American Negro"—the American Negro Academy was a pan-African institution. Its membership, although primarily African American, included black intellectuals from the African continent and the Caribbean. The academy's mission was twofold: to encourage scholarly research on Africa and Africans at home and abroad and to help to reproduce the black intelligentsia internationally. It was the physical setting in which the accumulated wisdom of nineteenth-century pan-Africanism and black nationalism was, quite literally, passed from the generation led by Alexander Crummell to that led by W. E. B. Du Bois (see Moss 1981; Moses 1989:258–75; Lewis 1993:168–74).

In 1911, with the American Negro Academy existing little more than in name, a second unsuccessful attempt was made to institutionalize the vindicationist tradition with the formation of the Negro Society for Historical Research (Moss 1981:192–93). Firmer foundations came in 1915 with the establishment of the Association for the Study of Negro Life and History (ASNLH) by Carter G. Woodson, a coal miner turned history Ph.D. Vindicationist scholarship subsequently became much better organized, placed on a professional and "scientific" basis, and guided by the canons of the historical craft as they had been elaborated in the nineteenth-century German academy and imported to the United States.

Central to the professionalization of vindicationist scholarship was the establishment of regularly published organs for the dissemination of research done by scholars working under the aegis of the ASNLH or elsewhere. Thus in 1916 Woodson established the *Journal of Negro History*; that publication and his more popular *Negro History Bulletin,* as well as other black-run organs such as the *Journal of Negro Education* and *Phylon,* became the leading outlets in the United States for scholarly research on the black experience in both the diaspora and in Africa. In 1926 Woodson—seeking to popularize black history and in the process to expand the market for the journals, monographs, and books published by the ASNLH—created the Negro History Week, which would later become Black History Month (Meier and Rudwick 1986; Goggin 1993).

The early vindicationist writers generally adhered to a cyclical theory of history, which they tended to view as something akin to a relay race, with one nation or people passing the baton of civilization to another. Thus the Egyptians—whom the vindicationists insisted were a black African people—had passed the baton to the Greeks, who then gave it to the Romans, who in turn entrusted it to the modern Europeans. But Africa's day, the vindicationists believed, was coming again: its redemption—a word always on the lips of nineteenth-century pan-Africanists and around which they wove an elaborate theory of global black emancipation—was drawing nigh.

A fundamental characteristic of vindicationist scholarship from the outset was its transnational and transcontinental perspective. Rejecting the dichotomies on which Africanist and to a lesser extent continentalist scholarship would later be constructed, the vindicationists connected ancient Africa to modern Africa, Africa north of the Sahara to Africa south of the Sahara, and especially the African continent to the African diaspora. They tended to concentrate on broad political, religious, and cultural themes that transcended national and continental boundaries in the black world. These hallmarks of nineteenth-century vindicationism continued to inform the work of professionally trained African American scholars well into the twentieth century, including Woodson, Du Bois, and William Leo Hansberry (see Du Bois 1947; Harris 1974, 1977), the Howard professor who influenced two generations of black students from all over the world, including Nnamdi Azikiwe, who had the Institute of African Studies at the University of Nigeria at Nsukka named after Hansberry (Azikiwe 1970:115–20).

Another important feature of the transcontinental school was the social and intellectual diversity of its practitioners and audience. As the premier body in the United States for the coordination and dissemination of research on the global black experience, the ASNLH was, from its foundation until the end of World War II, a big tent. It included academicians (most of them located at the historically black colleges) as well as scholars based outside the academy, professionally trained as well as amateur scholars, and schoolteachers as well community-based public intellectuals.

The Africanist enterprise, which supplanted the transcontinental school in the postwar period, was by contrast much more firmly centered in the academy, with a strong policy orientation befitting its close association with the extension of U.S. power across the world. The Africanist audience accordingly consisted primarily of white scholars, policymakers, and university students. Epistemologically and methodologically, the Africanist school also represented a sharp break with the transcontinental paradigm. Whereas the transcontinentalists specialized in broad surveys and grand sweeps, Africanist scholarship took as its object of analysis nation-states or tribes and was grounded in the intensive language training and field research made possible by foundation and federal funding.

Within the United States, then, the rise of the Africanist enterprise resulted in dramatic shifts in the definition of *Africa* and *Africans,* the scale of and priorities for research, the institutional location of the study of Africa, and the audience for Africa-related research, all of which were accompanied by a reversal in the racial composition of the research community. Just as most scholars working in the transcontinental tradition had been black, so now the great majority of Africanists were white.

The establishment in 1957 of the ASA symbolized the Africanist triumph over the transcontinental tradition in the United States, for the new organization shortly replaced the ASNLH as the premier professional organization concerned with the study of the African continent. A thoroughgoing intellectual transformation had taken place, a genuine change of paradigm. The segregation of the study of Africans at home and abroad was further solidified, it must be noted, by the emergence of the continental school, which never overcame the Africanists' insistence on the separation of continental Africa and continental America.

Although rigidly excluded from the higher reaches of the Africanist enterprise, the transcontinental paradigm and its exponents were never fully eclipsed. Five of our contributors reveal the breadth and vitality of the transcontinental tradition from both sides of the Atlantic: Elliott Skinner, C. Tsehloane Keto, Horace Campbell, Micere Mugo, and Jacques Depelchin. Of the five, Skinner is closest to this tradition in its classic form and bridges across its complicated relationship with the Africanist enterprise. Skinner, who holds the Franz Boas professorship in anthropology at Columbia University and was the U.S. ambassador to Burkina Faso (then called Upper Volta) from 1966 to 1969, has set much of his scholarly work in the Africanist paradigm, and he has over the years been closely affiliated with the ASA, which in 1985 gave him its Distinguished Africanist Award.

In his more recent writings, however, Skinner has been emphasizing a variety of transcontinental issues (e.g., Skinner 1992). His contribution to this volume returns to his roots in the older tradition as he tackles the contemporary revival of transcontinental perspectives. With the deft hand of a distinguished elder, he moves from the early vindicationist tradition through the rise of European and North American entanglements with Africa to the contemporary debates over the unity of African cultures and philosophy. This seamless treatment has the distinct advantage of tracking shifting locations and perspectives from within a single tradition. It moreover engages contemporary political and ideological struggles over "Africa" by tracing the constant battle of African peoples and intellectuals against European–North American domination.

Moving to the present, Skinner engages two central currents of intellectual and popular debate: the search by philosophers for a common African ontology and, in a more indirect fashion, Afrocentrist assertions of a universal African culture that knows no oceanic, much less intracontinental, boundaries. As his analysis of the work emanating from Placide Tempels's *Bantu Philosophy* to current debates among African scholars such as Hountondji, Appiah, and Mudimbe demonstrates, these contemporary discussions are rooted in an older and now resurgent search for a paradigm to facilitate the self-assertion of African peoples. In this regard it is revealing to note that Skinner's representation of debates among Africans leaps over, without much notice, two generations of Africanist scholarship. This is consistent with his concluding position—namely, that although ontological claims of a single African culture are difficult to sustain, a common "Africanity" has been forged by the existential position of Africans worldwide in their confrontation with racism and the "paradigmatic hegemony" emanating from the West. Skinner thus continues to hold to a common heritage even while he posits "Africanity" as a counter to Afrocentricity and other new or reemergent pan-African intellectual traditions.

Whereas Skinner's intellectual primogenitor is the transcontinental approach in its classic form, C. Tsehloane Keto belongs to the more recent expression of transcontinental perspectives associated with the notion of Afrocentricity. As the most visible and vilified contemporary expression of African revivals in the United States, Afrocentricity has been equated by its detractors with almost any statement of African pride and assertion, no matter the provenance or validity. As Keto is careful to point out, however, Afrocentricity as developed by the Temple University school is no proponent of melanin-based, biological, or racial theories of human culture, much less simple denunciations of oppression. In the words of Molefi Kete Asante, its leading academic exponent and formerly Keto's Temple University colleague, the core of Afrocentricity is "a radical critique of Eurocentric ideology that masquerades as a universal view in the fields of intercultural communication, rhetoric, philosophy, linguistics, psychology, education, anthropology and history" (1987:3). In his more politically assertive moments, Asante presents Afrocentricity as "the center piece of human regeneration," an intellectual and cultural antidote to white supremacy (1988:1). As Keto affirms in chapter 8, however, "the African-centered paradigm, unlike the Afrocentrism proclaimed by some scholars, is not a political ideology."

Afrocentricity echoes the transcontinental tradition in its rejection of the Africanist and continentalist schools' separation of the African continent from the African diaspora. In contrast to the transcontinentalist, Africanist, and continentalist paradigms, however, it accepts as part of this project the legitimacy of Eurocentric and Asiacentric paradigms for peoples of European and Asian descent. As Keto, Asante, and others have emphasized, the task of Afrocentric scholarship is to produce knowledge for Africans that originates or is centered in the global African community. And this means recovering the origins of African knowledge in ancient Kemet and demonstrating their relevance today for all African peoples. As Keto writes in his essay in this volume: "The Africa-centered paradigm is the original paradigm that Africans used to create knowledge about themselves, for themselves, and about the physical and social milieus in which they lived. This paradigm dominated African discourse about Africans from the time of ancient Kemet 5,000 years ago until the autonomy of African communities was snuffed out" by European colonialism. In contrast to the Africanists, Afrocentrists have anchored their efforts in a wider public constituency, targeting in particular primary and secondary schools. In addition to the Temple University–based scholarly organ *The Journal of Black Studies,* Asante's publishing arm, Peoples Publishing, has produced a series of textbooks and the associated newsletter *Nommo.*

By charting in detail the central tenets of the Temple school in comparison to Eurocentric and Asiancentric paradigms, Keto's chapter greatly clarifies the coherence of the Afrocentric agenda. He concludes that "the whole enterprise of Africa-centered scholarship should be about the reconstruction of the African's place in world history and the acceptance of all the world's people as actors in their own right and on their own terms, subject only to the recognition of the rights of others."

Thus the Afrocentric agenda, as defined by Keto, clearly separates its practitioners from many in the transcontinental tradition. Indeed, to those situated within the longer pan-Africanist stream, such a position appears as nothing less than an acceptance of political quiescence and idealism (see Lemelle 1993; Lemelle and Kelly 1994). Horace Campbell's chapter falls squarely within this pan-Africanist camp. Although acknowledging that "Afrocentrism does raise fundamental issues with respect to knowledge and power," Campbell takes the Afrocentric scholars to task for their focus on ancient empires and especially for their unwillingness to engage with the political struggles of Africans, including black feminists, in the diaspora or on the continent.

This assessment is derived, however, from a much larger task that Campbell tackles: the attempt to situate current pan-African scholarship within the long history of the pan-African movement, including its popular as well as intellectual expressions. As is readily apparent, this historical understanding of the study of Africa differs greatly from those offered by Africanists or, for that matter, Skinner and Keto's Afrocentric school. Central to Campbell's analysis is the long history of African scholars' struggle against "deeply rooted paradigms that have justified and covered up colonialism, militarism, and underdevelopment." Such a project entails tracing the intertwined work of black scholars and movements—before, during, and after the cold war—as they confronted the repressive activities of the U.S. government in Africa and at home.

In looking forward, Campbell seeks not only to counter new extensions of U.S. militarism in the academy and Africa but also to bring black scholars on the continent and in the diaspora closer together on questions of intellectual freedom, accountability, and the democratization of information and knowledge production. By turning to continental struggles, Campbell addresses, if only in part, two central quandaries for contemporary pan-Africanists. First, how can they rebuild their paradigm to suit a postnationalist and increasingly globalized world? Even setting aside its lack of any significant institutions, journals, and so forth, how might pan-Africanism, so triumphant in the phase of decolonization and national liberation struggles, be reforged in the light of contemporary realities? Second, how might scholar-activists rooted in pan-Africanist agendas ground their work in relation to popular movements and particularly black youth and women? Marginalization in the academy and from those who control power and resources is not the only explanation for these dilemmas: Campbell notes that Afrocentrism has an institutional base but has also been rather successful in its popular reach in the United States. Further, as Tadesse argues in her chapter, the postcolonial construction of African universities has left students and scholars isolated from contemporary African struggles. How feminist perspectives in the United States and continental Africa, and the broader wave of black nationalism (as exemplified by the Million Man March, Million Youth March, and Million Women March), might be incorporated remains an open question—although it is explored in new collections by African feminists and pan-Africanists (Imam, Mama, and Sow 1997; Abdul-Raheem 1996).

Micere Mugo's chapter takes up these challenges from an original position rooted in African cultural praxis. Drawing on her own work with orature-based community theater in Kenya and Zimbabwe, Mugo seeks to reveal the power of the performed word as the most readily available mode of African peoples' self-expression, cultural practice, and resistance to arbitrary power. This approach is set explicitly against Africanist writings on drama and art, which she unearths as but one instance of the "invasion of dominating paradigms," whether in colonial, neocolonial, or multicultural guises. In so proceeding Mugo roots her work in the long pan-Africanist tradition, drawing on, for example, the seminal contributions of Frantz Fanon and Amilcar Cabral. Rising to the call to move beyond the liberal-nationalist frameworks that were forged during the late colonial period, Mugo goes on to fashion a paradigm that can advance contemporary popular African resistance to "invasion from above," whether it takes the form of commercialization of culture or service to the state and neocolonial elites, including the World Bank and IMF.

This is no triumphalist exercise. As Mugo demonstrates with concrete examples drawn from the experience of community-based theater, the attempt to democratize the stage and root theater in the concerns of workers and peasants has had as many failures as successes. Problems of staging, language, the meeting place of oral and written work, and the equality of practice between community and academy-trained artists abound. The goal remains quite clear, however: to forge "a paradigm that creates space for democratic participation, involvement, and collective work."

Although they move from the heights of Africanist and pan-Africanist academic paradigms to local realities, Mugo's arguments do not extend to theater and art in the diaspora. Readers might be inspired to ask whether similar constructions could be investigated in the light of the explosion of performed orature and theater in the Americas and Europe, from reggae and rap to community-based Africa-centered groups (such as Chicago's MPACT troupe).

Indeed, one of the more interesting academic developments of the last decade has been the search for new conceptions to bridge such transcontinental cultural and political phenomena. The study of multiple diasporas has steadily grown, propelled in no small part by the increasing migration of peoples and the demise of assimilationist hopes and expectations in North America and Europe. This trend helps to explain the popularity of Gilroy's work on the "black Atlantic" (1993), the birth of new journals such as *Diaspora,* and the reemergence, through its relocation from Makerere to Boston, of the journal *Transition.* As many of our contributors imply, however, such projects remain far too wedded to the division between Africa and its dispersed peoples, often ignoring gender, class, and generational divisions, and are too committed to notions of a fundamental historical and cultural rupture in the post–cold war period.

The contribution by Jacques Depelchin takes up this challenge of producing the conceptual tools suitable for a historical understanding of the relationship between Europe and Africa. Setting himself against contemporary paradigms that stress a global cultural rupture in the present on the one hand and fragmented, localized cultures on the other, Depelchin's openly states what is today a novel premise, namely, that "history holds together and that purported ruptures, although appearing as such to those who are close to them, are more like fissures or cracks when seen from a distance." No less surprising is the model he interrogates: Fernand Braudel's highly influential conception of the *longue durée*, with its emphasis on forging transcontinental cultural engagements and hierarchies.

From such a foundation Depelchin engages Africanist and multiculturalist paradigms as they have permeated Western academic discourse, ranging across discussions of slavery, revolt, and the birth and expansion of capitalism on a world scale. As he strips away Braudel's universalism layer by layer, Depelchin demonstrates that even in this case the heavy hand of European historical conceptions serves to erase not only African historical realities but the horrors of the spread of European capitalism. Nevertheless, Depelchin concludes that a project of world history is feasible—indeed, necessary—but would have to move well beyond the dead end of Eurocentric versus Afrocentric perspectives and grapple with the irrationality and destructiveness that have bound Europeans and Africans together over the past five centuries.

Looking Forward: Many Africas?

What might the future hold for the study of Africa? Given all the varied perspectives and histories, what intellectual approaches will set our research agendas in the next century? Where will they be located in the academy? And how will students with a passion for Africa be nourished, trained, and employed?

Of one thing we may be certain: there is no single path before us. Gone are the days of imposing hegemonic definitions of Africa and Africans and a concomitant paradigm by which to study them. Yet the future is also unlikely to be one of a multitude of equal voices and perspectives. As in the past, the study and meaning of Africa will be shaped by upheavals in the positions of the United States and Africa on the world stage, by continuing struggles over resources and power in the production of knowledge as the national and global educational systems are restructured, and especially by movements of Africans in the widest sense.

One quite plausible future may be derived from an extrapolation from the dominant center of the cold war epoch, the programs and paradigms associated with the major Africanist institutions. As was charted previously, most Africanists not only were unprepared for current intellectual and institutional upheavals but appear to be unwilling to confront them. If continued, the Africanist disengagement could well lead to the retrenchment of African studies to a much smaller research specialty within the academy. Purely defensive responses by Africanists to external challenges—whether they emanate from Afrocentrists, the core disciplines, black scholars, or the funding establishment—could easily result in an encirclement of the major African studies programs and centers. Survival and reproduction of a rump Africanist establishment might well be ensured, but only at the cost of the Africanist enterprise's irrelevance to both popular and powerful constituencies.

Part of such a scenario would be an ongoing struggle by Africanists to contain "Africa" within its current channels, countering the increasing incorporation of "Africa" and "Africans" within the new streams of academic and even popular discourse. The flourishing of cultural, gender, Africa-centered, pan-Africanist, and global studies indicates the contest already underway, as scholars associated with these perspectives seek their own break with the dominance of the traditional disciplines and area studies.

Left unchecked, this process could produce the fragmentation and dissolution of the study of Africa as we have known and experienced it for two generations. Such trends are clearly strongest in cultural and global studies, where African subject matter has become dissolved in larger intellectual frameworks. In the new perspectives associated with cultural studies, such as postcolonialism and postmodernism, Africa finds its place as but one among many nonterritorial spaces for cultural imaginings and identity formation. In the case of global studies, there is equally little space for Africa, given the rejection of area boundaries and the competition for resources—even when senior Africanists have moved into leading administrative positions in global studies programs, as has occurred in a few instances.

Africanists could respond to these external, transcontinental challenges by embracing a wider vision of Africa. A first step would be to dissolve the rigid barrier between Africanists and black scholars. Indeed, this has already occurred in a few instances around the country as a new generation has begun to replace those hired in the 1960s and select continental African and, to a lesser extent, African American scholars have been incorporated into African studies proper, often in the wake of student protests. The primary intellectual foundation for such an alliance is Africanists' and continentalists' shared premise of the separation of the African continent from Africa overseas and the ability of the richer Africanist institutions to entice continental African scholars via salaries now impossible at African universities.

The limits of such a defense of the Africanist enterprise are considerable.

First, as the Curtin debate revealed and several essays in this volume chart, the dominant consensus among Africanists remains wedded to a racialized vision of Africa and African studies, and thus it is difficult to imagine the admission of any more than a few black intruders to positions of real authority. Second, such a movement would not address funders' and university administrations' concerns with global rather than area studies. Finally, this solution does not address the growing call from transcontinental scholars, black students, and the wider black public to abandon the separation of continental Africa and the diaspora.

Africanists' tentative explorations along these lines are moreover being rapidly outpaced by those energized by a broader African perspective. Whether rooted in the pre-Africanist, transcontinental, and pan-Africanist traditions or in the present-day renaissance of black cultural studies, new groups of scholars are establishing themselves as important intellectual and even institutional forces. Indeed, individuals inspired by Africa-centered methodologies, which seek to break down the division between the continent and the larger black world in the Americas, have attracted a large popular constituency, in addition to establishing important footholds in K-12 schools.

A related transformation emanates as well from established programs in Afro-American studies, where the generation-old narrowing of black studies (i.e., the study of Africa and its diasporas) to African American studies (i.e., the study of the black experience in the United States and perhaps the Caribbean) is now being reversed. The most celebrated and well-funded instance is the Harvard Department of Afro-American Studies and the W. E. B. Du Bois Institute for Afro-American Research, where Henry Louis Gates has promoted, in a highly celebrated if limited way (see Benjamin 1995; Kilson 1995), black studies programs' original concern with Africa—coalescing a constellation of faculty with transcontinental interests. Other black studies centers have also expanded their Africa-related programs, often with new federal or private foundation funding.

These initiatives signal a new and different path for the study of Africa in the United States: the potentially increasing centrality of black or African American studies. As with the Africanists before them, those pursuing these new agendas continue to confront the parochial concerns of the disciplines, the academy, and the state; the most successful programs, in purely material terms, have fashioned their agendas to these concerns, displaying high levels of cultural and political entrepreneurship in a national environment riven by concerns over multiculturalism and the growing polarization of rich and poor and black and white. This has predictably led to open discussions among black scholars, often instigated and highlighted by mainstream press solicitations and accounts. The attack on Afrocentrists may be the best known of the latter phenomena, but press and academic coverage now regularly bridges continental and African American divides. In the most prominent and highly controlled op-ed pages, there is a clear preference for black writers who can express, or be interpreted as expressing, the great white hope of universal values and standards and, in today's language of multiculturalism, the elision of racism by the celebration of cultural difference and the denunciation of "racial essentialism." The Harvard program's appeal to powerful white constituencies, for example, primarily rests on these strains in the views and policies promoted by Gates and his colleagues, including Anthony Appiah, Orlando Patterson, and William Julius Wilson, whom Gates recently enticed away from the University of Chicago, thereby completing his Harvard "dream team" of black talent.

Yet as the highly charged debates on op-ed pages suggest, African American scholars and programs confront not just cultural and racial power but many of the same institutional forces—and opportunities—as the Africanist and continental schools. This conundrum has moreover been openly debated over the last decade, with the discussions engaging such topics as the history and achievements of the field, the value of centers allied to core disciplines as opposed to the pursuit of degree-granting department status, and the broader issue of appropriate responses to institutional racism, internal intellectual and political debates, and national priorities related to multiculturalism, diversity, and cultural conflict. Ongoing evaluations and rankings of the field and its programs over the last decade reveal the evolution of these strategic concerns in far greater detail than have similar assessments of any of the three paradigms related directly to Africa.[9]

From such deliberations several trends may be discerned: a steady broadening of African American to diasporan studies through the inclusion of the Caribbean, Brazil, and other regions and countries; the pursuit of departmental status, including degree-granting capacities; an engagement with policymakers within and outside the university; and an appeal to a wider public audience, ranging from the corporate world to grassroots movements. It remains uncertain, however, whether these trends prefigure a wholesale movement to incorporate continental Africa. To move in this direction would entail an engagement with the themes and agendas of the broader transcontinental school, key parts of which—for example, the role of the Nile Valley civilizations and institutional linkages with African scholars and centers—many established African American centers have great difficulty approaching.

An alternative is, of course, the expansion of the pan-African tradition, including most notably those scholars and smaller programs that have kept alive a key component of the original struggles to establish black studies programs: a dedication to a global black emancipatory agenda. Yet these scholars and programs, resting as they do on a small resource base and standing in opposition to dominant corporate and university agendas, are unlikely to be blessed with the institutional resources to expand their instructional, research, and professional activities. The institutional division on many campuses between African and Afro-American units, developed in the wake of the 1960s rebellions, also remains a major obstacle to any transcontinental agenda. Even where such divisions do not exist, or are being breached, the incorporation under one house of continental African and African American courses, faculty, and institutional resources—much less professional associations and links with Africa-based scholars—remains quite tentative.

As is already evident, we believe that a far more positive vision of the future of the study of Africa rests on one fundamental theme: the end of the post–World War II division between the African continent and the African diaspora. One key benefit of the end of the cold war and the current upheavals in the worlds of education and culture is the demise in Africa, Europe, and the Americas of the political, ideological, and cultural maps that have so strictly demarcated the place and meaning of Africa for two generations. Thus the trajectory of the meaning and study of Africa can hardly be limited to academic conceptions or even to institutional configurations within the academy. Indeed, as we have already suggested, the most uncertain and unacknowledged factor by academicians, pundits, and even government officials may prove to be the development and direction of popular movements—whether of black youth, women, or elders—in the United States and abroad.

In this sense, we have indeed returned to the formative period of the Africanist enterprise, having entered an epoch where the old intellectual order is in disarray and cultural and political movements are likely to play a far more direct role. The current intellectual order was formed amid the intertwined history of pan-Africanism, negritude, and decolonization on the one hand and the civil rights and black power movements on the other, and it is entirely possible that contemporary conflicts and movements will assume a much larger role in refashioning the study and meaning of Africa than is commonly realized. Against such a backdrop, we may well be surprised by the form the study of Africa takes in the coming millennium.

Notes

1. Three contributions to the conference are not included here but remain important to an understanding of our subject. They are Carol Boyce Davies's essay "Uprooting the 'Posts': From Post-Coloniality to Uprising Discourses," which has been published in revised form as chapter 4 of her most recent book (1994:80–112); Ayesha Imam's presentation "Gendering Studies of Africa" may be found in a more developed form in Imam, Mama, and Sow 1997 (see also Imam and Mama 1994); and Tiyambe Zeleza's paper "Trends and Inequalities in the Production of Africanist Knowledge," which appears as chapter 4 in Zeleza 1997 (44–69).

2. The letter to the editor was signed by fifty black historians, including one of the authors of this introduction (the other author sent in a separate letter). The *Chronicle*

refused the group access to the prominent "Opinion" page, restricting the response to the space-limited "Letters to the Editor" page.

3. The original *Chronicle* materials, as well as the ASA's statements and the roundtable materials, are gathered together in *ACAS Bulletin* (1996), vol. 46.

4. Although a prominent scholar, member of the SSRC's African program, and the current head of the Program in African Studies at Northwestern, Guyer herself noted in the first draft of her report (a point omitted in the published version [Guyer, Virmani, and Kemp 1996]): "I am not as insightful on the ASA as I would like to be, having never served on the [ASA] Board" (Guyer, Virmani, and Kemp 1995:45). This is also the situation of the editors of this volume, who have also never served on the SSRC or any similar committe or held administrative responsibilities in any African studies program.

5. A recent work that explicitly employs the continental approach is Paul Tiyambe Zeleza, *A Modern Economic History of Africa, Vol. 1: The Nineteenth Century* (Dakar: CODESRIA Books, 1994); see the reviews by Manning (1995) and Martin (1996), which highlight the contest between Africanist generalizations and the pursuit of continentally grounded insights and comparisons.

6. Mamdani's critique was followed by responses in the *CODESRIA Bulletin* by Jane Guyer, Richard Joseph, and Edmond J. Keller (no. 3, 1990); Göran Hyden and Pearl Robinson (no. 4, 1990); and Jimi O. Adesina, who offered a summary critique, "Critique and Anti-critique in the 'Governance in Africa' Discourse" (no. 2, 1993:24–27).

7. Thus the SAREC evaluation reports that SAPES in the early 1990s received 85 to 92 percent of its income from such sources (Sawyer and Hyden 1993:36); CODESRIA, in its response to SAREC's evaluation team, notes that "it has always been the wish of CODESRIA to increase the African share of its funding. . . . the situation was difficult enough even in the heydays of relative prosperity and is now daunting given the austerity programmes being implemented in much of Africa. For the forseeable future, we do not, therefore, expect to see much change in the picture" (CODESRIA 1991:11–12).

8. On this critical point see the essays in Diouf and Mamdani 1994, including, for example, Claude Ake's contribution (1994).

9. This is too large a topic to explore here. See, among others, Asante's (1986) critique of the Ford Foundation report by Huggins (1985); the collection in the Winter 1993–94 issue of *Black Books Bulletin*, including essays by Molefi Asante, Vivian Gordon, Joyce Ann Joyce, and Robert Perry; the personal assessments in the *Journal of Blacks in Higher Education* 1994–95, as well as Benjamin 1995, Kilson 1995, and Kelley 1997; Marable 1995, on "multiculturalism" and black studies; the papers from a 1991 conference on Afro-American Studies in the Twenty-First Century in the *Black Scholar* 22, no. 3 (1992); Cruse 1984; McWhorter and Bailey 1984a, 1984b; and Staples 1984.

References Cited

Abdul-Raheem, Tajudeen. 1996. *Pan-Africanism: Politics, Economy, and Social Change in the Twenty-first Century.* New York: New York University Press.

Ake, Claude. 1994. "Academic Freedom and Material Base." In *Academic Freedom in Africa,* ed. Mamadou Diouf and Mahmood Mamdani, 17–25. Dakar: CODESRIA.

Alpers, Edward. 1995. "Reflections on the Studying and Teaching about Africa in America." *ISSUE* 23, no. 1 (Winter/Spring): 9–10.

Asante, Molefi K. 1986. "A Note on Nathan Huggins' Report to the Ford Foundation on African-American Studies." *Journal of Black Studies* 178, no. 2:255–62.

————. 1987. *The Afrocentric Idea.* Philadelphia: Temple University Press.

————. 1988. *Afrocentricity.* Rev. ed. Trenton, N.J.: Africa World.

Association of Concerned Africa Scholars (ACAS). 1997. *The Case against DOD and CIA Involvement in Funding the Study of Africa.* Leaflet.

Atkins, Keletso, John Higginson, Atieno Odhiambo, et al. 1995. "Letter to the Editor." *Chronicle of Higher Education,* Apr. 7, pp. B3–B4.

Azikiwe, Nnamdi. 1970. *My Odyssey: An Autobiography.* New York: Praeger.

Bates, Robert. 1997. "Area Studies and Political Science: Rupture and Possible Synthesis." *Africa Today* 44, no. 2:123–42.

Benjamin, Richard M. 1995. "The Revival of African-American Studies at Harvard." *Journal of Blacks in Higher Education* 9 (Autumn): 60–68.

Bernal, Martin. 1987. *Black Athena: The Afroasiatic Roots of Classical Civilization.* Vol. 1, *The Fabrication of Ancient Greece, 1785–1985.* New Brunswick, N.J.: Rutgers University Press.

————. 1991. *Black Athena: The Afroasiatic Roots of Classical Civilization.* Vol. 2, *The Archaeological and Documentary Evidence.* New Brunswick, N.J.: Rutgers University Press.

Chege, Michael. 1992. "Remembering Africa." *Foreign Affairs* 71, no. 1:146–63.

Chideya, Farai. 1997. "Africa's Hip Hop Generation: South African Youth and American Youth Live in Parallel Universes." *VIBE,* April, p. 67.

CODESRIA. 1991. *Response by CODESRIA to the Report of the SAREC Evaluation Team.* Stockholm: SAREC.

————. 1996. "The Future of the Social Sciences in Africa." *CODESRIA Bulletin* 1:1.

Cruse, Harold. 1984. "Contemporary Challenges to Black Studies." *Black Scholar* 15:41–47.

Curtin, Philip. 1995. "Ghettoizing African History." *Chronicle of Higher Education,* Mar. 3, p. A44.

Davies, Carol Boyce. 1994. *Black Women: Writing and Identity.* London: Routledge.

de Vylder, Stefan, and Anders Hjort af Ornäs. 1991. *Social Science in Africa: The Role of CODESRIA in Pan-African Cooperation.* Stockholm: SAREC.

Diouf, Mamadou, and Mahmood Mamdani, eds. 1994. *Academic Freedom in Africa.* Dakar: CODESRIA.

Drake, St. Clair. 1987. *Black Folk Here and There: An Essay in History and Anthropology.* Los Angeles: Center for Afro-American Studies, University of California.

Du Bois, W. E. B. 1947. *The World and Africa: An Inquiry into the Part Which Africa Has Played in World History.* New York: Viking.

Gadir, Ali A. 1994. "Donor's Wisdom versus African Folly: What Academic Freedom and Which High Moral Standing." In *Academic Freedom in Africa,* ed. Diouf and Mamdani, 109–17.

Gilroy, Paul. 1993. *The Black Atlantic, Modernity, and Double Consciousness.* Cambridge, Mass.: Harvard University Press.

Goggin, Jacqueline Anne. 1993. *Carter G. Woodson: A Life in Black History.* Baton Rouge: Louisiana State University Press.

Gregoire, Henri. 1957 [1810]. *An Enquiry Concerning the Intellectual and Moral Faculties and Literature of Negroes.* Trans. D. B. Warden. College Park, Md.: McGrath.

Guyer, Jane I., with Akbar M. Virmani and Amanda Kemp. 1995. *A Perspective on African Studies in the United States, 1995. A Report Submitted to the Ford Foundation.* Chicago: Northwestern Program of African Studies.

————. 1996. *African Studies in the United States: A Perspective*. Atlanta: African Studies Association Press.

Harris, Joseph, ed. 1974. *Pillars in Ethiopian History. The William Leo Hansberry African History Notebook, Vol. 1*. Washington, D.C.: Howard University Press.

————, ed. 1977. *Africa and Africans as Seen by Classical Writers. The William Leo Hansberry African History Notebook, Vol. 2*. Washington, D.C.: Howard University Press.

Heilbrunn, Jacob. 1996. "The News from Everywhere." *Lingua Franca* 6, no. 4:48–56.

Herskovits, Melville J. 1958. "Some Thoughts on American Research in Africa." (Presidential Address, First Annual Meeting, African Studies Association, Evanston, Ill., Sept. 8, 1958.) *African Studies Bulletin* 1, no. 2:1–11.

Hodder-Williams, Richard. 1986. "African Studies: Back to the Future." *African Affairs* 85, no. 341 (Oct.): 593–604.

Hopkins, A. G. 1987. "From Hayter to Parker: African History at Birmingham University, 1964–86." *African Affairs* 86, no. 342 (Jan.): 93–102.

Hountondji, Paulin J. 1995. "Producing Knowledge in Africa Today: The Second Bashorun M. K. O. Abiola Distinguished Lecture." *African Studies Review* 38, no. 3 (Dec.): 1–10.

Huggins, Nathan I. 1985. *Afro-American Studies: A Report to the Ford Foundation*. New York: Ford Foundation.

Imam, Ayesha, and Amina Mama. 1994. "The Role of Academics in Limiting and Expanding Academic Freedom." In *Academic Freedom in Africa*, ed. Diouf and Mamdani, 73–108.

Imam, Ayesha, Amina Mama, and Fatou Sow, eds. 1997. *Engendering African Social Sciences*. Dakar: CODESRIA.

Johnson, David. 1994. "Reconstructing the Study and Meaning of Africa." *South Asia Bulletin* 14, no. 1:122–25; repr., *CODESRIA Bulletin* 2 (1995): 22–25.

Journal of Blacks in Higher Education. 1994/1995. "The Lasting Contributions of African-American Studies," 6:91–4.

Kaplan, Robert D. 1994. "The Coming Anarchy." *Atlantic Monthly*, Feb., pp. 487–506.

Katsouris, Christina. 1997. "Sharp Fall in Resource Flows to Africa." *Africa Recovery* 11, no. 2:1, 4.

Kelley, Robin D. G. 1994. "Kickin' Reality, Kickin' Ballistics: 'Gangsta' Rap and Postindustrial Los Angeles." *Race Rebels*, 183–227. New York: Free Press.

————. 1997. "Introduction: Looking B(l)ackward: African-American Studies in the Age of Identity Politics." In *Race Consciousness*, ed. Judith Fosset and Jeffrey Tucker, 1–16. New York: New York University Press.

Kilson, Martin. 1995. "Forging Afro-American Studies at Harvard: Autobiographical Reflections." Unpublished paper.

Kirk-Greene, A. H. M., ed., 1995. *The Emergence of African History at British Universities*. Oxford: WorldView.

Lefkowitz, Mary R. 1996. *Not out of Africa: How Afrocentrism Became an Excuse to Teach Myth as History*. New York: Basic.

Lemelle, Sidney. 1993. "The Politics of Cultural Existence: Pan-Africanism, Historical Materialism and Afrocentricity." *Race and Class* 35, no. 1: 93–112.

Lemelle, Sidney, and Robin D. G. Kelly. 1994. *Imagining Home, Class, Culture, and Nationalism in the African Diaspora*. London: Verso.

Lewis, David Levering. 1993. *W. E. B. Du Bois: Biography of a Race, 1868–1919*. New York: Henry Holt.

Lowe, Christopher. 1997a. "Unexamined Consequences of Academic Globalism in African Studies." *Africa Today* 44, no. 3:297–308.

————. 1997b. "Resurrection How? A Response to Michael O. West and William G. Martin's Article 'A Future with a Past: Resurrecting the Study of Africa in the Post-Africanist Era.'" *Africa Today* 44, no. 4:385–421.

Mabaso, Thabo. 1997. "'Gangsta' War Hits Cape Townships." *Argus* (Cape Town), Aug. 23–24.

Mamdani, Mahmood. 1990. "A Glimpse at African Studies Made in USA." *CODESRIA Bulletin* 2:7–11.

Manning, Patrick. 1995. "Escaping the Tyranny of Theory." *Journal of African History* 36, no. 1:145–47.

Marable, Manning. 1995. "Black Studies, Multiculturalism, and the Future of American Education." *ITEMS* 49, nos. 2–3:49–56.

Martin, William G. 1996. "The End of Africanist History? Considerations on Tiyambe Zeleza's *A Modern Economic History of Africa, Vol. 1: The Nineteenth Century.*" *Comparative Studies of South Asia, Africa, and the Middle East* 16, no. 1:1–4.

————. 1998. "Waiting for Oprah and the New US Constituency for Africa." *Review of African Political Economy* 75:9–24.

Martin, William G., and Michael O. West. 1995. "The Decline of the Africanists' Africa and the Rise of New Africas." *ISSUE* 23, no. 1 (Winter/Spring): 24–27.

McCracken, John. 1993. "African History in British Universities: Past, Present, and Future." *African Affairs* 92, no. 367:239–353.

McWhorter, Gerald A., and Ronald Bailey. 1984a. "Black Studies Curriculum Development in the 1980s: Its Patterns and History." *Black Scholar* 15, no. 2 (Mar.–Apr.): 18–31.

————. 1984b. "An Addendum to Black Studies Curriculum Development in the 1980s, Its Patterns and History." *Black Scholar* 15, no. 6 (Nov.–Dec.): 56–58.

Meier, August, and Elliott Rudwick. 1986. *Black History and the Historical Profession, 1915–1980.* Urbana: University of Illinois Press.

Michaels, Marguerite. 1993. "Retreat from Africa." *Foreign Policy* 72, no. 1:93–108.

Miller, Christopher. 1985. *Blank Darkness: Africanist Discourse in French.* Chicago: University of Chicago Press.

————. 1990. *Theories of Africans: Francophone Literature and Anthropology in Africa.* Chicago: University of Chicago Press.

Mkandawire, Thandika. 1995. "Three Generations of African Academics: A Note." *CODESRIA Bulletin* 3:9–12.

Moses, Wilson Jeremiah. 1989. *Alexander Crummell: A Study of Civilization and Discontent.* New York: Oxford University Press.

Moss, Alfred, Jr. 1981. *The American Negro Academy: Voice of the Talented Tenth.* Baton Rouge: Louisiana State University Press.

Mudimbe, V. Y. 1988. *The Invention of Africa: Gnosis, Philosophy, and the Order of Knowledge.* Bloomington: Indiana University Press.

Parpart, Jane. 1995. "Is Africa a Postmodern Invention?" *ISSUE* 23, no. 1 (Winter/Spring): 16–18.

Rubin, Amy Magora. 1996. "National Security Education Program May Halt Grant Awards." *Chronicle of Higher Education,* May 17, p. A45.

Said, Edward. 1978. *Orientalism.* New York: Pantheon.

————. 1993. *Culture and Imperialism.* New York: Knopf.

Sanger, David E. 1997. "Analysis: Asian Economic Turmoil Will Reshape U.S. Policy." *New York Times,* Nov. 24.

Sawyer, Akilagpa, and Göran Hyden. 1993. *SAPES Trust: The First Five Years, an Evaluation Report Submitted to SIDA and SAREC.* Stockholm: SAREC.

Seddon, David, with Makoto Sato. 1997. "Japan, the Emerging 'Giant' of International Aid." *Review of African Political Economy* 24, no. 71:153–56.

Shepperson, George. 1974. "The Afro-American Contribution to African Studies." *Journal of American Studies* 8, no. 3:281–301.

Skinner, Elliott P. 1992. *African Americans and U.S. Policy toward Africa, 1850–1924.* Washington, D.C.: Howard University Press.

Spear, Thomas. 1995. "Letter to the Editor." *Chronicle of Higher Education,* Apr. 14, p. B4.

Staples, Robert. 1984. "Racial Ideology and Intellectual Racism: Blacks in Academia." *Black Scholar* 15, no. 2:2–17.

Taiwo, Olufemi. N.d. "International Dimensions of Knowledge Production in African Studies." Unpublished paper.

Twaddle, Michael. 1986. "The State of African Studies." *African Affairs* 85, no. 340 (July): 439–45.

Vansina, Jan. 1994. *Living with Africa.* Madison: University of Wisconsin Press.

Wallerstein, Immanuel. 1995. "Africa in the Shuffle." *ISSUE* 23, no. 1 (Winter/Spring): 22–23.

West, Michael. Forthcoming (1999). "Like a River: The Million Man March and the Black Nationalist Tradition in the United States." *Journal of Historical Sociology.*

West, Michael O., and William G. Martin. 1997. "A Future with a Past: Resurrecting the Study of Africa in the Post-Africanist Era." *Africa Today* 44, no. 3:309–26.

———. 1998. "Return to Sender: No Such Person in the House (Being a Reply to Christopher C. Lowe)." *Africa Today* 45, no. 1:63–69.

Williams, Cynthia. 1994. "Funders Rethink Priorities. New Era Requires Innovative Approaches to Area and International Studies." *Communiqué* 4, no. 2 (Nov.–Dec.): 1–3.

Zeleza, Paul Tiyambe. 1997. *Manufacturing African Studies and Crises.* Dakar: CODESRIA Books.

PART I

The Study of Africa and African Studies:
Reflections on the *Longue Durée*

1   The Rise of Francophone African Social Science: From Colonial Knowledge to Knowledge of Africa

Catherine Coquery-Vidrovitch

At the dawn of the colonial era a new science was born in western Europe: *ethnography*. Although the word appeared in France in 1823, the corresponding profession, that of the ethnographer, dates from 1835. At that time the principal meaning of the word *ethnic* was "pagan" as opposed to "Christian" (*Dictionnaire Littré*).[1] It was the intent of careful, inquiring observers to describe the customs and languages of exotic peoples who were thought to be different from those of "civilized" societies, that is, from Western Judeo-Christian culture (Mercier 1984; Guichaoua and Goussault 1993). As Hegel affirmed in 1831: "The peculiarly African character is difficult to comprehend, for the very reason that in reference to it, we must give up the principle which naturally accompanies all *our* ideas—the category of Universality. . . . The Negro . . . exhibits the natural man in his completely wild and untamed state" (1944:93).

The pseudoscientific ramblings at the end of the nineteenth century did not help matters. "Primitive" peoples were described in a static way: in tribes, clans, and so on, often subdivided to the maximum. Confusion reigned between racial, linguistic, and psychosocial meanings. People were classified by their material possessions. One of the first scientific manifestations of this new interest was France's Museum of Ethnography, created by Jules Ferry in 1880, at the moment of colonial expansion: primitive arts were approached from the ethnographic perspective, a particularly enumerative field of inquiry that progressively acquired respectability in the form of *ethnology*, or the schematization of these ethnographic descriptions. The first society devoted to ethnology appeared in France in 1838. The profession of ethnologist appeared in 1870, strongly marked by the beginning of the period of "colonial imperialism." Nonetheless, the discipline was not formally institutionalized until the creation of the Institute of Ethnology of the University of Paris in 1925. Under the direction of Marcel Mauss, the institute asserted the primacy of the study of social bonds over the enumeration of customs. Ethnographers became scientific on-site ethnologists.

This bastion was composed mainly of linguists, ethnologists, and to a lesser extent, archaeologists. Geographers made up a small minority, and in contrast to its counterparts in the British world, historians were practically absent. The few historians who did work at the institute concerned themselves with colonial history. Thus, in anticipation of the International Colonial Exhibition, which was held in Paris in 1931, G. Hanotaux and A. Martineau began in 1925 to prepare their *Histoire des colonies françaises et de l'expansion française dans le monde.* This work was to affirm the extent and diversity of the empire. Within it, the history of western Africa compiled by the former colonial administrator Henri Delafosse exemplifies this goal. It sought to reconcile the intervention of the "French peace" with an image of a motionless and ossified precolonial world set within a "Negro-African" civilization defined by its ethnographic, linguistic, and ecological origins. Once the anarchic episodes of decadence characterized by internal rivalries between princes and "rebels" were overcome, a return to a lost paradise would be achieved through the recovery of a bond with primal Africa. The whole collection appeared in 1931,[2] followed shortly by the publication of P. Vidal de la Blanche's *Géographie universelle,* several volumes of which were devoted to overseas territories; the great *Atlas des colonies françaises* by G. Grandidier (1934); and the treatise *Cartographie coloniale* by de Martonne (1935). This body of work resulted from over a quarter-century of efforts by the colonial military geographic and cartographic services. At approximately the same time the first inventory of the geologic wealth of the overseas territories was made.[3] The Society of Africanists (Société des Africanistes), founded in 1930, became the first French learned society devoted to the African continent, alongside the International African Institute, which was founded by the British in 1926.

These first observers made significant contributions, and they provide today's historians an eye-witness source for deciphering a past that would otherwise be largely unavailable. Toward the end of the colonial period, however, the changes in mentality resulting from World War II made it improper to study human beings in the manner of an ornithologist classifying species. In a significant change of terminology, the ethnography museum had became the Museum of Man (Musée de l'Homme) in 1938. During the 1950s the science was redefined, giving itself a more noble name: *anthropology,* a word that is etymologically unquestionable since it means a "science concerned with man."

Georges Balandier, although not a Marxist himself, became the leader of an "iconoclastic" school of young Marxist-oriented anthropologists whose work transcended his own goal, which was to reintroduce the dynamics of time—that is, history—into a process that until then had been bogged down in an atemporal present. The analyses of this school (especially dealing with the unequal relationships within kinship groups, with the practice of exchanging gifts, or with the enumeration of modes of production) were invaluable, for they enabled one to understand truly original mechanisms that were henceforth integrated into thought. African history, however, remained the "poor relative" whose students were mostly former colonial administrators, with the exception of Henri Brunschwig, who in 1961 became the first person to receive an advanced studies position in African history, winning a post at the École Pratique des Hautes Études. Until 1963 the Sorbonne still offered only the history of colonization, even though after World War II the chair had been given to Charles-André Julien, a major anticolonialist activist since his first article in 1914 and a specialist in the history of North Africa.

It was therefore anthropologists who showed French historians that oral sources are usable and that African societies, like all others, had been acquainted with and adapted political, economic, legal, and ideological systems—in short, that Africans were participants, like other societies, in the whole gamut of the social sciences. What worth would we accord today to a study dealing with African economy that failed to consider the realities of the "informal" sector? Or to a study dealing with African demography that failed to take into account the relevance of attitudes toward fertility? Or to a work that treated African law without taking into account theoretical references or traditional practices inherited from the past (Coquery-Vidrovitch 1988)?

Georges Balandier actually created the French Africanist school in the 1950s as a result of his teaching at the Hautes Études and his articles in the *Cahiers Internationaux de Sociologie,* written mainly between 1951 and 1962. It is not by chance that anthropology blossomed during the time of decolonization; during this period the struggle for desegregation emerged with equal vigor in the United States, as did the American Indian movement. This was the era when Western scholars discovered that the "native" is first and foremost a human being and consequently deserves as much attention as Western peoples.

Yet anthropology, which focuses on understanding other cultures, was also initially attracted by exoticism, that is, by the qualities of foreign human groups defined as being less developed than Western peoples (always based on the underlying Enlightenment concept of progress). Although he intended to reveal the fundamental characteristics common to all social life, Claude Lévi-Strauss, the founder of structuralism and an adversary of Balandier, contrasted the "cold" (ossified) history of archaic societies with the "hot" (vibrant) history of modern societies. He contributed to the spread of theories of this kind with works that in their time caused a sensation, such as

Mythologiques: le cru et le cuit (1964). In these works the gap between the savage and the civilized would be defined again and again through the language of myths.

In the name of Cartesian philosophy, anchored in the French logical mind, the notion thus remained strong that primitive societies were in effect privileged research laboratories precisely because these societies were homogeneous and hence easier to study than "complex" Western societies. Balandier's dynamic anthropology, in clearly different ways, also made reference to the admitted opposition of tradition versus modernity, since the affirmed primacy of history permitted one to retrace the evolution from nature to culture.

The other human sciences in France at this time studied only Indo-European societies, while history continued to focus solely on peoples that had attained the knowledge of writing. Jean Suret-Canale (1958) was the one exception to this state of affairs, playing in the French world the same role of the disseminator of African history that Basil Davidson played in England. Sociology dealt at this time only with societies that were considered to be civilized, and philosophy remained the quintessence of Western thought. Anthropology therefore gained great credence by incorporating non-Western societies into the general field of human sciences. Meanwhile Fernand Braudel showed initiative in breaking with tradition at the École des Hautes Études, where his implementation of the concept of cultural areas brought together minority and other hitherto excluded specialists. These scholars wished to devote their efforts to these poorly perceived and little-known zones, which until then had been reserved for linguists, geographers, or others interested in eccentric subjects denoted by geographical terms (orientalists, Americanists, and later, Africanists). Historians, sociologists, demographers, political scientists, jurists, economists, or philosophers rarely worked as scholars of the non-Western world, showing no interest in a subject they considered useless or impossible. The field was therefore left to the anthropologists, who scattered out across the terrain. Their work enabled the educated Western public to discover that the ways of life, systems of thought, and political and social models of other peoples were equal to ours, or at least as complex, moving, contradictory, and coherent in their own way.

The work and legacy of the French anthropological school (Claude Meillassoux, J. Copans, J.-L. Amselle, Marc Augé, etc.), widely translated into English, are not to be neglected. The work of these scholars attempted to restore to marginalized and ignored peoples their dignity, richness, and cultural identity. It was all the more important that at the same time the process for Afro-Asian independence was moving in the same direction politically, as illustrated by the Bandung Conference of 1955.

Nonetheless, French social scientists are now realizing that this rehabilitative work risked distorting its subject. By struggling to make the identity of the natives known, and by proclaiming the originality of their studies to accomplish this, the anthropologists turned their field of study into a private reserve inaccessible to the uninitiated. The manner of dealing with "Africanist" history and economics exemplifies this turn of events. Faced with the incomprehension of "professional historians" who, stricken by a strange but fleeting blindness, thought no history could exist in the absence of written records,[4] the first French Africanists thought it wise to invent a new discipline, "ethnohistory."[5] Within ethnohistory the closed field of kinship was treated as an abstract place of exchange where filial relationships, marriage, and women were viewed as objects—or at best as wagers [*enjeux*]—and not as subjects. Women's own personal view of themselves were accordingly excluded, if only because of the difference between men and women (Zimmerman 1993).

The field of economics presented a double obstacle. The first derived from an observation of the Africanists: Westerners were in general unable to conceptualize the Third World. The presupposition was that there is only one kind of development, which could be understood as a process leading to an economic situation comparable to that existing in the West. The concept remained therefore locked in a strictly economic sense, that of an economy that could be used to explain a whole society since it is the expression of a culture. How could these rigorous economists understand a notion such as the "global development"—that is, both economic and cultural—of a culture based on different terms that could generate new forms of development? It is basically impossible for a classical economist to understand the validity of a question such as "Must one refuse development?" (Latouche 1986) or even "What if Africa refused development?" (Kabou 1989). It is therefore understandable that the anthropologists, especially those who were Marxists, sought to counter this perverse doctrine of economics. This often led them to reformulate the economics of development as the application of economic analysis to a concrete geographical area.

Yet this procedure led anthropologists to another impasse. Their purpose was to show the autonomous and therefore specific—indeed, unique—nature of the economic logic of "native" societies. The effect was, perversely, to isolate the discipline from the developmentalist project, which was rejected as being founded on "overexploitation" (Meillassoux 1981), dependency (Amin 1974), or even "ethnocide" (Jaulin 1974). The analysis was judicious, but a degree of dogmatism resulted in cutting off anthropologists from realities as the concept of "traditional societies" crumbled and the peoples concerned, eager for the modern way of life, refused to view themselves as isolated from the contemporary world.

Many French researchers had trouble accepting the fact that they were no longer the only ones to control a domain that was in the process of decolonization. A number of them returned home to France. The disillusionment of the "generation of 1968" (Bruckner 1986; Copans 1990) was added to the "recruitment crisis" that was brought about—in France as in Great Britain—by a lack of positions, which resulted in a slow turnover in personnel. The latter trend has been bolstered by publishers who claim that "Africa does not pay" (at least the Africa of the Africa specialists). Good historical works thus remain undisturbed in specialized libraries in mimeograph form, whereas media coverage is generally absent or weak.

As for the anthropologists, they discovered by necessity that it was unnecessary to leave France to carry out their research. As independent African states emerged, French scholars returned home with the concepts and techniques they had developed in exotic regions and gave birth to French rural anthropology. It was determined, for example, that the circulation of dowries within a restricted circle of rural lineages from generation to generation controlled, in the French countryside as elsewhere, matrimonial exchanges until at least the end of the nineteenth century, if not longer. This was a major contribution to social history, thereby undermining anthropology as a separate human science.

Following the lead of scholars writing in English (Anderson 1983; Hobsbawn and Ranger 1983; Mudimbe 1988), the French discovered quite clearly over a ten-year period that by being too structured, they had forgotten history. Their excessive differentiation had led them to "invent" and "create" an Africa of traditions, communities, and ethnic groups where there existed, as elsewhere, social processes inherited from a complex and turbulent past (Amselle and Mbokolo 1985; Amselle 1990; Chrétien and Prunier 1989). These phenomena are both universal and specific; in brief, if sub-Saharan Africa is a "cultural area," then Europe is one as well. Moreover, the globalization of economic phenomena has in the West led to the creation of forms of exclusion and informality that derive directly from Third World countries. What matters henceforth is to take cross-cultural relations into account in every way.

It has become common today to speak of the crisis of Africanist anthropology. This may be traced to the globalization of phenomena, which has given a planetary dimension to social reactions. These range from the tribalisms of Yugoslavia, Zaire, or Ireland to the fundamentalist temptations and forms of intolerance and exclusion existing in Iran, India, or the United States—to say nothing of Europe. The subject of anthropology as it has developed over the past fifty years—in the broadest sense, from 1935 to 1985, with its peak phase between 1950 and 1970—has thus disappeared. It has yielded to an extremely complex and varied series of interwoven phenomena, local, regional, national, supranational, or nonnational. As a result of various factors (historical, geographic, economic, legal, etc.), this series repeatedly produces in field observations different forms that echo one another. In this sense, anthropology, an essential stage in the scientific discovery of the world, has fulfilled its role in Africa. And from this stems the confusion of the French researchers, a confusion that expresses their own disenchantment more than that of their field of study: exoticism is dead; long live modernity (Copans 1990). Redeployment is occurring. Yet the institutions (Centre National de la Recherche Scientifique, Office de la Recherche Scientifique et Technique Outre-Mer [ORSTOM], École des Hautes Études en Sciences Sociales [EHESS], Musée de l'Homme) retain the heritage of a great number of professional researchers, which the following generation will inevitably absorb to some extent. For the later scholars devote themselves especially to precise local analyses whose microregional fragmentation obscures the principal focus of twenty years earlier:[6] the conceptual intelligence of social systems. They call for a rapprochement between anthropology and history, but since most of them devote themselves to microhistory, the synthesis will occur to the advantage of the historians.

Influenced by the research thrusts opened in the United States (Cooper 1983, 1987), the historians brought about a renewal of comparative research on Africa. A good example is research on the town, something that French Africanists had shunned for a long time because it contradicted their rural perception of nondeveloped societies. The challenge had been raised in France first by geographers[7] and economists,[8] then by sociologists and historians, and finally by political scientists, since power is created in the town.[9] The substantial arrival of African politics on the international scene, from the massacres in Rwanda to Mandela's assumption of power, has lent impetus to this research. It is interesting to note that in just the last five years, university history departments in Paris and elsewhere in France—which up until then had devoted almost all their efforts to European history—have recruited a good dozen professors or research specialists of African history. This is a new and promising development that represents a decision to no longer make ghettos of scholarly fields.

Francophone Africans

One sign is quite revealing: Francophone African researchers are never anthropologists, except those who do fieldwork in France. Even this is still too rare. Fifteen years ago a positive experiment took place, one that was unfortunately little noted because of its lack of financial support: three African researchers were "dropped" into different rural or urban areas in France. The most successful experiment among these involved an observer of a small village of the southwest where the people had almost never encountered blacks. Similar encounters occur in an informal way when, through links established between French villages and African villages or quarters, nongovernmental organizations allow the partners to discover their similarities. Yet these experiments remain largely independent of the university circles.

French-speaking African social scientists have evolved quite differently from their English-speaking counterparts. The fact is that the two countries' relationships with the urban African milieu followed different chronologies. Following World War II, the French provided less instruction in their colonies than did the British in West Africa, where Nigerian and Ghanaian researchers, in particular, had become rather numerous. The major difference is that France encouraged the creation of African universities in only a limited way: the only university founded prior to its country's independence was that in Dakar—and then only toward the middle of the 1950s. Young African university students all graduated from French universities until a late date.

Curiously, ideological relations between Francophone intellectuals of European or African origin appear to have developed quite differently from those between Anglophone intellectuals. On the English-speaking side, the intellectual divorce was never significant, because everyone, the English as well as the Africans, had been trained at home yet within the same university ambiance, whether it was in London or Birmingham or in Ibadan, Dar es Salaam, or Kampala. As in the United States, only today is the demand for emancipation making itself heard clearly in these regions. On the French side, the break was almost radical at the beginning. Before the 1970s only a handful of African researchers could, strictly speaking, be found on the university map. Only a minority of the first generations, still colonized or scarcely decolonized, reproduced the Francophone assimilationist model; most opposed it violently. Academicians or not, their reaction was, as was normal, brutal. These young nationalist activists fervently wished to construct a national history separate from their French heritage. A recently published study dealing with *Présence africaine* (Mudimbe 1992) shows how much the often innovative articles published in this journal were—even in Paris, where it was and still is published—seen as marginal or irrelevant by French Africanist academicians, who with few exceptions did not participate in the journal or read it.

The major works by the first generation of Francophone African scholars were exceptional and sometimes controversial (e.g., Cheikh Anta Diop [*Nations nègres et culture,* 1955], whose role is discussed by Elliott Skinner in chapter 3 of this volume; Ki-Zerbo, who in 1972 published the first history of Africa written by a French-speaking academician). The young intellectuals of that time, activist and committed yet very few in number, were especially concerned with nation building. Their efforts were carried forward with a lot of goodwill if sometimes a bit demagogically.[10]

A second, still small generation devoted itself essentially to the useful restoration of unknown or overshadowed regional monographs that focused especially on precolonial history (see Loucou 1984; Cissoko 1986; Bathily 1989) or to the necessary rehabilitation of opposition to colonization (see, among others, Metegue N'nah 1981; Nzabakomada 1986). These efforts were, however, a little like a historical restoration done backward, as Tsehloane Keto points out in chapter 8 of this volume. Nevertheless, some opened the way to new themes and subjects, such as that of the town, including its marginal elements (see Kipré 1985; Bah 1985; Semi-Bi 1979; Mworoha 1977).

These intellectual encounters have developed only during the past decade. They date from the time when independent universities were created; when the instructional personnel became almost all nationals, even though they were trained in France; and especially when graduate-level studies became permanently established at the African institutions. Indeed, Africans were trained in Western knowledge. Yet this stage is being overtaken today by the new generations of those who, because they have been born in the independent states, have not known the cultural heartbreaks of their elders. This new generation sometimes accuses its elders of having become bogged down in the propitious neoprimitivism of their French Africanist friends (Kabou 1989:102). Today the "Senegalese school" (e.g., Boubacar Barry, Abdoulaye Bathily, Mamadou Diouf, Ibnou Diagne, Mamadou Fall, Mohamed Mbodj, Ibrahima Thioub; see the theses published by Harmattan or Karthala) is expanding rapidly. Its members are now part of a pan-African social science network, CODESRIA, based in Dakar. It is striking that two major scholars of this school, Mamadou Diouf and Achille Mbembé, were trained in France. They clearly aim to promote and develop an independent, autochthonous history of Africa. The creative contributions of Cheikh Anta Diop have been assimilated, while the excesses have been eliminated (although they have come back among the younger generation under the influence of Diop's rediscovery by African Americans). Others are now following this lead, especially in Madagascar (e.g., Faranina Esoavelomandroso and Lucile Rabearimana, who recently completed their "French-style theses" [*thèses d'État*]).

There are still too many in France who refuse to recognize that Africa has solid intellectuals whose revisionist approach is new and original. The works of French-speaking Africans, however, permit us not only to analyze the developments but also to chart the contradictions of preexisting societies and nationalist movements. These works allow us to understand the disillusionment that followed independence and to unearth strategies of resistance and collaboration and the weakest point in the power-holding elites' neutralization of the masses. Unfortunately, the lack of resources and of African publishing houses means that most of their work is not widely published or, in the case of the young, not published at all.

The View from the Other Side

A new school and vision may still be quite difficult to define, but the use of a cross-cultural perspective (*le regard croisé*)[11] is clearly evident. The construction of global comprehension systems, on which anthropologists not long ago set their sights, now appears to be a task assumed by African philosophers. The French-language philosophical school is particularly rich: let me mention, among others, Paulin Hountondji of Benin (1997), Harris-Memel Fote of the Ivory Coast, Béchir Souleïmane Diagne of Senegal, and Valentin Mudimbe of Congo, even though the latter is now based in the United States. Their insider perspective is particularly enriching to the outward gaze of the anthropologists who formerly spoke in their name.

In several countries (as in Senegal), African intellectuals publish and speak without fear. In others they face exile, for the free individual who intends to stay free is forced to wander. These new individuals, these "African intellectuals" (see the special issue of *Politique africaine* [1993] with that title), do not know the taboos and fears of those who preceded them. No longer having any immediate political ambitions, they affirm, like others, their freedom of decision and speech:

> Notwithstanding, I had never imagined that one day I would go away. . . . It is this night of the postcolonial African world that stirs me and shakes what is a provisional place of "identity" for me. . . . This is what reminds me constantly that what is real in Africa is complicated, and that we must reflect on this complexity. . . . I do not know whether what one calls an "African intellectual" in these closing years of the century is one whose job it is to listen to and decipher this "singing coming forth from the shadows" and its masks, to "read" it and to "write" it. I do not know what an "intellectual" is. Letting myself be stirred by the night of the postcolonial African world, I am not certain that I wish to become the mirror in which people look at themselves. . . . I don't care about any of that since, in any case, I have never been anything but a "vagabond." In the meanwhile, let them leave me alone and stop asking me to be everything, indeed all things, except myself. . . . (Mbembé 1993:74, 97)

The cross-cultural view between Africans and foreigners clearly implies that African researchers are starting from their own vision, which is today more national than continental: the vision of an African is necessarily "Afrocentric" in the sense that each departs from the point of view that is his or her own—whether this vision comes from Africa, the United States, or Europe. This involves not a mythical "Africanness" but rather a perspective that is political and cultural, based on research carried out in centers set up and controlled by continental authorities. The construction of a knowledge divorced from the constraints and imperatives imposed by Western institutions has begun; it is also, and perhaps especially, dependent on autonomy in the matter of the direction and financial support for research, that is, on a national scientific policy. It is therefore above all a political problem, and it is this problem that present-day democratization, founded on still difficult and groping procedures enacted by internal political and social forces, is attempting to address effectively. The "Francophone" translation of this situation has been the vigorous thrust of the "popular national conventions" against the existing autocratic regimes supported by France, among others.

In the final analysis, what is needed today are capable specialists of every kind who know their territories and know not to impose on one geographical location what they have learned elsewhere. This is a rare kind of research, it is true, but one that puts little faith into the former kind of anthropology, whose assumed focus was encyclopedic. What is needed is rather good sense and knowledge deprived of ethnocentrism, which today is indeed Eurocentric. Nonetheless, we must ask whether it would be healthier to replace it by another, even if it were radically Afrocentric. Is this possible? Is this reasonable? Still, I agree with Anthony Appiah or Valentin Mudimbe (1994) that this change is necessary.

The fact is that beyond these proximities and exchanges, there is a greater need than ever in all areas for interdisciplinary and intercultural teams, with each person doing his or her part in the common field, matched to a permanent process of comparison suitable to global processes. This is why in France one can no longer, except in an old-fashioned way, conceive of the possibility of research in African social sciences without the preliminary and joint implementation of Franco-African teams.

Such teams do not seem, at least for the present, to be subject in France to black/white oppositions. This is not to say that such oppositions do not exist or that a demand for history viewed from the inside (Afro-centered) has not been expressed. Without a doubt this state of affairs is due to the nature of racism in France, which is expressed differently than it is in Britain or the United States: in the former, racism is based much more on cultural and social issues than simply on color. The anecdote told by Elliott Skinner at the conference from which this volume stems is typical in this respect: in Paris, people will mistake a black intellectual for a cab driver because, socially, most unskilled workers are immigrants and often immigrants of color. Once the social misunderstanding has been cleared up, however, the color is forgotten (at least by the white, naturally).

Another fact comes into play: unlike people in the English-speaking world and especially America—which was profoundly marked by slavery and segregation—the French do not devalue interbreeding. In contrast to its English equivalent (*halfbreed*), the word *métis* has no pejorative connotation and can even be culturally positive. This is why Keto's proposed division of knowledge into three distinct points of view—Africa-centered, Asia-centered, and Europe-centered—which indeed played an effective, combative role in the time of Cheikh Anta Diop, now appears demeaning to many Francophone Africans, for such an analysis thumbs its nose at the history of this accumulated heritage. As Anthony Appiah states, Africans, and not only African intellectuals, will from now on be increasingly involved in one way or another in the world-system; they have become, like all the inhabitants of the world, *cultural métis*. The Francophone Africans of today (such as the historian Mamadou Diouf, scientific officer of CODESRIA) do not consider this state of affairs— or rather no longer consider it—to be a simple amputation, as is the pan-African heritage transmitted to the African Americans, which Elliott Skinner discusses in chapter 3. Most Francophone Africans have decided for the future to view these multiple viewpoints as a complementary richness, for this triple heritage gave rise to a new African syncretic culture. From this perspective ancient Africa is one root among others, an essential one indeed, but one that has been transformed by history. This evokes fully the Francophone perception of *métissage* as an advantage and not a defect. This also explains why there is no debate over "multiculturalism" in France. French Africanist scholars and antiracist intellectuals plead for "interculturalism," which is a quite different endeavor. The purpose behind interculturalism is not to look equally at all minorities but to promote reciprocal, cross-cultural exchanges rather than homogenization and its attendant assimilationist excesses. This was splendidly symbolized by the popular Francophone enthusiasm provoked by the "métis" victory of the French soccer team in the 1998 World Cup.

As for racism in France, it exists especially against North Africans and Jews, that is, against the whites, against a culture brutally assimilated into a religion. It is still expressed in France with a disturbing harshness: this viewpoint, held especially by Le Pen's nationalist party, is capable of securing 15 percent or more of the votes in French elections. Curiously, however, in the previous period, toward the end of the 1960s and in the 1970s, African and West Indian students, especially in the local universities, began to develop a xenophobic antiwhite movement. This moment coincided with a precise political struggle: the attempts to transform the content of the agreements of cooperation established with the home country at the moment of independence, still frankly tainted with paternalistic neocolonialism. This was the period, too, when the open expression of antiblack racism by the last colonists became impossible. Since then in France, in the case of the young, students or not, the political movement "SOS-Racisme" has had a real impact. In spite of a resurgent racism today, the motto "Don't touch my buddy" ("Touche pas à mon pote"), whatever his or her national origin or skin color, has had a truly consolidating effect in the wake of the struggle for an interracial culture, called "*beur*," a struggle led by young people of North African origin. The recent growth in the threat posed by Le Pen may, one hopes, provoke a militant reaction against racist temptations.

Likewise, the oppositions or divergences in the area of African studies in France take on aspects that are more political than racial. I believe that this aspect, which is rather difficult to understand from British or American points of view, is positive, for it allows one to approach problems in an activist rather than an emotional fashion.

Notes

This text was translated from the French by Ed Montgomery of Interlink Translations. An earlier and different version of this essay was published in French as "L'Anthroplogie ou la mort du phénix?" *Le Débat* 90 (1996): 114–28.

1. Littré was born in 1801, and his dictionary was completed in the 1860s.

2. Volume 3 of the *Histoire des colonies françaises,* devoted to Morocco and Tunisia, was written by Georges Hardy in 1830.

3. *La Géologie et les mines de la France d'Outre-Mer,* Conference of the Office of Colonial Geological and Mining Studies (1932), comprises 664 pages.

4. They maintained this blindness in spite of the early warning by Marc Bloch, for whom everything was a source: "The diversity of historical evidence is almost infinite. All that man says or writes, all that he creates, all that he touches can or must tell something about him" (1949:27; written in 1941–42).

5. This term was coined by Hubert Deschamps, a former administrator who came to history after a rather long overseas career and who, in 1963, became the recipient of the first chair in African history at the Sorbonne.

6. Among the best studies of this type were those by Georges Dupré (1982, 1985), which focused on the Nzabi and Beembe, two Congolese groups not exceeding several thousand individuals. The first group was practically destroyed by the colonial impact, whereas the second more or less succeeded in integrating itself into the colonial economy.

7. Geographic monographs addressing certain historical periods are a French specialty that sprang up at the beginning of the 1950s, particularly in innumerable monographs concerning towns and urban quarters published in the *Cahiers d'Outre-Mer*. One of the first theses published was by Guy Lasserre (1958).

8. See Isabelle Deblé (demographer) and Philippe Hugon (economist) (1982).

9. Notice how well the journal *Politique africaine* has succeeded, since 1981, in the area of "the invention of a political culture," to use the phrase of Jean-François Martin (1988).

10. See, among others, the critical reviews of J. A. Mbembé and of Mamadou Diouf in the *Revue de la Bibliothèque Nationale* 34 (1989) on the rereading of the colonial past through the prism of the nation-state.

11. *Le regard croisé* has no precise English translation. The author's use of this term in the heading for this section was therefore problematic. "The View from the Other Side" was devised by the editors (with thanks to Immanuel Wallerstein for assistance).

References Cited

Amin, Samir. 1974. *Accumulation on a World Scale: A Critique of the Theory of Underdevelopment.* New York: Monthly Review. (Originally published in French in 1971.)

Amselle, Jean Loup. 1990. *Logiques métisses: anthropologie de l'identité en Afrique et ailleurs.* Paris: Payot.

Amselle, Jean Loup, and Elikia Mbokolo, eds. 1985. *Au coeur de l'ethnie: ethnies, tribalisme, et état en Afrique.* Paris: Maspero.

Anderson, Benedict. 1983. *Imagined Communities: Reflections on the Origins and Spread of Nationalism*. London: Verso.

Bah, Thierno. 1985. *Architecture militaire traditionnelle et poliorcétique dans le Soudan occidental du XVIIe siècle*. Yaoundé: Clef/ACCT.

Barry, Boubacar. 1972. *Le Royaume du Waalo*. Paris: Maspero. Repr., Karthala, 1988.

————. 1989: *Histoire de la Sénégambie*. Paris: L'Harmattan.

Bathily, Abdoulaye. 1989. *Les Portes de l'or: le royaume de Galam (Sénégal) VII-XVIIIe siècles*. Paris: L'Harmattan.

Bloch, Marc. 1949. *Apologie pour l'histoire ou Métier d'historien*. Paris: Colin. (English-language edition, *The Historian's Craft* [New York: Knopf, 1953].)

Bruckner, Pascal. 1986 (French ed., 1983). *The Tears of the White Man: Compassion as Contempt*. New York: Free Press.

Chrétien, Jean-Pierre, and Gérard Prunier, eds. 1989. *Les Ethnies ont une histoire*. Paris: Karthala-ACCT.

Cissoko, Sekene Mody. 1986. *Contribution à l'histoire politique du Khasso dans le Haut-Sénégal, des origines à 1854*. Paris: ACCT/Harmattan.

Cooper, Frederick. 1987. *On the African Waterfront. Urban Disorders an the Transformation of Work in Colonial Mombasa*. New Haven: Yale University Press.

Cooper, Frederick, ed. 1983. *Struggle for the City: Migrant Labor, Capital, and the State in Urban Africa*. London: Sage.

Copans, Jean. 1990. *La Longue Marche de la modernité africaine: savoirs, intellectuels, démocratie*. Paris: Karthala.

Coquery-Vidrovitch, Catherine. 1988. *Africa South of the Sahara: Endurance and Change*. Bekeley: University of California Press.

————. 1991. "Colonial History and Decolonization: The French Imperial Case." *The European Journal of Development Research* 3, no. 2:28–43. (Special issue, "Old and New Trends in Francophone Development Research.")

Deblé, Isabelle, and Phillippe Hugon. 1982. *Vivre et survivre dans les villes africaines*. Paris: PUF.

Dupré, Georges. 1982. *Un Ordre et sa destruction*. Paris: ORSTOM.

————. 1985. *Les Naissances d'une société espace et historicité chez les Beembe du Congo*. Paris: ORSTOM.

Guichaoua, André, and Yves Goussault. 1993. *Sciences sociales et développement*. Paris: Colin.

Hegel, G. W. F. 1944. *The Philosophy of History*. New York: Wiley.

Hobsbawn, Eric, and Terence Ranger, eds. 1983. *The Invention of Tradition*. Cambridge: Cambridge University Press.

Hountondji, Paulin. 1997. *Combats pour le sens: un itinéraire africain*. Cotonou: Les éditions du Flamboyant.

Intellectuels africains. 1993. Special issue of *Politique africaine*, no. 51 (Oct.).

Jaulin, Robert. 1974. *La Décivilisation: politique et pratique de l'ethonocide*. Brussels: Complexes.

Kabou, Axel. 1989. *Et si l'Afrique refusait le développement?* Paris: L'Harmattan.

Kipré, Pierre. 1985. *Histoire des villes en Côte d'Ivoire, 1896–1940*. 2 vols. Abidjan: Nouvelles Éditions Africaines.

Ki-Zerbo, Joseph, 1972. *Histoire de l'Afrique*. Paris: Hatier.

Lakroum, Monique. 1992. "De l'histoire coloniale à l'histoire africaine, 1912–60." In

L'Afrique occidentale au temps des Français: colonisateurs et colonisés c. 1860–1960, ed. C. Coquery-Vidrovitch and Odile Goerg, 36–47. Paris: Découverte.

Lasserre, Guy. 1958. *Libreville, la ville et la région.* Paris: Colin.

Latouche, Serge. 1986. *Faut-il refuser le développement?* Paris: PUF.

Loucou, Jean-Noël. 1984. *Histoire de la Côte d'Ivoire.* Vol. 1: *La Formation des peuples.* Abidjan: CEDA.

Martin, Jean-François. 1988. *Tanzanie: l'invention d'une culture politique.* Paris: Karthala.

Mbembé, Achille, 1993. "Écrire l'Afrique à partir d'une faille." *Politique africaine,* no. 51:69–97.

Meillassoux, Claude. 1981. *Maidens, Meal, and Money: Capitalism and the Domestic Community.* Cambridge: Cambridge University Press.

Mercier, Paul. 1984. *Histoire de l'anthropologie.* Paris: PUF.

Metegue N'Nah, Nicolas. 1981. *Domination coloniale au Gabon: la résistance d'un peuple (1839–1960).* Paris: L'Harmattan.

Mudimbe, V. Y. 1988. *The Invention of Africa.* Bloomington: Indiana University Press.

———. 1994. *Les Corps glorieux des mots et des êtres: esquisse d'un jardin africain à la bénédictine.* Montréal: Humanitas.

Mudimbe, Valentin, ed. 1992. *The Surreptitious Speech: "Présence africaine" and the Politics of Otherness, 1947–1987.* Chicago: University of Chicago Press.

Mworoha, Emile. 1977. *Peuples et rois de l'Afrique des Grandes Lacs.* Dakar-Abidjan: Nouvelles Éditions Africaines.

Nzabakomada, Raphaël. 1986. *L'Afrique centrale insurgée: la guerre du Kongo-Wara, 1928–1931.* Paris: L'Harmattan.

Semi-Bi, Zan. 1979. *La Politique française des travaux publics en Côte d'Ivoire.* Abidjan: Mémoires de l'Université d'Abidjan.

Suret-Canale, Jean. 1958, 1964, and 1972. *L'Afrique noire (occidentale et centrale).* 3 vols. (vol. 1., *Géographie civilisations, histoire;* vol. 2, *L'Ère coloniale, 1900–1940;* vol. 3, *De la colonisation aux indépendances).* Paris: Éditions Sociales. (English-language trans. of vol 1., *French Colonialism in Tropical Africa, 1900–1945.* London: Heineman, 1971.)

Zimmerman, Francis. 1993. *Enquête sur la parenté.* Paris: PUF.

2   The Emergence and Evolution of African Studies in the United Kingdom

Christopher Fyfe

African studies emerged in the United Kingdom as an adjunct of the British Empire and has evolved in step with the successive changes in British overseas involvement.

In days of empire, African studies meant studies that might be of use to those who were going to Africa in government service or as missionaries. The School of Oriental and African Studies (SOAS) of the University of London, founded in 1916, received government funding for this purpose. In its early years the main emphasis was on the study of African languages. Around language study grew up the more widely conceived Department of Africa, whose research findings—particularly in the study of anthropology, which in those days was dominated by the investigative functionalist tradition—were intended to be of use to colonial administrators (Philips 1967:1–4).

This is well illustrated in Lord Hailey's monumental *African Survey* (1938), with chapter 24 entitled "The Future of African Studies." Hailey saw African studies primarily as a means of providing useful information for administrators—for instance, investigating African legal concepts and land rights in order to adapt them to the official legal systems, examining the effect of what he called "native habit" on problems of nutrition and disease, estimating the social effects of labor migration, or discovering whether solar radiation affects European adaptability to the tropics. The task of African studies, as he saw it, was to conduct research that would assist and improve the government of the African territories. He did not see it as any kind of academic discipline.

There were also nongovernmental bodies concerned with the study of Africa. The African Society, founded in 1901 in memory of Mary Kingsley and renamed the Royal African Society in 1935, published a journal (renamed

African Affairs in 1945) that included scholarly contributions but was intended for a general rather than an academic readership. The academically oriented International Institute of African Languages and Culture, however, founded in 1928 (and in 1945 renamed the International African Institute), along with its journal *Africa,* specifically aimed to co-ordinate the work of international scholars doing African research and to relate their findings to the needs of those who were working in Africa (Lugard 1928:2).

These two organizations and their journals were intended for those very few people in Britain who took any interest in Africa. In the days of empire most British people were unconcerned with Africa and took not the slightest interest in it. Africa was rarely mentioned in the British press.

Then, in the 1950s, decolonization began, and there was a sudden and quite new public interest in Africa. Africa was in the news, as it had never been before. Suddenly it began to be realized in Britain that Africans were people (not just remote "tribes")—moreover, people with ideas, histories, and economic aspirations of their own. Africans were now appearing on the world stage, and it was important to find out what they were likely to do there.

This could be done only by systematic study of Africa, hence the emergence of African studies as a branch of academic inquiry. Substantial government funds were made available to enlarge SOAS and to start up centers of African studies in the Universities of Birmingham and Edinburgh (Great Britain 1961). African studies quickly attracted interest. British teachers and students were excited by the new dynamic forces being generated in Africa and wanted to study them. Many were in any event becoming bored by the old Eurocentric boundaries of their disciplines and wanted something more stimulating. African studies thus became fashionable.

It would be wrong, however, to see the emergence of African studies in the United Kingdom as a purely academic enterprise that arose in the universities through the imaginative efforts of professional university teachers, although there are those who have presented it in this way (Fage 1989; Kirk-Greene 1995). There was also stimulus from outside academia. The late Thomas Hodgkin (one of the inspiring pioneers in the African field and not in his earlier career an academic) once recalled what *he* saw as the start of serious African studies in Britain: a 1950 gathering of publicists and political figures of the left, African as well as British and none of them professional teachers, who were anxious to study and publicize the new developments in Africa (Fyfe 1976:6). One of them was Basil Davidson, by profession a journalist, whose subsequent writings have done more than anyone else's to present the history of Africa to the world.

In the new African studies programs in the British universities, the teachers and the majority of students were British. African students (chiefly graduate students) came from Africa to study there but then returned to teach in the new universities being rapidly founded throughout British Africa. Indeed, part of the role of British African studies was to service these new African universities with teachers and expertise. British academics and "experts" (it was the great age of the "expert," a class of person somewhat discredited today) were encouraged by attractive salaries and conditions of service to take jobs in Africa. At least fifteen academics returned from teaching in African universities to hold professorial chairs in Britain (Fage 1989:406). Graduate students, too, hurried to Africa to do fieldwork and returned to jobs in the new centers and other academic institutions.

Thus in Britain, as in the United States, money suddenly poured into African studies in the early 1960s. But the two countries differed greatly in their motivations for this funding. In the United States, as William Martin and Michael West show in chapter 4 of this volume, the goal was primarily to prevent an unknown "Dark Continent" from falling into the clutches of the Soviet Union. In Britain, by contrast, it was to ease the transition from empire to independence.

As a discipline, African studies in Britain emerged with a bias toward history. It first came into the limelight with three conferences (1953, 1957, 1961) organized at SOAS by a historian, Roland Oliver, in which the contributions, though covering diverse fields including agriculture, linguistics, and serology, were linked through a historical focus. Moreover, the proceedings of the 1961 conference appeared in the newly launched *Journal of African History* (3, no. 2 [1962]). In addition, when the African Studies Association of the United Kingdom (ASAUK) was founded in 1964, a high proportion of the members were historians (Fage 1989:409).

Over the succeeding decades, starting at a time when Hegel's assertion that Africa had no history was generally believed, British historians published a mass of original work that I would be invidious to exemplify. Their productions include the eight-volume *Cambridge History of Africa,* and most of them worked in the British empirical tradition; we have tended to leave theory to our French colleagues. British Africanist historians began with political and economic narrative, the necessary groundwork in a new field, and then branched out into studies of the family, food production, poverty, disease, gender, and so on.

At this period many younger British archaeologists were seeking to escape from the narrow traditions of classical archaeology, and Africa opened many untouched fields. Peter Shinnie and Merrick Posnansky inaugurated archaeological work at the University of Ghana; Thurstan Shaw, drawing on work already begun in Nigeria, did the same at the University of Ibadan. All of them combined their own research with the training of African archaeologists. Here, too, there was fruitful collaboration with historians, of a kind that the old-school archaeologists and historians of Europe had always shunned. In

East Africa, moreover, archaeologists working in the British Institute in Eastern Africa, notably Mark Horton in recent years, have helped to transform the historiography of the East African coast.

Africanist anthropologists, freed by Evans-Pritchard from the antihistorical narrowness of functionalism, were also ready to draw on historians' findings and give their work a historical focus, while historians gladly drew on the work of anthropologists. The leading British Africanist journals—the old, established *Africa* and *African Affairs* and the newer *Journal of African History, Journal of Modern African Studies* (founded and edited for over thirty years by David Kimble, an astonishing feat), *Journal of Southern African Studies,* and the librarians' *African Research and Documentation*—all have a historical slant. The study of African literature in Britain also was given a historical dimension by one of its pioneers, the late Paul Edwards, with his editions of the works of eighteenth-century African writers, notably Olaudah Equiano.[1]

The leading part played by historians in the development of African studies in Britain contrasts strikingly with developments in France. There, as Catherine Coquery-Vidrovitch rather ruefully demonstrates in this volume, it was the anthropologists who ruled the roost.

The introduction of African studies (also Asian and other area studies) in Britain was part of the great educational expansion of the 1960s, an era of optimism and apparently irreversible economic growth, when money was lavished on British universities. Many of the new universities founded during that period—notably York, Kent, Warwick, Sussex, and Stirling—had African studies programs, and some of the older universities—including Cambridge, Manchester, Liverpool, and Leeds—added them. In the 1970s, however, as the economic climate changed, the money for expansion began to dry up. Meanwhile, the wave of enthusiasm that had greeted the first years of decolonized Africa was being replaced by the growing "Afro-pessimism" that has now become familiar.

Hence in Britain, as in the United States, investment in African studies began to decline. Government funding was reduced, and African studies had to retrench. Funds for travel, a lifeline for Africanists, were cut, and jobs became scarce. In a new discipline where most of the teachers were still in the prime of life, this trend meant that there were few opportunities for promotion. Graduate students were deterred from embarking on African research for fear of finding themselves unemployable. At the same time conditions of employment in the new African universities became less attractive as the African economies began to decline—nor, obviously, was there the same demand for British teachers in Africa as more and more Africans became qualified for university posts. Inevitably, therefore, African studies lost the appeal it had enjoyed when it was a great growth subject in the 1960s.

Africanists began to move instead into the newly fashionable disciplines of "development studies" or "Third World studies."

This change was reflected at a conference organized in Edinburgh in 1974 on the theme of "African studies since 1945," a retrospective survey of the way that African studies had emerged during the era of decolonization—how it had developed, as Professor Lalage Bown put it, "from a cottage industry to a multi-national enterprise" (Fyfe 1976). The phrase "state of crisis" was regularly repeated by the participants. Many of the papers spelled out that the confident paradigms of the early days were no longer usable: the historians' uncritical assumption that they were somehow going to reveal the existence of a glorious African golden age of the past; the political scientists' teleological fantasies of "nation building"; the economists' weak "dependency theory"; and theories that upheld the African educational systems, installed at great expense, which had become objects of widespread disenchantment. There were even hints of the coming crises that social anthropologists seem to have been enjoying in recent years.

By the 1970s it was becoming clear that the era of British decolonization was being followed by an era of British disinvolvement. Whereas the successive governments in France (and particularly the successive presidents of France) preserved close ties with their former African dependencies, British governments lost interest. Africa faded out of the news in Britain. Only military coups and famines were reported. Aid money declined.

Then came the devastating Thatcher years, which were devastating for African studies in two ways. First was Thatcher's own unconcealed lack of interest in black Africa and her avowed preference for the white regime in what was then Rhodesia (until she had to accept Lord Carrington's Zimbabwe settlement) and for the white apartheid regime in South Africa (a preference perhaps not unconnected with her husband's substantial investments there). Her vendetta against the concept of the Commonwealth also tied in with disinvolvement from Africa. While she was in charge, African studies had little hope of government sympathy.

Second, and far more important, was Thatcher's onslaught on the autonomy of the British universities and her determination to bring them under direct government control and to run them on bureaucratic and accountancy principles of cost-effectiveness, imposing, to quote Tony Hopkins, the government's own "legitimating ideology" of insularity, chauvinism, and philistinism (Hopkins 1987:94). The British universities will never recover from the irreversible damage she inflicted on them, which, as is well known, drove many leading British scholars to a more humane atmosphere on campuses in the United States. African studies was an obvious victim. Who in the new disinvolved Britain cared for Africa?

This decline became dramatically clear at SOAS, where total staff numbers fell from 234 in 1970 to 166 in 1984 (Dalby 1984b:2). In the Department of African Languages and Culture they fell from a peak of thirty-three to nine during those years (Dalby 1984a:1).[2] The African studies centers at the Universities of Edinburgh and Birmingham faced closure. In an atmosphere where all British academics suddenly woke to find their own precious departments and institutions under threat and in need of justification simply to continue, it was a world of dog eat dog. Who in the universities was going to stand up for African studies if their own interests were equally under threat ?

As it happened, moreover, during the 1980s the only two holders of chairs specifically designated for African history, Roland Oliver in London and John Fage in Birmingham, retired. Neither was replaced. Similarly, when John Hargreaves retired from Aberdeen, and Paul Hair from Liverpool, neither was replaced by a historian of Africa. Denied promotion, some scholars moved to the United States or to South Africa, today the dynamic location for African history. In addition, some of the South African exiles who had made an important contribution to the development of African studies in Britain returned home. No British historian was available to fill editorial vacancies on the *Journal of African History,* so in 1990 two American editors were appointed, leaving only two British ones. With no new posts for Africanists, it looked as if African studies would die away as the present Africanists retired. One historian lamented at a conference that when his children grew up and were old enough to go to university, there would be no one left to teach them African history.

When Thatcher was ousted, there was some small improvement, although her successor's government was basically (if I may use the word) as disinvolved from Africa as was hers. When I retired from the University of Edinburgh in 1991, government money was available to provide a successor. New posts have been created at SOAS and elsewhere. The universities have now settled down under the changed regime, and the African studies centers are no longer under any immediate threat, although their survival depends on their being able to fight for scarce resources and to raise outside funding. The present Labour government, although better willed toward Africa, shows no sign of providing more funds for studying it. At the end of the day, however, African studies has survived, battered but still alive and well. Students are still attracted, although they tend to be undergraduates, not graduate students who might supply teachers for the future.[3]

Meanwhile a new constituency of students is being attracted to African studies, the black British. The children of those who migrated from the Caribbean in the 1950s and 1960s in search of manual employment or of those in the new African diaspora who have made their homes in Britain are now entering the universities. White British teachers are now liable to be confronted, as white Africanists in the United States have long been confronted, by black students who question their right to teach the history of Africa.

Three conferences on black British history have been held in London (1981 [see Gundara and Duffield 1992], 1985, and 1991) where black participants voiced their uneasiness—indeed, in some cases angry resentment—at what they saw as an unjustifiably predominant white academic presence from which they felt excluded. In reaction, the Association for the Study of African, Caribbean, and Asian Culture and History in Britain (ASACACHIB) was started in 1991, attached to the Institute of Commonwealth Studies of the University of London.

Outside the universities, too, black heritage groups have started up in recent years, inspired by the Afrocentrist doctrine expounded by such African American teachers as Molefi Kete Asante (Howe 1998). In some British cities locally based groups celebrate a "Black History Month" akin to the old African American model. The antagonisms long played out in North America between African studies and black studies are now beginning to be enacted in Britain.

In Britain, however, the population of African descent is small compared with that of the United States (it is outnumbered by those of Asian descent). Nor has the black British population the political leverage that the African American community can exert on U.S. universities. Afrocentrist black studies are thus likely to remain well outside the African studies curriculum.

Notes

1. Paul Edwards was commemorated at the conference entitled "Africans and Caribbeans in Britain: Writing, History, and Society" and held in his memory on March 21–23, 1994, at the Centre of African Studies, University of Edinburgh.

2. For details in the African history field, see McCracken 1993:242–43.

3. For a general survey, given as the Presidential Address at the African Studies Association of the United Kingdom (ASAUK), Annual General Meeting, Sept. 10, 1992, see McCracken 1993.

References Cited

Dalby, David. 1984a. "The Study of African Languages in the United Kingdom: Part II." *African Research and Documentation* 34:1–10.
———. 1984b. "The Study of African Languages in the United Kingdom: Part III, and Proposals for a London School of Languages and Literatures." *African Research and Documentation* 35:1–11.
Fage, J. D. 1989. "British African Studies since the Second World War: A Personal Account." *African Affairs* 88, no. 352:397–413.
Fyfe, Christopher, ed. 1976. *African Studies since 1945: A Tribute to Basil Davidson.* London: Longman.
Great Britain, University Grants Committee. 1961. *Report of the Sub-Committee on Oriental, Slavonic, East European, and African Studies.* London: HMSO. (Hayter Report.)
Gundara, Jagdish S., and Ian Duffield, eds. 1992. *Essays on the History of Blacks in Britain: From Roman Times to the Mid-Twentieth Century.* Aldershot: Avebury.
Hailey, Lord, William Malcolm. 1938. *An African Survey: A Study of Problems Arising in Africa South of the Sahara.* London: Oxford University Press.

Hopkins, A. G. 1987. "From Hayter to Parker: African History at Birmingham University, 1964–86." *African Affairs* 86, no. 342:93–102.

Howe, Stephen. 1998. *Afrocentrism: Mythical Pasts and Imagined Futures.* London: Verso.

Kirk-Greene, A. H. M., ed. 1995. *The Emergence of African History at British Universities.* Oxford: Worldview.

Lugard, Sir F. D. 1928. "The International Institute of African Languages and Cultures." *Africa* 1, no. 1:1–12.

McCracken, John. 1993. "African History in British Universities: Past, Present, and Future." *African Affairs* 92, no. 367:239–353.

Philips, C. H. 1967. *The School of Oriental and African Studies, University of London, 1917–1967: An Introduction.* London: University School of Oriental and African Studies.

3   The African Presence:
In Defense of Africanity

Elliott P. Skinner

African peoples have yet to recover from the consequences of that bloody encounter in 1441, when Nuño Tristao and Antam Gonçalvez attacked the local people around Mauritania in the name of "Portugal" and "Santiago," taking a number of them to Lisbon as captives (Beazley and Prestage 1896:39). Over the next five and a half centuries much—and for a long period, most— of the African continent was hostage to foreigners, while the descendants of African captives in the diasporas were denigrated. With the election of Nelson Mandela as president of South Africa in 1994, Africa may now be said to have achieved independence politically, if not economically and culturally. Meanwhile, Africans in the diasporas are battling to overcome centuries of oppression based on alleged biological and cultural inferiority. The struggle for the complete emancipation of Africa and African peoples must thus continue. Until people of African origin are viewed as equal in capacity to other *Homo sapiens,* both individually and collectively, and until the interrelated culture complex that arose on the African continent is respected, African peoples will be unable to contribute to the emerging global civilization.

Scholars of African origin have not failed to notice that the major Western paradigms invented to understand humankind—whether the earlier biblical, evolutionary, diffusionist ones or more recent ones such as structural-functionalism, structuralism, structural Marxism, hermeneutics, and even postmodernism—have invariably denigrated Africa, its peoples, and their cultures. Repeatedly stung by these assaults, African peoples have attempted to defend themselves by resorting to "Afrocentrism," a kind of "symbolic estate" by which their intellectuals, often using biophysiological or cultural features, challenged global Europe by developing competing ideas in the battle for equality. Unfortunately, however, this has forced African peoples into a reactive mode, thereby frustrating the use of their own cultural background—that is, "Africanity"—as a source of tradition or as a means of developing original ideas about the world, its peoples, and their cultures. The time has now come to change this situation and to enlist Africanity to help much of the still-dependent world defend itself in what has been seen as an almost inevitable future cultural war (Huntington 1996:28).

As portrayed through various texts and discourses, many members of the early generations of Africans who were sent away to Europe for education, or were taken as captives to the New World, accepted the existential superiority of the West. For example, Philip Quaque, from Cape Coast, Ghana, who in 1754 was sent to England to be trained as an Anglican priest (he returned home, with an English wife, to serve as official chaplin at Cape Coast Castle), wrote back to England that the customs of his people were "detestable," "barbarous and inhuman," and generally unbelievable (in Curtin 1967:129). Likewise, in 1773 Phillis Wheatley, who became a slave in British North America, wrote the following lines in the poem "On Being Brought from Africa to America":

> 'Twas mercy brought me from my Pagan land,
> Taught my benighted soul to understand
> That there's a God, and there's a Saviour too:
> Once I redemption neither sought nor knew.
> Some view our sable race with scornful eye,
> "Their colour is a diabolic die."
> Remember, Christians, Negroes, black as Cain,
> May be refin'd, and join th' angelic train.
> (Wheatley 1786:13)

Although many of these early Africans started the process of vindicating their humanity and African civilizations in a countertextual "radical critique of the Eurocentric ideology" (Asante 1987:3), their "Afrocentric" visions were refracted through European lenses—perhaps an unavoidable outcome given that the powerful Europeans controlled the available discourse. Thus Equiano of Benin, who had been sent to Barbados as a captive in 1756 and who subsequently bought his freedom, used the Bible as a canon to compare African behavior and civilizations with those of the ancient Hebrews. Noting the actions of "Abraham and the other patriarchs," Equiano wrote, "We also had our circumcision (a rule I believe peculiar to that people); we had also our sacrifices and burnt-offerings, our washings and purifications, on the same occasions as they had" (in Curtin 1967:82). Drawing parallels between Africans and the venerated Israelites, substantial elements of whose religion the Europeans adopted, Equiano demanded to know what right European Christians had to criticize African dances as lewd and savage since King David had danced before the Lord.

Operating in the same vindicationist tradition, in 1792 Benjamin Banneker, a freeman and possibly a "freethinker," sought to convince Thomas Jefferson, then secretary of state of the emerging United States, that a member of "the African race, and in that color which is natural to them of the deepest dye," was capable of astronomical and mathematical accomplishments (1951:24). Banneker knew that Jefferson disdained Phillis Wheatley's poetry but hoped that a man of positivist French philosophical inclinations would see in his (Banneker's) almanac evidence of African intellectual capacity.

Banneker conceded, "We are a race of beings, who have long labored under the abuse and censure of the world; . . . we have long been looked upon with an eye of contempt . . . [and have] long been considered rather as brutish than human, and scarcely capable of mental endowments" (1951:24–25). He urged Jefferson, however, to consider the "state of degradation, to which the unjustifiable cruelty and barbarism of men" had reduced African Americans. The irony was that while making an appeal for intellectual parity, Banneker invoked the very image he sought to neutralize. He presented himself as the transformed "brute" who had been redeemed through the cleansing powers of Western epistemology, the same epistemology that denied him recognition. Banneker's appeal to Jefferson unwittingly exposed an Afrocentric conundrum that centuries later has still not been reconciled, namely, how to adequately represent and apprehend Africa through the eyes of a Western epistemological and *hegemonic* tradition that itself has been deployed as an active agent of the colonial and Western imagination.

The nineteenth-century intellectual heirs to Equiano and Banneker attempted to defend themselves and Africa by using the concept of a "black nationality," a concept whose major trope invoked the glories of Egypt and Ethiopia. These scholars protested that slaveholders expected African Americans to be morally irreproachable even while held in bondage and subjected to hostility and discrimination. "Why will you look for grapes from thorns, or figs from thistles?" they asked, adding, "It is in our posterity enjoying the same privileges with your own, that you ought to look for better things" (Allen and Jones 1951:37). These persons consoled themselves that God works in mysterious ways, His wonders to perform. They prayed that African Americans might be instruments of His scheme "until the princes shall come forth from Egypt and Ethiopia stretch out her hand unto God" (Allen and Jones 1951:38).

Since these early African Americans used the biblical Exodus as a metaphor for ending slavery, their "promised land" became identified with Africa—the biblical Eden. It was quite an easy yet bold step for them to voice the idea that the first human beings appeared in Africa and that Africa was the source of all civilization. Thus the Reverend Henry Highland Garnet, in a spirited defense of African peoples and African civilization, resorted to an Afrocentric argument.

Garnet complained that by almost common consent, the modern world appeared determined to pilfer Africa of its glory. He noted that not only had Africa's people been "scattered over the globe, clothed in the garments of shame—humiliated and oppressed—but her merciless foes weary themselves in plundering the tombs of [their] renowned sires, and in obliterating their worthy deeds, which were inscribed by fame upon the pages of ancient history" (Garnet 1848:6). Garnet implied that white skin was a divine punishment for the biblical Miriam's murmuring against her brother, Moses, for marrying an Ethiopian woman. He claimed that when the representatives "of [the African] race were filling the world with amazement, the ancestors of the now proud and boasting Anglo-Saxons were among the most degraded of the human family" (1848:12). Garnet was determined to recapture for Africa the "glory that was Egypt" and to assert the superiority of African culture. He, like others of his cohort, sought to unravel "the Sphinx of African history."

Edward Wilmot Blyden, born of allegedly unmixed African parentage in St. Croix in the Virgin Islands, attempted to deal with this paradox. Seeking to trump the contemporary European hegemonies, Blyden insisted that the Sphinx—believed to have been modeled on the head of a prominent pharaoh from Old Kingdom times even before the basic outlines of Egyptian civilization had been established—vindicated Africa. Blyden, who would later be hailed as the "father of negritude" and of the "African personality" (Mudimbe 1988:99), wrote: "Her features are decidedly that of the African or Negro type, with 'expanded nostrils.' If, then, the Sphinx was placed here—looking out in majestic and mysterious silence over the empty plain where once stood the great city of Memphis in all its pride and glory, as an 'emblematic representation of the king'—is not the inference clear as to the peculiar type of race to which the king belonged?" (in Du Bois 1915:34). Likewise Alexander Crummell, steeped in the biblical prophecy of "Egyptian princes" and "Ethiopia's hands," used the Sphinx to explicate the odyssey of African peoples (Stuckey 1972:1–29). Crummell called on African American intellectuals to go to the aid of the ancestral continent. Du Bois's classic studies of the Atlantic slave trade and urban African Americans were equally didactic in tone and sentiment. In an essay written for the American Negro Academy, an organization founded by Crummell in 1897, Du Bois (1996) challenged the social Darwinists who argued that Africans had made no contributions to world civilization. Egyptian civilization, he asserted, clearly demonstrated that Africans and their descendants had made significant contributions to world cultures.

Du Bois had "a visceral faith in the historic significance of Africa" (Lewis 1993:352). His 1915 book, *The Negro,* was regarded as one of the first serious American works on African cultures and described Africa in Afrocentric, lyrical, and visionary terms. Although Du Bois desired to help blacks break the mental shackles of a white-imposed inferiority in an overwhelming white and hostile America, he was aware that Eurocentricity saddled African Americans with a "double-consciousness." As Du Bois wrote in *The Souls of Black Folk*, he did not wish African Americans to lose either their African or their European tradition. He had no desire for the African American to "Africanize America, for America has too much to teach the world and Africa. He would not bleach his Negro soul in a flood of white Americanism, for he knows that Negro blood has a message for the world. He simply wishes to make it possible for a man to be both a Negro and an American, without being cursed and spit upon by his fellows, without having the doors of Opportunity closed roughly in his face" (1979 [1903]:3).

Consider also the case of Marcus Garvey, who in 1916 left Jamaica for Harlem, then emerging as a mecca for African peoples (much as European migrants viewed the rest of New York City as their mecca). Garvey had earlier traveled in Central America and Europe, and he had read about the African American situation. He subsequently decided to establish the Universal Negro Improvement Association (UNIA), with the aim of redeeming Africa. Garvey described his epiphany: "I had read 'Up From Slavery,' by Booker T. Washington, and then my doom—if I may call it—of being race leader dawned upon me in London after I had traveled through almost half of Europe. I asked, Where is the black man's Government? Where is his King and his kingdom? Where is his President, his country, and his ambassador, his army, his navy, his men of big affairs? I could not find them, and then I declared, I will help to make them" (Garvey 1983:166).

Garvey boldly proclaimed that "Africa belonged to Africans at home and abroad" and planted politically charged UNIA cells wherever blacks lived (Skinner 1992:381). Around him in Harlem there was a veritable cultural revival. Poets reveled in their "blackness" and celebrated the dialect poetry that enlivened the singing sermons of black preachers, rhapsodizing about "hibiscus in the snow." Rivers of the Old World were conflated with those of the New, the poets recalling how Africans had built the pyramids along the banks of the Nile and loaded cotton on the Mississippi. Countee Cullen raised and answered the question of his relationship to Africa in his poem "Heritage," while jazz, an original synthesis of African and European musical styles, came of age. "Le Jazz Hot" won adherents among expatriate Americans in Paris as well as among the native French and African students there (Davis 1989).

Continental Africans also participated in the Afrocentric cultural wars to redeem Africa. J. E. Casely Hayford, in his books *Gold Coast Native Institutions* (1903) and *Ethiopia Unbound* (1969 [1911]), systematically compared African institutions with those of the Europeans. Perturbed by reports that a former British governor of the Gold Coast had "declared that the Gold

Coast was neither 'fit' for a white man, nor a black man, nor a Chinaman, nor yet for dog," Hayford responded that as far as the local people were concerned, "The Gold Coast is, and will always be, 'fit' for the Gold Coast man. So has God ordained it" (Hayford 1903:238). Then, echoing Equiano before him, Hayford declared:

> It is a matter of history that, at the beginning of the Christian era, you were worse off than we are to-day; greater darkness brooded over your intellectual horizon. By the absorption of Grecian and Roman culture and the science of the Eastern world, you gradually emerged from darkness into light, and were able to develop what was natural and innate in you, and to, in time, contribute your quota to the world's work. In a word, given the conditions of development, you developed on your own lines, until you became the great nation you are today. (1903:239–40)

While concealing Egypt and Ethiopia behind the "science of the Eastern world," Hayford proudly proclaimed his ambition: "We are anxious to take part in the race of nations towards the attainment of higher ideals, if you will give us a chance to work out our own salvation" (1903:7).

Scholars of African origin not only wanted an opportunity to assert themselves; they welcomed the help of sympathetic whites. Du Bois invited Franz Boas of Columbia University to give a commencement address at Atlanta University on May 31, 1906. The distinguished anthropologist noted regretfully, "We have no place in this country where the beauty and daintiness of African work can be shown; but a walk through the African museums of Paris, London and Berlin is a revelation" (Boas 1945:64). He sought to convince the young graduates that the lowly status of blacks in America was not immutable:

> To those who stoutly maintain a material inferiority of the Negro race and who would dampen your ardor by their claims, you may confidently reply that the burden of proof rests with them, that the past history of your race does not sustain their statement, but rather gives you encouragement. The physical inferiority of the Negro race, if it exists at all, is insignificant when compared to the wide range of individual variability in each race. There is no anatomical evidence available that would sustain the view that the bulk of the Negro race could not become as useful citizens as the members of any other race. . . . Your advance depends upon your steadfastness of purpose. (Boas 1945:66, 69)

On the other side of the Atlantic, African students in Paris welcomed the views of Maurice Delafosse, a French colonial administrator turned ethnographer, who argued that Africans were not intellectually inferior to whites and that the African Middle Age was comparable to that of Europe. Delafosse felt certain that the bronzes of Benin are worthy of comparison with "corresponding products of several famous civilizations" (Delafosse 1922:92). He concluded:

When peoples . . . have been able by means of their own resourcefulness alone
to organize states, . . . to create and maintain education centers like Timbuctoo,
for example; to produce statesmen like the Mansa Congo-Moussa or the Askia
Mohammed, . . . scholars and educated men who, without the aid of dictio-
naries or any vehicular language, have grasped Arabic sufficiently well to read
it fluently and write it correctly, to form idioms which could—by the normal
play of their morphological laws and without foreign interpolation—furnish
the required instrument to those speaking these idioms . . . then these people
do not deserve to be treated as intellectual inferiors. (1922:159)

Similarly, Leo Frobenius, a German ethologist who traveled widely in West
and Central Africa in the 1930s, felt that Africans produced works of "art
worthy of comparison with creations in the Roman-European style" (Frobenius and Fox 1936:15). Elliot Smith and William Perry were also convinced
that the brilliant early Egyptian "children of the sun," whose culture was
based on pyramids and gold, left their homeland in the attempt to civilize
the rest of Africa and the world (Perry 1923).

Colonized African intellectuals always welcomed the views of colonial
scholars. When confronted with famous professors who had little interest in
the African "mind" and who used a structural-functionalist approach to
discover how "primitive" African societies actually worked (Harris 1968:514),
however, some African students sought to defend Africa. Jomo Kenyatta, of
Kenya, who studied under Bronislaw Malinowski at the London School of
Economics, and Kofi Busia, of the Gold Coast, a student of Radcliffe-Brown
at Oxford, asserted their own brand of Afrocentricity. In his monograph
Facing Mount Kenya (1938), Kenyatta stoutly defended Kikuyu culture against
its detractors, whereas Kofi Busia (1951) analyzed the changing position of
traditional rulers among the Ashanti. Both Kenyatta and Busia later became
presidents of their respective countries.

It was, however, the traditional French interest in the characteristics of the
human mind, first broached by Gustave Le Bon, and continued in the 1930s
by Marcel Griaule (1948), that would stimulate interest in African philosophy. Griaule published brilliant essays and monographs about the symbolism and religious systems of the Dogon and Mande. Long aware of Griaule's
work, Father Placide Tempels, a Dominican monk missionizing the Baluba
people in the then Belgian Congo, published a small book entitled *Bantu
Philosophy* (1959). In this work he proposed "no more than an *hypothesis,* a
first attempt at the systematic development of Bantu philosophy" (1959:40).
He suggested that ontologically, "Bantu speak, act, live as if, for them, beings
were forces. Force is not for them an adventitious, accidental reality, force is
even more than a necessary attribute of beings: *Force is the nature of being,
force is being, being is force*" (1959:51).

Tempels argued that for the Bantu, not only is the "origin, the subsistence or annihilation of beings or of forces . . . expressly and exclusively attributed to God," but "the term 'to create' in its proper connotation of 'to evoke from not being' is found in its full signification in Bantu" ontology (1959:57). Furthermore, "all force can be strengthened or enfeebled. That is to say, all being can become stronger or weaker" (1959:55). From this followed what Tempels considered to be "general laws of vital causality": "Man (living or dead) can directly reinforce or diminish the being of another person"; "the vital human force can directly influence inferior force-beings (animal, vegetable or mineral) in their being itself"; and "a rational being (spirit, manes, or the living) can act indirectly upon another rational being by communicating his vital influence to an inferior force (animal, vegetable, or mineral) through the intermediacy of which it influences the rational being" (1959:67–68).

While welcoming what appeared to be an explanation of aspects of the supernatural in African societies, many African intellectuals were frustrated and annoyed by Tempels's contention that Bantu ontology "penetrates and informs all the thought of these primitives; it dominates and orientates all their behavior" (1959:21). Moreover, Tempels felt that although this ultimately "primitive" philosophy was not formulated by the Bantu-speaking peoples themselves (since it was unrealistic to "expect the first African who comes along, especially the young one, to be able to give us a systematic exposition of his ontological system"), their ontology was not difficult for Europeans to grasp (1959:21). Tempels claimed that his methodology was based primarily on empathy or sympathy. He was convinced that neither folklore, ethnology, linguistics, psychology, jurisprudence, sociology, nor religion could yield full insights into African cultures; only a thorough study of Bantu philosophy could do that.

The ensuing debate on Bantu philosophy involved William Abraham, a Ghanaian philosopher; Léopold Sédar Senghor, a prominent Senegalese scholar-politician; and many Catholic clerics, among others (Mudimbe 1988:180). Abbé Alexis Kagame, a Rwandan cleric, had little difficulty with the notion of a "silent philosophy" among the Bantu, but he advocated a comprehensive study of Bantu languages (Mudimbe 1988:187), without which any study of African culture would be questionable. More important among African leaders and scholars was to say how and why the notion of an African philosophy or "ethnophilosophy (as some preferred to call it) was raised just when Africans were agitating for national independence (Mudimbe 1988:157–58).

A number of Francophone African professional philosophers, such as Paulin Hountondji, a graduate of the prestigious École Normale Supérieure, felt that ethnophilosophy is no more than an imaginary, intoxicating interpretation. Ethnophilosophy, Hountondji believed, is unsupported by textual authority, too dependent on the interpreter's whims, and not amenable to a search for truth. He warned that if Westerners accepted ethnophilosophy, they would be guilty of an ethnocentric bias intended to placate Africans, since it contradicts the theoretical implications of Western philosophical practices. He rejected the notion that Bantu philosophy is determined by the geographical origin of the authors rather than by an alleged specificity of content. African philosophy was therefore being deprived of "a methodological inquiry with the same universal aims as those of any other philosophy in the world" (Hountondji 1983:66). Hountondji's colleague Marcien Towa agreed that ethnophilosophers seeking to rediscover traditional reality were making no more than a "militant profession of faith, 'authenticated' in terms of their so-called Africanity" (Towa 1971:32).

Yet supporters of an "African philosophy," whether ethnologically based or otherwise, condemned Hountondji and Towa for their neocolonist dependency on the West. The critics resented the claim that African cultures are backward, static, and nonliterate and that contemporary Africans must practice "revolutionary iconoclasm" and destroy "traditional idols" to use and "assimilate the spirit of Europe" according to a Hegelian world-historical process in which all peoples, Western and non-Western alike, are engaged (Mudimbe 1988:39–41). The notion that a literary tradition is necessary for philosophy was also questioned, with the suggestion that the early Greek philosophers should not have been deemed philosophers because originally they had no written texts. The view of Henri Frankfort, among others, was championed because he recognized that each civilization has its individual and recognized character that is maintained throughout its development. Moreover, there will be "a certain coherence among its various manifestations, a certain consistency in its orientation, a certain cultural 'style' which shapes its political and its judicial literature, its religion as well as its morals" (Frankfort 1949:63).

Valentin Mudimbe, a philosopher from Congo-Zaire, admitted that there were "complex questions about knowledge and power in and on Africa" and admitted that the discourses about "African worlds have been established as realities for knowledge. And today Africans themselves read, challenge, rewrite these discourses as a way of explicating and defining their culture, history and being" (Mudimbe 1988:xi). From these discourses arose a *gnosis* about both African discourses and ideologies of alterity of which negritude, black personality, and African philosophy were examples. Mudimbe refused to deal with the unphilosophical discourses about philosophy and an "invented" Africa and insisted that the real issue was being an African and also a philosopher. He concluded that from a methodological viewpoint, "discourse in general[,] and scientific discourse in particular, is so complex a reality that we not only can but should approach it at different levels and with different methods" (1988:xi).

What this debate about ethnophilosophy demonstrates is the continued difficulty African scholars have had in delinking the issues of Afrocentricity and Africanity. This was particularly true of Kwame Anthony Appiah, a philosopher of British-Ghanaian origin. In his contribution to the debate, he admitted that historical factors led to "the invention of Africa" among peoples of African descent. Moreover, he enlisted Du Bois and others in his contention that "racism" and European cultural chauvinism generated a "racial" and "Afrocentric" response. Nevertheless, Appiah challenged the value of the enterprise. He asserted that a racial response, or Afrocentricity, is "disabling" because it leaves people unprepared "to handle the 'intraracial' conflicts that arise from the very different situations of black (and white and yellow) people in different parts of the economy and of the world" (Appiah 1992:176).

With respect to Africanity, Appiah believed that the notion of an "African culture" arose only when "Africans" were contrasted to "Europeans." He objected to viewing specific African cultures as variants of an almost universal African culture. His only concession was to suggest that any similarities seen in African cultures should at best be related to possible evolutionary levels or grades in the universal culture of our species. Appiah was more impressed by the difference among African cultures than by their similarities. He defended his ideas in a book with the provocative title *In My Father's House* (1992). Since this title was taken from a biblical verse that ends "there are many mansions" (John 14:2), one wonders whether Appiah unconsciously accepted the view that there are indeed variations within the overall definition of "African culture" in his parent's house (1992:180).

Davidson Nicol, a close friend of both Appiah's African father and his English mother, suggested that this young scholar's "mixed racial ancestry" did in fact "affect his outlook, as he confesses" (Nicol 1993:109). Nicol did not object to Appiah's criticism of both Afrocentricity and negritude as a "reaction to exogenous European imperialism and not a metaphysical continental consensus with its own individuality." He also agreed with Appiah that the notion of "African particularism" is too parochial. Nevertheless, Nicol was not prepared to "discard racial solidarity and the emotional appeal of Pan-Africanism altogether or immediately" (1993:115). Nicol believes that these are common reactions to economic and psychological injustices that "many of African origin continue to suffer everywhere from other groups. In the perfect world of the future these would cease to exist and with them Pan-Africanism" (1993:115).

Nicol was equally cautious about the issue of the cultural unity of Africa, or Africanity, an issue that had started to subvert the conflict between Afrocentricty and Eurocentricity. He acknowledged the dangers of "oversimplification" when considering the underlying cultural unity of Africa but maintained that "there are certain cultural events which seem too general and common to the sub-Saharan region and bind blacks together in Africa and elsewhere—rhythmic singing and movement, ancestor worship, spirit possession and, one has observed, an unusual readiness to forgive racial injustice" (1993:111).

Nevertheless, the issue of the relationship between Eurocentricity, Afrocentricity, and Africanity refused to go away. Some European scholars such as Frobenius and Delafosse, although contributing to the dialectic between Eurocentricity and Afrocentricity, appeared more interested in plumbing the nature of Africanity. While writing about his respect for the mentality of Africans, Frobenius was obviously more interested in the traces of a common civilization that he suspected to have existed throughout Africa, from Egypt to the Sudan, Senegal, Dahomey, Nigeria, the Congo, and South Africa. Almost Hegelian in methodology, he felt that everywhere he recognized a similar "spirit," a "characteristic" and essence that "dominates *all of Africa* and is the very expression of its essence. It is manifest in the gestures of all Negro peoples as well as in their plastic arts. It speaks in their dances and in their masks, in their religious feelings as in their mode of existence, in their forms of government and in their destiny as peoples. It lives in their fables, their fairly tales, their legends and myths" (Frobenius and Fox 1936:17–18). Marcel Griaule, too, though primarily interested in African philosophy, noted both the similarities and variations of African culture traits as he contemplated the history of migrations. He was especially struck by the cultural sequences in West Africa and believed that he had established to his own satisfaction "the existence of a ramified but coherent culture area he later portrayed as one of three major division of sub-Saharan Africa: the Western Sudan, Bantu Africa, and an intermediate zone in Cameroon and Chad. Each region was characterized by a traditional *sophie* or science—a mode of knowledge inscribed in language habitat, oral tradition, myth, technology and aesthetics" (Clifford 1983:57).

No doubt aware of these views, Melville J. Herskovits, a student of Boas at Columbia, brought an eclectic and nondogmatic Boasian approach to his subject. Herskovits profited from the then contemporary hypothesis of archaeologists and paleontologists that "the early date of pebble tools threw quite as new a light on the role of Africa in the development of human culture as the fossil finds did for its role in the evolution of man's physical form" (Herskovits 1962:38). He also felt that there was a remarkable continuity in African prehistory and that what he termed a "culture area approach" is a particularly effective "scientific" way to study African cultures. Looking specifically at "ecological and institutional factors," Herskovits concluded that it is possible to classify whole ways of life and to see the similarities and differences between African cultures in continental perspective. He identified ten culture areas (the Congo, two cattle areas, Khoisan, Western Sudan and North Africa, and the like), but faced with criticisms that his alien paradigm distorted the African data, Herskovits all but abandoned it.

Profiting from Herskovits's work, but also instructed by the "culture circle," or *Kulturkreislehre*, concept of the Austrian school, Baumann and Westermann (1948) identified smaller groupings of African cultures, but they could not escape the criticism that historical factors distorted the comparability of their circles. Similarly, George Peter Murdock, an American anthropologist using a scheme not too different from that of Baumann and Westermann, identified some forty-seven cultural provinces (Murdock 1959). Once again, however, the cultural history of the continent played havoc with his paradigm. Jacques Maquet, a Belgian scholar, sought to avoid the historical dilemma by identifying such African civilizations as those of the "clearings," "cities," and the like, but by so doing he lost some of the dynamism and especially the ethos that characterizes the sources of the African tradition (Maquet 1972).

Working independently of the anthropologists but aware of their concerns about aspects of African civilization, the British historians Roland Oliver and John Fage declared that, after a lifetime studying African history, they had concluded that a divine king complex was the basis of a civilization whose institutions were so similar that they must have derived from a common source. This source, they argued, extended from "the Red Sea to the mouth of the Senegal, and right down the central highlands spine of Bantu Africa from the Nile sources to . . . [Zimbabwe]" (Oliver and Fage 1966:44). The traits of the complex included divine honors, seclusion, sowing of the first seeds, the idea that the fertility of the land depends on the physical well-being of the ruler, immunity from natural death, embalming after ritual death, ceremonies involving sacred fires, and the like (1966:44).

William Y. Adams, an anthropologist whose historical work on Nubia led him to examine that region within the larger context of African archaeology and history, was so intrigued by the stylistic similarity of the prehistoric rock art of Africa and "the great Magdalenian cave paintings of France and Spain" that he suggested a "historical connection by way of the Straits of Gibraltar." He noted that the Nubian rock art not only resembles that of contemporary "Bushman hunters" but apparently dates from all periods, from the prehistoric to the fairly recent past. The prehistoric drawings show the typical savanna game animals found today in Central and South Africa (and presumably found also in Nubia at the time they were drawn), whereas cattle are the favorite theme of most later periods. There are also a number of motifs, such as a large boat with masts and steering oar, of unmistakably Egyptian derivation. Similar drawings are found all over the Sahara and are thought to be associated with specific mortuary beliefs (Adams 1977:115–16).

Igor Kopytoff, a student of Herskovits, impressed with the similarities of African cultures through space and time, attempted to account for these by using Frederick Jackson Turner's paradigm of the American frontier. In his "African frontier thesis," Kopytoff not only noted a "pan-African cultural unity" but claimed that it was time to begin analyzing this cultural unity (even if implicitly, as implicitly as European cultural commonalities are treated in the writing of European history). Unfortunately, however, Kopytoff was pre-pared to make "cultural and historical analyses of [only] Sub-Saharan Af-rica" (Kopytoff 1987:76).

Essentially agreeing with the work of most of the linguists and archaeolo-gists, Kopytoff holds that during the Neolithic era, sometime between 5000 and 2500 B.C., "the populations ancestral to the present populations of Sub-Saharan Africa" were concentrated in the north of the continent, in the then fertile Saharan-Sahelian belt that spans east to west. He adds further that "these populations—ancestral linguistically, culturally and preponderantly biologically—were living in association and contact with one another in the kind of setting in which regional cultural syntheses and patterns are usually evolved. It is here that we must assume that the 'incubation' of the ancestral pan-African culture patterns took place, often under frontier conditions and in contact with the kindred patterns of pre-Islamic Near-East" (1987:9).

Kopytoff believes that from this ancestral "hearth," a pan-African culture spread southward in two movements, during which its carriers encountered small groups of Pygmoids, Bushmanoids, and Cushites. The first movement came after 2500 B.C. with the desiccation of the Saharan-Sahel region to the Equatorial zone, and the second spurt came during the first millennium B.C. with the spread of the Bantu-speaking peoples to the southern and relatively inhabited parts of the continent (1987:10). He concluded that "as the initial tidal frontier crept across Africa, the frontiersmen were bringing with them a basically similar kit of cultural and ideological resources. It is thus not sur-prising that Sub-Saharan Africa should exhibit to such a striking degree a fundamental cultural unity" (1987:10).

Kopytoff separated himself from those scholars who sought to see all of Africa as the scene of action, accusing them of engaging in "the mechanistic assumptions of continent-wide diffusions and the nearsighted vision of pa-rochial functionalism" (1987:34). He criticized such ethnologists as Frobenius and Murdock and such historians as Oliver and Fage, among others, who attempted to link cultural traits from all over Africa and not only among the societies of sub-Saharan Africa. Kopytoff was unhappy with Murdock, who viewed a certain kind of pan-African political culture "as the result of the diffusion of what he calls 'African despotism'" (1987:33). Similarly, he was highly critical of Oliver and Fage, who "also attributed to diffusion the preva-lence in Africa of 'divine kingship' (which Murdock subsumes under his 'despotism')—with the improbable touch of deriving it from ancient Egypt" (1987:33). Still, Kopytoff was forced to admit that the "similarities across Africa are too complex to have simply arisen from direct diffusion, yet they are too great to have developed through repeated coincidence, again and again, independently. The explanation must be sought in some kind of functional historicity" (1987:34).

Kopytoff could deal with the possibility that some kind of functional historicity would best explain the African data only by suggesting, in contrast to his own frontier theory, the adoption of a "functionalist analysis *within* the givens of a culture-historical tradition." This, he argued, is "an essentially Boasian view of culture as a sociological variable which is a historical product. . . . Cultures and societies are historical and regional products, local variations of regional patterns. We take this for granted when we deal with Europe" (1987:34). This approach is possible, he felt, because "in Europe, where we know there was a history, we automatically begin with the region and see communities in it as local, sometimes idiosyncratic, expressions of the regional culture and history. In Africa (and wherever else we had to 'discover' history) we had been forced by necessity to proceed in reverse order" (1987:34).

The result was that he had to use the "tribe," the unit that he believed to be knowable from firsthand fieldwork, and then speculate about data on a regional level whose patterns he recognized. What Kopytoff was not prepared to do was to use as much data as he could gather from archaeology, linguistics, physical anthropology, and even history to deal with areas outside sub-Saharan Africa.

Intriguingly, Jan Vansina, who like Kopytoff worked in Congo-Zaire, refused to limit his assessment of African cultures to the sub-Saharan part of Africa. Like Herskovits, Vansina was impressed with the relationship between the regional art styles found within Africa, leading him to remark: "Two thousand years and more before the first Pharaoh was enthroned, hunters and pastoralists in the Sahara were both engraving and painting on rock. Indeed, ancient Egyptian graphic art owes something to the great Saharan tradition that both preceded it and ran parallel to it for most of its history" (Vansina 1984:6). Vansina speculated that the engravings and paintings typical of nomadic peoples were probably practiced "all over the continent before the spread of settled life" (1984:6).

Africanity as the Source of Tradition

It was always the notion of a possible early or "ur-cultural" horizon that intrigued scholars and tempted some of them to link this idea with Afrocentricity. A central protagonist in this debate was Cheikh Anta Diop, a

Senegalese scholar imbued with a Senghorian desire to bring a *"présence africaine"* to the elaboration of a universal civilization. Diop resented what he believed was Europeans scholars' tendency to refuse to deal fairly with Africa and then to compound this problem by refusing to consider Egyptian civilization as a high point in the evolution of African cultures. Like many of the scholars he criticized, Diop, conflating race and culture, asserted that the "Egyptians perceived of themselves as Blacks," thereby challenging the notion that blacks made no contribution to world civilization. Diop insisted that for postcolonial or (more correctly) contemporary Africans, the return of Egypt in all its domains is the necessary condition for reconciling African civilizations with history, with that reconciliation itself necessary to construct a body of modern human sciences to rehabilitate African culture. Far from this being a case of reveling in the past, an appreciation of ancient Egypt is the best way to conceive and build our cultural future, Diop argued. Egypt should play the same role for Africa that Greco-Latin antiquity plays in Western culture (Diop 1991).

Coming as it did during the decolonization of Africa, Diop's assertive stand had two results: it encouraged non-African scholars to review their stand on Africa and Egypt and gave weight to those interested in using a symbolic estate to help rehabilitate African peoples. Basil Davidson was among the first to concede that "with one or two exceptions," source books for the study of Africa still conceived of that "subject as no more than an extension to the study of Europe or the New World" (1991:4). He viewed these books as "strictly European in standpoint, and their value lies less in any light they may throw on African life than in the movement they reveal of European penetration and conquest" (1991:4).

With respect to Egypt and Africa, Davidson believed that scholars had to "right the balance" by dealing with Egypt as part of Africa. He noted that "the records of ancient Africa begin with Egypt, yet the Egyptian contribution has been little studied on its African side. A familiar habit has considered old Egypt merely and strictly in her relationship to the civilizations of Asia and the Mediterranean . . . If the history of early Africa is unthinkable without Egypt, so too is the history of early Egypt inexplicable without Africa. Ancient Egypt was essentially an African civilization" (1991:49).

Diop's provocative stance blinded some persons to his diffusionist methodology in dealing with Africanity, or the cultural unity of Africa. He focused on such common factors as the "structure of African royalty" (including the dual monarchy and regicide), circumcision rites, totemism, cosmogonies, and similarities in art, architecture, musical instruments, and the like. In addition to attributing the widespread variants of this African civilization to diffusion, Diop asserted that the movement of peoples was also due to climatic factors (Diop 1987:20). What he insisted on, however, was a strong connection between Egypt and Ethiopia (as Nubia was called):

As a matter of fact, the Negro characters of the Ethiopian or Abyssinian race have been sufficiently affirmed by Herodotus and all the Ancients; there is no need to reopen the subject. The Nubians are the accepted ancestors of most African Blacks, to the point that the words Nubian and Negro are synonymous. Ethiopians and Copts are two Negro groups subsequently mixed with white elements in various regions. Negroes of the Delta interbred gradually with Mediterranean Whites who continually filtered into Egypt. (Diop 1991:15)

Diop's assertion that the Negroes of the Delta region of Egypt interbred with Mediterranean whites suggests he had no difficulty understanding the factors that led to biological and cultural features of the contemporary inhabitants of Egypt and North Africa. Nevertheless, he objected to any denial of a persisting continental substratum to which have been added elements from neighboring countries of the Middle East, from across the Mediterranean, and later, even from Western Europe. Conversely, he insisted that Egyptian and therefore African elements found their way into the Middle East, across the Mediterranean to Greece and Rome, and eventually to the regions these civilizations conquered.

The United States and Afrocentricity

There is little doubt that the racial and cultural chauvinism of Western European peoples not only fueled a belief in their civilizing mission but led to their denial that their ancestors received aspects of high civilization from Egypt through Greece and Rome. It is perhaps significant to note that the site of the greatest contestation between Afrocentrism and Eurocentrism is the United States of America, the uncontested global power and a place where African Americans appear determined to free themselves from "mental slavery." Joseph R. Washington once observed that black awareness, or in this case Afrocentricity, is a two-edged sword: if it was designed to achieve complete social, economic, and political equality through the development of black identity and a sense of peoplehood, it then struck at the root of white racial dominance (Washington 1972:134).

Arthur M. Schlesinger Jr. has railed against the use of Afrocentricity as a symbolic estate by African Americans, for he believes that instead of healing racism, it disunites America. His contention is that the emerging nation held out the promise and premise of a "unique American Creed that explicitly expressed the ideals of the essential dignity and equality of all human beings, and their inalienable rights to freedom, justice and opportunity" (Schlesinger 1991:8). Schlesinger noted, parenthetically, that not many among the Founding Fathers found it amiss that Africans were not party to the social compact that created the United States. He drew from this omission the lesson that "America is continuously struggling for its soul." Schlesinger objects to the current use of the processes of the "symbolic estate" (also affirmative action) as tools by which African Americans can attempt to achieve equality within the society. He views such movements as detrimental to the social health of the republic because the "bonds of cohesion in our society are sufficiently fragile . . . that it makes no sense encouraging and exalting cultural and linguistic apartheid" (1991:8).

What Schlesinger failed to realize is that what he termed "cultural and linguistic apartheid" is a purely defensive reaction of people of African origin in the face of paradigmatic hegemony. It is significant that those contemporary African American and African scholars of African origin who use the work of Cheikh Anta Diop for its Afrocentricity rather than its Africanity value are changing their strategies as they discover that it is Africanity that will help them achieve their goal, that is, using the African tradition as a source of liberation (Ben-Jochannan and Clarke 1991). For example, although it is fitting to use Egyptian civilization, a high point in African civilization, to combat Greece and Rome, scholars of African origin should not make the same mistake as the Western Europeans who appropriated the Elgin Marbles as the relics of their ancient culture while remaining indifferent to, or even scornful of, the contemporary inhabitants of Greece.

This approach of Africanity is not as simple as it seems, however, because it challenges its practitioners in North America to shift the focus away from Europe and the Afrocentricity of black Athena and to come to grips with the experience of African peoples, including those of West and Central Africa, the home of many of their proximate ancestors. This approach must also take into consideration that over the past five centuries African peoples have been subjected to severe sociocultural, genophenotypical, historical, and linguistic pressures. It must also be understood that during this period, Africans as well as other human beings have continued to use old paradigms by which to live, invented new ones, and synthesized the new with the old, all in the battle of survival.

Moreover, although the requirements of the modern world clearly entail that African peoples cannot rely exclusively on our own paradigms and traditions as guides for action, our paradigmatic achievements must not be undervalued as we seek to assert ourselves. One should never forget that just one hundred years ago, in his 1897 essay with the intriguing title "The Conservation of Races," Du Bois insisted that "if the Negro is ever to be a factor in the world's history—if among the gaily colored banners that deck the broad ramparts of civilization is to hang one uncompromisingly black, then it must be placed there by black hands, fashioned by black heads and hallowed by the travail of 200,000,000 black hearts beating in one glad song of jubilee" (1996:234). Thus instead of simply talking about syncretism of African cultures with those of others, African peoples must emphasize redefinition and, more important, the "retrieval" of African cultural traits. For example, many persons of European descent, and perhaps those of African descent, were uncomfortable when an African praise singer appeared on the podium as Nelson Mandela took the oath of office to become the first black president of South Africa. They did not feel that this tradition was compatible with modern political culture (television news cameras showed that many Afrikaners in the stands were visibly upset, especially Mrs. F. W. de Klerk). How far these changes can proceed without severe paradigmatic shifts is unknown, but such shifts, if and when they take place, should emphasize African traditions if possible.

In an article entitled "Yoruban Astrophysics" in the *Washington Post* in 1995, Wole Soyinka, the Nobel laureate in literature, sought to explain how his Nigerian past prepared him for the "mysterious future." He noted: "The Yoruba respond to new, alien experiences by integrating them into the domain of the deities. Today, for instance, with the penetration of computer technology in everyday life, the only problem might be to decide whether the computer belongs to Ogun, the god of electricity, or to Sango, the god of metals. I suspect it will be Ogun of the Cyber-Superhighways!" Perhaps responding to those who lament the current low technological condition of Africa, Soyinka continued: "Technology is not considered alien in Nigeria. From childhood, I knew roadside mechanics adept at fixing almost any kind of mechanical contrivance, and I have no doubt that we shall soon produce our own computer experts." What intrigued him, however, was that so far Western scientific theories have no privileged answers to cosmic issues:

> Until a spacewalker brings back irrefutable evidence, the Big Bang theory, black holes, time warps and allied originating motions of space, eons of light years away, convulsing in labor pains or collapsing inwards—they occupy the same realms of mystification as the most outlandish myths. A truly rational explanation seems, for now, beyond the most sophisticated instruments or inspired projection of the mind. I remain optimistic however. One of these days, the darkest secret of space will be laid bare. Then the Yoruba cosmic view of interlocking worlds, ancestor, living and the unborn—will find a triumphant correlation in the universe of astrophysics.

Closer to home, in the contemporary United States, there is an example of how African Americans invent traditions to suit their needs. With tongue in cheek, and with its Oxbridge nose in the air, on December 17, 1994, the *Economist* ran a story on end-of-year holidays in the United States, stretching from "Thanksgiving through Hanukkah and Christmas, all the way to Kwanzaa." It explained to its British readers that Kwanzaa is a "festival of African America heritage, celebrated for seven days starting the day after Christmas" and that it now receives "equal holiday-season treatment in many schools and museums. Not bad for an upstart." After all, the *Economist* said, Hanukkah was 2,159 years old, and Christmas, 1,194 (or thereabouts), whereas

Kwanzaa was "a mere babe of 28." What intrigued the *Economist* was that Maulana Karenga, the founder of Kwanzaa, had "concocted his festival by borrowing from a number of cultural sources. . . . His idea was to create a ritual for America's blacks to express pride in their African roots." The magazine noted that Kwanzaa cannot be found anywhere in Africa. It is "entirely African-American." Not being a religious festival, Kwanzaa can "happily co-exist with Christmas," and it has taken on local colorations in different places in the United States.

The article noted that many blacks and whites objected that Kwanzaa involves what they termed "mythmaking" that harks back to an "idealized African past" and that it ignores part of the black American tradition. Nevertheless, the festival is now celebrated by about five million African Americans, and it has spawned holiday expositions at which big American companies such as Pepsi Cola, AT&T, Revlon, and Hallmark exhibit their wares. The magazine quipped that those persons who did not believe that the tradition would last some 2,000 years were accused of having little faith, or "imani." Unfortunately, the article was published too early to report that President Clinton understood the meaning of this festival and wished African Americans "Happy Kwanzaa" when he offered year-end greetings to all Americans.

The events surrounding both Soyinka's "Ogun" and Kwanzaa demonstrate not only that it is possible for peoples of African origin to meld aspects of Africanity with modernity so as to deal with contemporary issues but that they can do so in novel ways. This is the real dream of Du Bois, Senghor, and others who have asserted that African peoples intend to bring their own brick to the construction of a universal civilization.

References Cited

Adams, William Y. 1977. *Nubia—Corridor to Africa.* Princeton, N.J.: Princeton University Press.

Allen, Richard, and Absalom Jones. 1951 [1794]. "Two Negro Leaders Reply to Slanders—and Denounce Slaveholding." In *A Documentary History of the Negro People,* vol. 1, ed. Herbert Aptheker, 32–38. New York: Citadel.

Appiah, Kwame. 1992. *In My Father's House: Africa in the Philosophy of Culture.* New York: Oxford University Press.

Asante, Molefe Kete. 1987. *The Afrocentric Idea.* Philadelphia: Temple University Press.

Banneker, Benjamin. 1951 [1792]. "Copy of a Letter from Benjamin Banneker to the Secretary of State." In *A Documentary History of the Negro People,* 3 vols. (1951, 1973), ed. Herbert Aptheker, 1:23–26. New York: Citadel.

Baumann, Hermann, and D. Westermann. 1948. *Les Peuples et les civilisations de l'Afrique.* Paris: Payot.

Beazley, Charles Raymond, and Edgar Prestage, eds. and trans. 1896. *The Chronicle of the Discovery and Conquest of Guinea by Gomes Eanes de Azurara.* London: Hakluyt Society.

Ben-Jochannan, Yosef, and John H. Clarke. 1991. *New Dimensions in African History.* Trenton, N.J.: Africa World.

Boas, Franz. 1945. *Race and Democratic Society.* New York: J. J. Augustin.

Busia, Kofi A. 1951. *The Position of the Chief in the Modern Political System of the Ashanti.* London: Oxford University Press.

Clifford, James. 1983. "Power and Dialogue in Ethnography: Marcel Griaule's Initiation." In *Observers Observed: Essays on Ethnographic Fieldwork,* ed. George Stocking, 121–56. Madison: University of Wisconsin Press.

Curtin, Philip D. 1967. *Africa Remembered.* Madison: University of Wisconsin Press.

Davidson, Basil. 1991. *African Civilization Revisited.* Trenton, N.J.: Africa World.

Davis, Charles T. 1989. *Black Is the Color of the Cosmos: Essays on Afro-American Literature and Culture, 1942–1981.* Ed. Henry Louis Gates Jr. Washington, D.C.: Howard University Press.

Delafosse, Maurice. 1922. *Les Noirs de l'Afrique,* Paris: Payot.

Diop, Cheikh Anta. 1987. *Precolonial Black Africa: A Comparative Study of the Political and Social Systems of Europe and Black Africa, from Antiquity to the Formation of Modern States.* Westport, Conn.: Lawrence Hill.

———. 1991. *Civilization or Barbarism: An Authentic Anthropology.* New York: Lawrence Hill.

Du Bois, W. E. B. 1915. *The Negro.* New York: Henry Holt.

———. 1979 [1903]. *The Souls of Black Folk.* Nashville: University Press of Tennessee.

———. 1996 [1897]. "The Conservation of Races." In *Classical Black Nationalism: From the American Revolution to Marcus Garvey,* ed. William Moses, 228–40. New York: New York University Press.

Frankfort, Henri. 1949. *Before Philosophy: The Intellectual Adventure of Ancient Man.* Baltimore: Penguin.

Frobenius, Leo, and Douglas C. Fox. 1983 [1936]. *African Genesis.* Berkeley: Turtle Island Foundation.

Garnet, Henry Highland. 1848. *The Past and Present Condition and the Destiny of the Colored Race: A Discourse at the 50th Anniversary of the Female Benevolent Society of Troy, New York, February 14, 1848.* Troy, N.Y.: J. C. Kneeland.

Garvey, Marcus. 1983. "UNIA Memorial Meeting for Booker T. Washington." In *The Marcus Garvey and Universal Negro Improvement Association Papers,* 9 vols., ed. Robert Hill, 1:166. Berkeley: University of California Press.

Griaule, Marcel. 1948. *Dieu d'eau: entretiens avec Ogotommeli.* Paris: Chene.

Harris, Marvin. 1968. *The Rise of Anthropological Theory.* New York: Crowell.

Hayford, J. E. Casely. 1903. *Gold Coast Native Institutions.* London: Sweet and Maxwell.

———. 1969 [1911]. *Ethiopia Unbound: Studies in Race Emancipation.* London: Frank Cass.

Herskovits, Melville J. 1962. *The Human Factor in Changing Africa.* New York: Knopf.

Hountondji, Paulin. 1983. *African Philosophy: Myth and Reality.* Bloomington: Indiana University Press.

Huntington, Samuel. 1996. "The West: Unique, Not Universal." *Foreign Affairs* 75:28–46.

Kenyatta, Jomo. 1938. *Facing Mount Kenya.* London: Secker and Warburg.

Kopytoff, Igor. 1987. "The Internal African Frontier: The Making of African Political Culture." In *The African Frontier: The Reproduction of Traditional African Societies,* ed. Igor Kopytoff, 3–84. Bloomington: Indiana University Press.

Lewis, David L. 1993. *W. E. B. Du Bois: Biography of a Race.* New York: Holt.

Maquet, Jacques. 1972. *Civilizations of Black Africa.* New York: Oxford University Press.

Mudimbe, V. Y. 1988. *The Invention of Africa.* Bloomington: Indiana University Press.

Murdock, George Peter. 1959. *Africa: Its Peoples and Their Culture History.* New York: McGraw-Hill.

Nicol, Davidson. 1993. "Race, Ethnohistory, and Other Matters: A Discussion of Kwame Anthony Appiah, *In My Father's House: Africa in the Philosophy of Culture.*" *African Studies Review* 36, no. 3:109–16.

Oliver, Roland, and John Fage. 1966. *A Short History of Africa.* Baltimore: Penguin.

Perry, William J. 1923. *The Children of the Sun.* London: Methuen.

Schlesinger, Arthur M. 1991. *The Disuniting of America.* New York: Whittle Direct Books.

Skinner, Elliott P. 1992. *African Americans and U.S. Policy toward Africa: 1850–1924.* Washington, D.C.: Howard University Press.

Soyinka, Wole. 1995. "Yoruban Astrophysics." *Washington Post,* Apr. 9, 1995, p. C3.

Stuckey, Sterling. 1972. *The Ideological Origins of Black Nationalism.* Boston: Beacon.

Tempels, Placide. 1959. *Bantu Philosophy.* Paris: Présence Africaine.

Towa, Marcien. 1971. *Essai sur la problematique philosophique dans l'Afrique actuelle.* Yaounde, Cameroon: Cle.

Vansina, Jan. 1984. *Art History in Africa.* London: Longman.

Washington, Joseph R. 1972. *Marriage in Black and White.* Boston: Beacon.

Wheatley, Phillis. 1786. *Poems on Various Subjects, Religious and Moral.* Philadelphia: Joseph Crukshank.

PART 2

Transcontinental Power and Resources
in the Production of Knowledge

4   The Ascent, Triumph, and Disintegration of the Africanist Enterprise, USA

William G. Martin and Michael O. West

To speak of the study of Africa in North America is almost invariably to enter into a discussion of the state and future of the field of African studies. Yet it has not always been so: less than fifty years ago, few would have imagined the existence of an extended national network of scholars and institutions focused on continental or, to be more precise, sub-Saharan Africa. And it may not always be so: as we and others in this volume argue, the present state of the field portends a far more exciting and diverse future than the one commonly charted by boosters of African studies.

This chapter contributes to the discussion by unearthing the origins and evolution of African studies in the United States, with an emphasis on its core intellectual and institutional pillars. There are many surprises along the way. Contrary to a generation of triumphalist narratives, African studies was not born out of thin air; rather, the emergence of this highly racialized field of study—the Africanist enterprise—required the purposeful displacement of a competing and older tradition of black scholarship. In looking forward we depart sharply from Africanist assessments that stress the field's assured place in the academic firmament. In our view the original intellectual, material, and racial pillars underpinning the Africanist enterprise are crumbling under pressure from academic and global restructuring on the one hand and insurgent intellectual and popular movements on the other, thereby opening up exciting prospects for a broader, more deeply engaging investigation of the African world. If the study of Africa is to survive, much less flourish, we need not only to reappraise the legacies we inherit but also to choose wisely among the multiple, alternative paths before us.[1]

The Study of Africa before Africanists

Africanist accounts of the genesis of African studies in the United States have much in common with European notions of life on the African continent before the onset of colonial rule: in the beginning, the intellectual landscape was without form, and knowledge of Africa was void. Then came the Africanists with the light, and they thought it was good, and they proceeded to divide the light from the darkness. Put in less biblical language, the Africanist creation narration claims that prior to the 1950s, interest in Africa was minuscule, knowledge about it even less significant, and serious scholarly inquiry into the subject virtually nonexistent.

This view of the beginning is as old as the U.S. Africanist enterprise itself, finding expression in Melville Herskovits's presidential address to the African Studies Association's (ASA) first annual meeting in 1958. Although heartily self-congratulatory about "the number of visitors from Africa and from Europe who comment on the seriousness with which Africanists in this country approach the problems they study, their competence, and the scope of their knowledge," Herskovits made no mention of any previous intellectual tradition in the study of Africa (Herskovits 1958b:2). Gray Cowan, Herskovits's immediate successor as president of the ASA, took much the same view (see, e.g., Cowan n.d.)

The silences of the older Africanist pioneers were elevated to the level of historical fact by those following in their footsteps. Thus Philip D. Curtin, their disciple and younger colleague, could declaim in his 1970 ASA presidential swan song: "At the end of the Second World War North America had no real community of scholars specializing on Africa" (Curtin 1971:358). Over ten years later Immanuel Wallerstein, another former ASA president, repeated the same refrain from the standpoint of a young researcher who first went to Africa in the late 1950s: "Scholars [of Africa] in the United States, who prior to 1945, had virtually been one man—Melville Herskovits—now began to invade every remote corner of the continent." This Africanist invasion of Africa, he was quick to add, was a multiracial affair: "Among these American scholars, there was an important contingent of Black American scholars" (Wallerstein 1983:12).

Conspicuously absent from these narratives is any mention of more than a century of work by African American scholars. The output of these scholars, working alongside other black scholars elsewhere in the diaspora and in Africa, had been a central element in pan-African thought since the time of the French, American, and Haitian revolutions. Labeled "vindicationist" by St. Clair Drake, this intellectual tradition was primarily historical and, to a lesser extent, ethnographic in focus, encompassing the great African kingdoms and civilizations in North as well as West Africa (Drake 1990). The vindicationist tradition had its origins in attempts by black intellectuals, writers, pamphleteers, and memorialists to vindicate Africa and Africans, to defend them against their traducers in Europe and the Americas who hurled calumnies about a "Dark Africa" devoid of history and culture. Vindicationism, in brief, was a project to negate the "whiting out" of the African past.

With the dawning of the new century, the study of Africa in the United States became increasingly more sophisticated as self-trained historians steeped in the vindicationist tradition gave way to university-educated scholars. Most of these new professional researchers and teachers found a home in the black universities and colleges that had been founded after the Civil War. In 1915 Carter G. Woodson, a professional historian based outside the academy, took the lead in establishing the Association for the Study of Negro (now Afro-American) Life and History, which soon became the premier U.S. organization concerned with the study of the African American and other Africa-related experiences (Goggin 1993; Meier and Rudwick 1986; Shepperson 1974). Journals published by these and other black intellectual networks, such as the *Journal of Negro History,* the *Journal of Negro Education, Phylon,* and the more popular *Negro History Bulletin,* became the leading outlets for scholarly research on Africa in the United States.

The founding of the ASA in 1958 signaled the coming eclipse of this intellectual network. Contrary to the silences fostered by various accounts of the development of African studies, however, the Africanist pioneers were highly cognizant of the earlier tradition of black scholarship. Indeed, to study Africa prior to the 1950s required participation in a nexus consisting of black scholars, journals, professional associations, and institutions such as Howard and Fisk, where courses on continental Africa, if not actual programs, had been established.

These interconnections are well exemplified by the career of Melville Herskovits, the founding father of the Africanist enterprise. Herskovits was a student of Franz Boas, well known for debunking previous white-supremacist anthropological cant, and his early work on people of African descent necessitated an engagement with African American scholars and scholarship. For example, he employed black assistants to measure the lips, pupils, noses, faces, skin color, stature, and craniums of "crossed individuals" in Harlem and at Howard University—research from which he produced over a dozen publications by the late 1920s on "the biological phenomenon of racial mixture" (Herskovits 1930:1, 282).

Herskovits's concern with race mixing and genealogy extended to publications in black-directed projects. Thus one of his earliest scholarly essays appeared in *The New Negro,* the foremost anthology to come out of the New Negro movement, or Harlem Renaissance, of the 1920s, where he addressed a leading theme in the preceding century's pan-African scholarship: the relation of Africans in the diaspora to Africans on the continent. In "The Negro's Americanism" Herskovits rejected the notion that there is a distinctive African heritage in the United States, arguing rather that African Americans are "just like any other American community. The same pattern, only a different shade!" (Herskovits 1986:353). "Of the African culture" he found "not a trace. Even the spirituals are an expression of the emotion of the Negro playing through the typical religious patterns of white America" (1986: 359). In short, blacks had assimilated the dominant Anglo-American culture "as all great racial and social groups in this country have absorbed it" (1986:359). Herskovits subsequently abandoned this idea, most notably in *The Myth of the Negro Past* (1958a), where he joined other scholars in arguing for a significant African component in black cultures throughout the Americas, including the United States. Significantly, in all these endeavors, those sympathetic to Herskovits's views (such as Lorenzo Turner) as well as his opponents (such as E. Franklin Frazier) were mainly black scholars.

Among the individuals in this scholarly network, however, Herskovits alone would move to a position of power and stature within the academy. As this occurred, his pivotal position endowed him with a gatekeeper role for the funding of U.S. scholarship on the African diaspora as well as on continental Africa—all of which, up to the end of World War II, remained primarily the province of black scholars. Although supporting limited assistance to black scholars such as Lorenzo Turner, whose position was more in line with his own evolving interpretations (Wade-Lewis 1992), Herskovits was far less chivalrous to men with opposing views and greater talents. Thus in the 1930s he sought to deny funding for what was then the most ambitious black scholarly project to date: W. E. B. Du Bois's *Encyclopedia Africana*. Herskovits curtly informed Rayford Logan, a Howard historian and keen supporter of the project, that "Dr. Du Bois was not a 'scholar'; he was a 'radical' and a 'Negrophile'" (Janken 1993:95). When the General Education Board (GEB) declined to support the encyclopedia, Herskovits took the credit, gloating, "I was the hatchet man" (in Janken 1993:95). This was in part an idle boast based on Herskovits's underestimation of the level of anti-Semitism in the upper echelons of U.S. society; Herskovits was not quite as influential as he thought, at least not at that time. As Janken notes, the GEB official who handled the application felt that "Jews had entirely too high a profile in the United States. Nevertheless, the decision to deny the funding of the Encyclopedia, which was made at the top of the philanthrophic ladder, borrowed something from the tone of Herskovits's crowing" (Janken 1993:95).

Nor was Herskovits the only Africanist pioneer to engage the predominantly black, pre-Africanist networks concerned with the study of global Africa. Consider, too, the case of William O. Brown, another founding fellow of the ASA, its third president, and creator of the Boston University African Studies Center. Brown, like Herskovits, taught at Howard University—in his case working in the Department of Sociology for more than five years. Then, in 1943, Brown left Howard and joined the State Department's Office of Strategic Services. The whitewashing of these histories reveals just how sharply the Africanist pioneers sought to separate their enterprise from African American traditions and scholarship and how African studies from its very origins was to be marked by a racialized intellectual tradition and hierarchy. As we will show, these features would bedevil Africanists until the present day.

African Studies: Ascendant and Resplendent

The Africanist enterprise in the United States experienced its greatest growth in the late 1950s and 1960s. The major signposts are well known: the founding of the ASA, the creation and proliferation of major African studies centers, and the establishment of new journals and book series. At the heart of these efforts stood a small cohort of scholars, symbolized by the activities of the individuals who met in New York on March 22–24, 1957, to launch the ASA. As the news release prepared by United States Information Agency (USIA) officer John Noon noted, this new "nonpolitical" body would "focus upon the problems of sub-Saharan Africa." Melville Herskovits became the first president, backed by vice-president Gwendolen Carter and six other members of the board of trustees.[2] Voting rights and board membership were restricted to the College of Fellows, with the credentials of aspiring fellows being screened by the board "to ensure the continued scholarly character" of the ASA and prevent its control by "action groups, dilettantes, or fadists" (U.S. Department of State 1958:6).

The rapid expansion of African studies is illustrated by ASA membership: the ranks grew from the 35 founders to 291 fellows and 866 total members in 1960 (African Studies Association 1960:36) and 1,400 members by 1970 (Bay 1991:3).[3] The institutions organized by Africanists followed a similar path, with the program established in 1948 by Herskovits at Northwestern University being joined by the Boston University program in 1953 and Howard's new program in 1954; perhaps another ten smaller programs were in existence by the time of the ASA's founding.

The 1960s were the real growth years, as many more small programs emerged and existing ones grew into what became known as comprehensive language and area studies centers. Lambert would count at least thirty-four major programs by the early 1970s (Lambert 1973:15).[4] The appearance of new journals followed a similar path, with the first issues of *African Studies Bulletin* (later *African Studies Review*), *African Historical Studies* (later the *International Journal of African Historical Studies*) and *Research in African Litera-*

tures appearing in 1958, 1968, and 1970, respectively. Ties to African scholars and institutions were also established as U.S. Africanists and their students, flush with funding, descended on the continent and its new, postindependence universities. Meanwhile, the number of African students in the United States increased rapidly, and they began to be channeled away from Howard and the historically black universities in the South to the new programs in the North, Midwest, and West.[5] In short, by the end of the 1960s the Africanist enterprise at the major historically white research universities had become rather well established.

Underwriting this impressive record was an outpouring of private and public funding. In the 1940s and 1950s the major foundations—Carnegie, Rockefeller, and especially Ford—mobilized to create the new fields of area, including African, studies. Ford began offering Foreign Area Fellowships in 1954, and Carnegie supplied the funds for the ad hoc committee whose deliberations led to the founding of the ASA. Ford subsequently donated $25,000 ($133,000 in 1994 dollars)[6] to cover the first two years of the ASA's operations and in the third year gave the organization another $100,000 ($500,000 in 1994 dollars) ("Ford Foundation Grant" 1961:50).

Public support was even more substantial than that provided by the foundations. The federal government is estimated to have invested $76 million in African projects between 1949 and 1964, and the Ford Foundation alone claims to have spent $20 million over a somewhat longer period (Staniland 1983:79). Moreover, area studies faculty were paid considerably more than most faculty in the country and supplemented their incomes to a greater degree with summer teaching, lecture fees, and research salaries (Lambert 1973:43–44). In ways unimaginable to both the previous generation of researchers of Africa and today's younger scholars, a career in African studies in the late 1950s and 1960s was indeed a rewarding one.

Federal and foundation support for the creation of African studies was, of course, only one small part of a much larger agenda: the rapid production of a body of experts on all major areas of the world. Underpinning this drive was the United States' startling new role on the world stage, the emergence of the cold war, and the decolonization of European empires. As Sputnik was launched and fear and loathing of the Soviet Union accelerated, the U.S. government propelled forward major new programs such as the National Defense Education Act (NDEA) of 1958, which created the Title VI area centers.[7] As one of the founders of the ASA aptly put it, African studies programs were "originally designed somewhat as crash programs to create requisite numbers of young African specialists for posts in government, industry, or in international public and private agencies" (Cowan 1969:5). This somewhat overstates the case; as Wallerstein has recently pointed out (1997), during and immediately after World War II, U.S. state, corporate, and foundation officials became increasingly concerned about the lack of experts on the contemporary dynamics of what would come to be called the "Third World." There is no question, however, that the cold war and nationalist movements propelled this concern onto center stage.

Leading government and foundation officials were quite blunt in linking the projection of U.S. power on the world stage, the defense of the "free world" against communism, and the creation of African and area studies programs to counter the Soviet threat (Staniland 1983:79). Such concerns mushroomed rapidly with the emergence of independent and often radical African states and, especially, cold war competition in Africa, as dramatically illustrated in the Congo crisis of 1960. Speaking at Tulane University in 1959, less than six months after his appointment, Joseph C. Satterthwaite, the first U.S. assistant secretary of state for African affairs, denounced "predatory international communism, the new imperialism of the USSR" (van Essen 1960:853).

Foundation officers heartily endorsed the crusade. The president of the Ford Foundation proclaimed in 1954: "Any program directed toward human welfare in this period of history must be concerned with the increased involvement of our country in world affairs, with our new responsibilities of international leadership, and, above all, with the deadly threat to any hope of human progress posed by wars and communism" (Sutton and Smock 1976:68). Similarly, Alan Pifer of the Carnegie Corporation urged Africanists to help fulfill the university's role as "a highly important instrument of policy-making and execution in America's international relations," pointing to Senator Henry Jackson's advocacy of NATO recommendations on the teaching of African languages (African Studies Association 1959:24).

Little systematic research has been done on the close relationships that developed between federal officials, military and security agencies, foundation officials, and leading area and African studies scholars. To a large extent, these hidden relationships began to be unearthed only in the wake of the 1960s rebellions, particularly through the revelations of the Church Committee in Congress and insurgent scholars' unmasking of direct Central Intelligence Agency (CIA) funding of such major organizations as the African American Institute and the Congress for Cultural Freedom (Africa Research Group 1970; Berman 1982; Ray et al. 1979; Schecter 1976; Staniland 1983–84). Yet the forging of common agendas extended back well prior to the 1960s, as in the private meetings and deliberations funded and hosted by foundation officials that led to the design of the ASA (African Studies Association 1958; Cowan 1957). Unexplored private archives suggest even covert solicitations, and not always from the federal government to area experts. Thus one of Herskovits's first acts on assuming the ASA presidency was to write to Allen W. Dulles, director of the CIA, on behalf of the ASA: "The Association, which represented the combined strength of those concerned with Africa in this country . . . would be happy to aid you in any way it can," Herskovits informed the spymaster (Herskovits 1958c).

Such individual actions reveal a much more significant and collective process: the creation of a set of shared assumptions, agendas, and interchanges at the higher levels of the academy and private and public agencies. These mutual understandings were a hallmark of U.S. hegemony as a common worldview was disseminated across academic, foundation, government, and popular institutions. Initiated by numerous planning conferences, shared personnel, and research projects, this process eventually took root in new academic, nongovernmental, and governmental organizations concerned with what was called the "Third World" (see, e.g., Berman 1982; Murphy 1973). By the mid-1960s common commitments and perspectives were so well dispersed that activities within a multilayered set of institutions could proceed along similar lines, without the necessity of a coordinating group or central institution.

Constructing the Africanist Household

Although firmly grounded in extended relations with policymakers and foundation officials, the nascent Africanist enterprise faced critical choices and difficulties within the academy, such as fixing the institutional location of the field and its personnel, recruiting and training experts on sub-Saharan Africa, and constructing "Africa" as an object of study. In all these areas, the Africanists and other area specialists confronted well-entrenched and parochial interests within the leading research universities. Aiding the new fields' advocates was the vast expansion of tertiary education in the 1950s and 1960s, which paved the way for the emergence of new and well-funded programs on the study of the world beyond the borders of Europe and North America.

Early postwar commissions, in tackling the pressing problem of U.S. policymakers' embarrassing lack of information on most parts of the world (see, e.g., Hall 1947; Fenton 1947), boldly argued for an altogether new structure within the academy: independent units staffed by faculty members ranging across the traditional academic disciplines and organized according to postwar geostrategic criteria. For reasons discerned in the late 1940s, however, the promise of new multidisciplinary perspectives was never to be fulfilled. Such an intellectual rearrangement was precluded by the academy's preexisting divisions along disciplinary lines, with each discipline vigorously defending its own methods, subject matter, and resources. As Fenton foresaw in his 1947 report: "Integrated area study threatens the regular departmental organization of the university since by its very nature it calls for a realignment of subject-matter fields and methodologies. . . . All threats to the reduction of the staff and the number of courses with a resultant drop in enrollments, loss of book fees, and decline in budget are resisted by heads of departments" (Fenton 1947:81). Taking the line of least resistance, the vast majority of the leading Africanists sought to locate themselves within the disciplines, a decision based on the power and prestige of the disciplines as well as on the Africanists' desire to distinguish themselves from what they regarded as the "unscientific" and eclectic interdisciplinary methods of black and pan-African scholars.

Herskovits was among the strongest exponents of this latter position, despite his own training, his early "scientific" work on "mixed races," and the difficulties he faced in his home discipline of anthropology. In concluding his opening address as first ASA president, he drew attention to a key point in a Ford Foundation report that had been distributed in advance to the conference participants:

> One point, made again and again in the Report that was laid before us, is eminently relevant here. I am convinced that our best insurance against the vagaries of academic faddism lies in the continuation of the policy so strongly urged there, that Africanists obtain their degrees in the disciplines, and that candidates for these degrees not only be good Africanists, but good economists, good anthropologists, good geographers, good historians, and the like. . . . The very fact that our Association has taken the form we have given it is perhaps the best augury of its permanence. (1958b:11)

The very definition of the term *Africanist* was distilled from this view. As Ford Foundation official Melvin Fox put it, "the Africanist—or Africa Specialist— is the individual whose advanced qualifications and status in a specific discipline have been obtained through extended Africa research, and who has the motivation and interest to continue to use Africa research and experience as a major means of advancing training and resources in his discipline" (Africa Studies Association 1959:19).

Herskovits and Fox were hardly alone in this view, which was widely shared within the Africanist community. Jan Vansina, one of the founders of the program at the University of Wisconsin at Madison, recalls in his autobiography:

> We [Philip Curtin and Vansina] had to decide [in 1961] whether the program should become a department of its own, as it was at SOAS and soon would be at UCLA, or whether the teaching of area courses should be done in existing departments. We decided for the second alternative because the goal was to spread awareness of African Studies throughout the university, rather than to create a ghetto for it. . . The African Studies Program was then merely to be a coordinating agency whose goal would be to place African specialists in the main departments of social sciences and humanities. . . The formula we developed for African studies (interdepartmental programs) was quickly imitated by most universities elsewhere in North America. (Vansina 1994:101, 103)

Although the Wisconsin program was hardly such a leader—following as it did on the older programs at Northwestern, Howard, and Boston—Vansina is correct in noting that centers and programs came to be small coordinating operations with few faculty lines.[8] This practice was consistent with the pattern in area studies generally, where fewer than 6 percent of the programs in the early 1970s reported that "some," "most," or "all" of their faculty members held appointments in the coordinating unit (Lambert 1973:211).

These decisions would later come to bedevil the founders of African studies and their protégés. As he notes ruefully throughout his autobiography, ethnohistorian Vansina was constantly confronted with the choice of being either an anthropologist or a historian (Vansina 1994). By the early 1970s Philip Curtin was noting the changing fortunes of historians, as other disciplines better suited to policy and development studies came into prominence (Curtin 1971). For younger scholars, the choices narrowed even further: promotion, tenure, and the other rewards of an academic career depended on the judgments of senior scholars deeply rooted in the disciplines, and with the possible exception of anthropology, the key disciplines were always dominated by scholarship and methods based on studying the United States and Europe.

The turn toward the disciplines also complicated the founding Africanists' search for scholars to fill the expanding number of faculty positions. Given the disciplines' historical lack of interest in areas outside Europe and North America, and the rigid exclusion of black scholars and their research agendas, the early years of the Africanist enterprise were marked by a scramble for personnel that ranged across the United States, Canada, Europe, and even Africa. Some U.S. Africanists, such as William O. Brown, founder of the Boston University program, came to African studies from government posts. Others shifted the focus of their research, as in the then ongoing transition among anthropologists—particularly the students of Boas—from the study of Native Americans along the now-closed frontier to the study of seemingly more pristine African "tribes." Still other budding Africanists went from Commonwealth or Caribbean studies to African studies, a path taken by historian Philip Curtin and political scientist Gwendolen Carter, among others. Absent by design, of course, were scholars such as Howard's William Leo Hansberry, whose courses on African kingdoms and empires were not welcome in the new program constructed by Franklin Frazier and funded by the Ford Foundation;[9] more distinguished pan-African scholars such as Du Bois were not only ostracized by academia but hounded by the U.S. government as well.

The talent scouts for the U.S. Africanist enterprise found a particularly rich pool of potential recruits among the European experts produced by colonial and settler powers, with extended and well-financed tours across Africa and

Europe pinpointing available personnel for recruitment.[10] Faced with the dismal prospects of postwar Europe, many European scholars found the more lucrative field of African studies in the United States irresistible; Vansina, recruited to Wisconsin, would innocently remark on unexpected tenure, promotions, funding, and competing offers from other universities (see Vansina 1994:93, passim). Leading Africanists, including expatriates, became academic gatekeepers, often in their capacity as directors of African studies programs. A few senior Africa specialists assumed even more powerful positions. For instance, C. W. de Kiewiet, an expatriate from the settler and colonial world, became president of Rochester University and a key consultant to private foundations (Murphy 1973:53, 90, 99–119). By 1969 one assessment reported that over 80 percent of the full professorships in African history were held by men recruited from overseas (Curtin 1971:362).[11]

Although it has been suggested that the recruitment of overseas personnel constituted a "brain drain" from both Europe and Africa (Curtin 1971), there is little evidence that Africans, particularly those engaged in pan-African networks, were recruited in any appreciable numbers in the 1950s and 1960s. Lambert's 1973 study reported that only 2.1 percent of U.S. African area specialists were born in Africa. Indeed, the flow during this period was most likely in the other direction. In the late 1960s, even with the process of "Africanization" in full swing, the full-time teaching staff at many leading African universities—including Nairobi, Dakar, Abidjan, and Makerere— remained predominantly expatriate (de Kiewiet 1971: table 14). Many European scholars were attracted to African universities by salary levels that were higher than those they could command at home. Historian John McCracken fondly remembered that during the buoyant 1960s, "to my own good fortune, salaries in African universities were actually higher than in Britain," and "there was a constant going between Britain and Africa with young African scholars making the pilgrimage to SOAS just as young British scholars set out to win their spurs in English-Speaking colleges, several of which were still taking the London degree" (1993:239–40).

Needless to say, direct northern funding of research by Africans or independent African institutions was minimal, with the exception of white scholars in the settler areas.[12] Even visits to the United States by politically active African students or scholars were rare. Writing from New York to colleagues at Fort Hare, Z. K. Matthews noted that foundations were uninterested in supporting institutions such as Fort Hare and added, "It is not easy to get into America, because the great bugbear here as elsewhere is the communist. The F.B.I. is on the lookout for them all the time, and they find them, to their satisfaction, in the queerest of places!" (Matthews 1952). Privileging white scholars also enabled North American funders and scholars to avoid confronting racism in the colonies or settler states, including the United States.

Reporting to the Fulbright Foundation in 1953, Alan Pifer addressed the question of whether it was "advisable to select American negroes to take teaching positions in the African colonies." The answer was predictable; colonial officials in East and Central Africa, he asserted, "frankly thought it was not advisable. Regardless of any attempts to make negro teachers feel welcome, they would find themselves subjected to the same social restrictions as Africans, similar in character to those obtaining in the southern states of the United States. As senior members of staff receiving salaries based on expatriate rates they would be entitled to expatriate housing, which could be most awkward" (Pifer 1953:86). In the case of South Africa, not covered by Pifer, the buttressing of racial discrimination in housing, education, and salaries was even greater.

As these comments suggest, the Africanist pioneers had strong relationships with European scholars and institutions.[13] Yet it would be a mistake to view the rise of African studies in the United States as simply the emergence of a new, wealthy, senior partner in the Anglo-American world, for central to the creation of the Africanist enterprise in the United States was a fundamental shift in the construction of "Africa" as an intellectual object. Whereas European scholars had long defined and studied Africa as part of larger imperial or orientalist networks stretching from Asia to the Caribbean, area and African studies were a U.S. invention, befitting a global hierarchy of nation-states grouped into newly defined regions atop which sat the United States (Palat 1996).[14] As one scholar from Sierra Leone noted in the late 1950s, "'area' programs were a peculiarly American idea. . . . British scholarship in the past tended to look on African studies as an aspect of the colonial relationship and therefore as of comparatively minor importance" (Africa Studies Association 1959:15).

The institutional and intellectual framework that emerged from these efforts marked a new "Africa," separated from the African diaspora and European colonial systems. The Africa thus created by Africanists was then further subdivided into the study of localities, whether in the older anthropological tradition or, increasingly, in the emergent nation-states model preferred by political science and the other social sciences dedicated to national integration and development (Wallerstein 1983). In practice, this almost always meant that "Africa" encompassed only sub-Saharan Africa, as openly stated in the ASA's founding news release. Such a definition marked, of course, a sharp break with the earlier generation of pan-African scholarship, which stressed ties across the boundaries of North Africa, sub-Saharan Africa, and the wider African world; the study of African civilizations and kingdoms, central to the vindicationist tradition, was studiously shunted aside.

The Africanist intellectual rupture moved hand in hand with the federal government's own institutional reorganization. Up through the mid-1930s responsibility for African issues was largely located, as befitted a colonial world, in the Bureau of European Affairs. This pattern changed slightly in 1943 when Africa came under an equally imperial construction called the Bureau of Near Eastern, South Asian, and African Affairs, although South Africa and Madagascar remained within the Bureau of European Affairs and therefore outside "Africa." Only in 1958 was an autonomous bureau of African affairs established (van Essen 1960:845–46), marking the new concerns with anticommunism, African nationalism, the birth of independent states, and eventually, development programs for U.S. allies.

African Studies and Unruly Africans

By the late 1960s the core features of the Africanist enterprise were in place. The key journals, centers, and national associations were all established, providing channels for the production of the first generation of scholars at the major research universities dedicated to the study of a newly defined Africa. No period is more fondly recalled by Africanists than the golden first decade, when all seemed possible and all, seemingly, was funded.

Yet all was not well, for there was trouble brewing on both sides of the Atlantic. From the African continent itself came increasing signs that African scholars were rejecting their subordinate status in the Africanist enterprise. As Robert Baum, acting director of the Office of Research and Analysis for Africa in the State Department's Bureau of Intelligence and Research, noted in a 1965 *African Studies Review* article:

> In recent years new obstacles have confronted Europeans and Americans, as well as Africans, who wish to pursue social science research in Africa. Europeans and Americans face increasing African annoyance and suspicion. Africans are disturbed at being regarded as guinea pigs and their countries as laboratories to test scientific hypotheses. They are wearying of visits by team after team of specialists, asking many of the same questions, probing many of the same people, with very little, Africans feel, being received in return for what some of them consider exploitation. The days are numbered when an Apter or a Coleman can go to Africa, find "virgin" fields of social science research, and be welcomed with open arms. (Baum 1965:43)

These warnings were echoed by others. In the wake of revelations about CIA funding of African studies, the ASA's Africa Research Liaison Committee held a small conference that addressed the issue of African resistance to visiting U.S. Africanists (Africa Studies Association 1966). Such concerns were also expressed in more public venues. Writing in the *African Studies Bulletin,* leading Africanists William Hance and Philip Curtin called for greater sensitivity and responsibility on the part of U.S. scholars (Hance and Curtin 1966), a view endorsed by Ford Foundation officials, who funded Hance and

Curtin's research into the matter (Sutton 1977). Still, a noticeable trend to-ward "total disengagement" from the Africanist enterprise among Africa-based African scholars continued unabated (Cowan 1972).

Particularly noteworthy was African scholars' and institutions' shunning, often by private arrangement, of Northern Africanists and their journals. In the case of the British, some Africans argued that it was their loss of control over journals in their former colonies (e.g., *Transactions of the Historical Society of Ghana*, the *Uganda Journal, Tanganyika Notes and Records*, and the *Journal of the Historical Society of Nigeria*) that led directly to the founding in the early 1960s of the *Journal of African History* and the *Journal of Modern African Studies* (Obichere 1976:30).[15] Increasingly, African and European–North American scholars went their separate ways, with well-funded U.S. Africanists bypassing African scholars and institutions.

Closer to home, an even more direct challenge to the Africanist enterprise was in the making. As the civil rights movement gave way to the Black Power era in the United States, African studies would confront a serious crisis ema-nating from a new round of intellectual resistance that drew on the African American traditions, commitments, and definitions of Africa that had been shunted aside by the Africanists. In sum, black studies was posited in oppo-sition to African studies.

The first open signs of trouble appeared during the 1968 annual ASA meeting in Los Angeles when a black caucus emerged, using as its rallying cry that great buzzword of the 1960s: relevance.[16] The emergence of a black caucus within the ASA should not have come as a surprise, for it followed a pattern of black self-assertion apparent around the world. As is well known, by the mid-1960s young black students and scholars were launching major assaults on the white academy, including the major disciplinary associations, where black caucuses were often formed (Guthrie 1976; Ladner 1973; Woodard 1977). Indeed, black scholars and students had an added incentive for form-ing a black caucus inside the ASA: not only was the Black Power movement in the United States greatly inspired by continental African political move-ments and intellectual currents, but many U.S.-based black scholars of Af-rica traced their academic lineage directly back to the pre-Africanist tradi-tion. Black scholars thus concluded that "when the ASA was formed in the late 1950's and large grants were made to this White-led organization, Blacks and Black organizations who had been interested in Africa were bypassed" (Payne 1970:22).

The ASA Black Caucus called on the organization to take steps "towards rendering itself more relevant and competent to deal with the challenging times and conditions of black people in Africa, in the United States, and in the whole black world." This the ASA could do by recruiting more blacks into the organization, "with particular emphasis on black youth, inside and outside the universities," and by giving black scholars a more visible role in the organization. A second major demand of the Black Caucus was that the ASA should encourage interaction between Africanists and the emerging field of black studies (Clarke 1969:7–8). These demands were formally presented to the ASA board, which responded by forming an ad hoc committee—the Committee on Afro-American Studies—under the chairmanship of James Gibbs, a Stanford professor, to look into the matter.[17]

Meanwhile, the Black Caucus established its own ad hoc committee and made plans for a meeting in New York at the end of the year.[18] This meeting was followed by a second one in June 1969 in Washington, D.C., where the Black Caucus was transformed into the African Heritage Studies Association (AHSA).[19] The AHSA reiterated the Black Caucus's demand for greater black participation in the ASA, including the election of more blacks to the College of Fellows; recommended the establishment of a journal; and spoke generally about black people having "control over [their] own history, its interpretation, etc." (Clarke 1969:8–9). Still, at this point the AHSA remained old wine in a new bottle, the Black Caucus under a new guise rather than an organization separate from and competing with the ASA, as it would soon become.

The road to separation was laid through Montreal, where in October 1969 the ASA, in its first foray outside the United States, held its twelfth annual meeting in conjunction with the Committee on African Studies in Canada. At the opening of the first day's session, a group of AHSA members, in an apparently well-orchestrated move, mounted the stage and seized the microphone from incoming ASA president L. Gray Cowan, who was about to introduce the guest speaker, Gabriel d'Arboussier, Senegal's ambassador to West Germany (Haynes 1969; Fraser 1969; Smith 1970).

The AHSA demands, which were elaborated later that day in another commandeered forum, centered on the usual issues of social relevance and black empowerment within the ASA and the field of African studies as a whole. Accusing the ASA of perpetuating "colonialism and neocolonialism through the 'educational' institutions and the mass media," the black activists demanded that the study of Africa "be undertaken from a pan-Africanist perspective . . . [which] defines that all black people are African peoples and negates the tribalization of African peoples by geographical demarcations on the basis of colonialist spheres of influence." Specifically, the AHSA demanded racial parity in the ASA, with a new board to consist of "six Africans and six Europeans," as well as a committee to allocate research funds, also to be made up of "equal numbers of Africans and Europeans." The AHSA further urged the ASA to denounce the detention by a "colonialist government" of black (mainly Caribbean) students who had been imprisoned in the wake of protests at Sir George Williams University in Montreal in 1968 and to provide them with financial support (Africa Studies Association 1969:1–2).

By this point the meeting had assumed a crisis atmosphere, with most of the planned academic deliberations and other business curtailed or suspended entirely. There was talk of calling in the riot squad to rout the black militants, but cooler heads prevailed, partly because Canadian Africanists, who had suspended their participation in the meeting when it turned raucous, feared a contagion effect on the volatile politics of Quebec: "Police activity might prompt outside trouble by local French-speaking militants" (Johnson 1969).

The crisis came to a head at the usually staid ASA business meeting, where Professor Chike Onwuachi officially presented the AHSA demands. The ASA board accepted the demand for a committee to look into the issue of research funds but doubted its authority to abolish itself and reconstitute a new board based on racial parity. Consequently a motion was introduced, and after heated discussion the ASA fellows, who were the only ones eligible to vote among the 1,600 people who registered for the meeting, defeated it by a vote of 104 to 93 (a vote comprising less than a third of the 614 fellows as of October 1, 1969). As the dismayed AHSA members, with a small group of white supporters in tow, withdrew to decide on their next strategy, Professor Fred Burke, of SUNY-Buffalo, rose to offer a way out of the quagmire.

Speaking on behalf of a group of twenty-five "concerned white liberals," Burke proposed the creation of a thirty-member racially balanced committee to draft a new constitution that would include a clause stating that "at least half of the members of the new Board of Directors must be Black" (Africa Studies Association 1969). Reversing their earlier decision, the fellows voted for the Burke amendment by a wide margin, and the AHSA accepted the proffered olive branch provided that it could appoint the committee's fifteen black members—a demand approved by the ASA leadership. The ASA also decided to select, by mail ballot of the entire membership and not just fellows, the other fifteen committee members, who could be of any race. With these arrangements in place, regular academic business resumed on the last day of the meeting, and Ambassador d'Arboussier, who had been patiently cooling his heels for the better part of two days, was finally able to hold forth at a banquet (Africa Studies Association 1969; Haynes 1969; Fraser 1969; Resnick 1969a; Burke 1969).

The truce did not last, however, the immediate reason for its demise being the actions of James Duffy, the ASA executive secretary and a former president of the organization. In response to attacks on the Burke amendment, Duffy unilaterally suspended the accord while he sought legal advice on its validity. The ASA attorney determined that the constitution had indeed been violated at the business meeting in Montreal, making any resolution passed there null and void (Duffy 1970). With the death of the accord went all hope of reconciliation between the ASA and AHSA.

Yet the death by legal technicality of the Montreal accord merely pre-empted a less decorous political execution orchestrated by ASA members, including representatives of the board. Besides challenging the legality of the accord, the rejectionists launched a campaign to put it to a referendum of the ASA membership. The result was decisive. With 1,040 of the approxi-mately 1,600 members voting, only 235 favored refashioning the board on lines demanded by the AHSA and proposed by the Burke amendment. A majority of respondents, 588, believed the ASA should maintain the "non-racial" status quo while at the same time working with the AHSA to recruit more blacks into the organization. A smaller group of "nonracialists," 148 with the conditional support of an additional 24, rejected all outreach to the AHSA "or any other special interest group" (Duffy 1970:3).

Although prominent Africanists such as John Marcum, Gwendolen Carter, and Ibrahim Abu-Lughod publicly defended the Montreal accord, its detrac-tors were far more numerous, high powered, and loquacious. The rejection-ists accused the ASA leadership of appeasing thugs bent on introducing ex-traneous political issues under the threat of violence, making the Montreal accord both legally and morally invalid. For instance, Henry L. Bretton, speak-ing "as a graduate of Hitler Germany," declared his unwillingness to appease the AHSA, saying: "I cannot ever bring myself to agree that dissent can be allowed to be stifled by violent means. Neither can I agree that meetings called for peaceful purposes can be allowed to be hijacked" (Bretton 1969:19–20). Arthur Keppel-Jones, claiming to have "spent much of [his] life opposing the white racist regime in South Africa," went further: "I recognize Nazi storm-troopers when I see them, and am no more willing to submit to bullying from black ones than from white" (Arthur Keppel-Jones 1969:27).

The most notable objection to the Montreal accord came from a group consisting of Harvard professors Rupert Emerson (a former ASA president), Martin Kilson (an ASA board member), and Joseph S. Nye, joined by MIT's Robert I. Rotberg. Addressing itself directly to L. Gray Cowan in his capac-ity as ASA president, the Cambridge quadrumvirate denounced the "almost incomprehensible gesture of concession" made to the "small minority" rep-resented by the AHSA, which had rejected "orderly democratic procedure" and sought instead to impose its will by "physical force." The ASA, the letter continued, had "been forced to accept racialist principles and to divide its membership into racial categories," a "flagrant violation of the 'one man one vote' principle which is properly insisted on in southern Africa" (Emerson, Kilson, Nye, and Rotberg 1969:22). The letter was endorsed by an additional ninety-six Africanists, including a number of founders and former presidents of the ASA (Letters from Members 1970:11).

It was in these circumstances that representatives of the ASA and the AHSA entered into what would prove to be futile discussions, with much mutual distrust and little goodwill on either side. As the negotiators would have been well aware, there was little left to salvage. The AHSA continued to insist that the Montreal accord had to be the basis of any discussion, but the accord was dead beyond resurrection, both legally and politically. The most substantive—and as it turned out, last—meeting between the two organizations took place in January 1970. The AHSA team consisted of its president, John Henrik Clarke, along with Nicholas Onweyu, Chike Onwuachi, Inez Reid, and Herschelle Challenor, while the ASA delegation included L. Gray Cowan, Absalom Vilakazi, Daniel McCall, and Philip Curtin, the latter two having signed the Emerson-Kilson-Nye-Rotberg letter to Cowan.

The ASA representatives emphasized recent moves to "democratize" the organization, notably the abolition of the College of Fellows and the consequent elimination of the two-tier membership system. An ASA invitation to jointly host its next annual meeting was rejected by the AHSA negotiators on the grounds that theirs was "too young an organization to undertake this responsibility," although individual members were free to participate. In fact, the AHSA was busy making plans for what was billed as its second annual meeting, which was held at Howard in May 1970. Finally, Curtin, in an obvious recognition of the de facto split, proposed the establishment of a "supra board" to deal with issues of "common interest" to both organizations, a proposal the AHSA agreed to consider (Cowan 1970a:2; Rowe 1970).

The ASA supra board proposal, worked out by Curtin, was formally submitted to the AHSA in March 1970. The board would consist of six members, three AHSA nominees who were also members of the ASA and three ASA representatives who were not members of the AHSA. It would have authority over two ASA committees—the Committee on Afro-American Issues and the Committee on Teaching about Africa—with a mandate to increase the number of blacks in the ASA and improve the teaching of Africa in the United States, including instruction at the historically black universities. These proposals were so far removed from the AHSA's minimal demands, however, that they inevitably invited rejection.

In the interim the Committee on Afro-American Issues, chaired now by Adelaide Cromwell Hill, intervened to stave off the coming rupture. With the ASA "facilitating" their efforts, sixteen black scholars of Africa representing a wide range of opinions met in Kingston, Jamaica, in April 1970 in a setting described by Hill as reminiscent of the first Pan-African Congress of 1900 and the Niagara Movement of 1905 (out of which the NAACP eventually emerged). Their numbers included four of the negotiators who had met in January: Challenor, Onweyu, and Onwuachi on the AHSA side and Vilakazi on the ASA side. The "Jamaica Gathering," which featured a pep talk by the venerable Amy Jacques Garvey, generally agreed that black scholars were not being well served by the ASA and the Africanist enterprise in the United States as a whole. The gatherers were, however, powerless to reverse developments that had now developed their own internal motion (Hill 1970:5–8).[20]

Two days after the Jamaica Gathering concluded its deliberations, John Henrik Clarke, acting on behalf of the AHSA executive committee, sent a letter to L. Gray Cowan officially replying to the ASA-Curtin proposals. The proposals had been "unanimously rejected," principally because they failed to address the fundamental issue of power and resources within the ASA and African studies generally. The only meaningful supra board, Clarke allowed, would be one encompassing "all vital matters relative to African Studies: conferences, research planning, African Studies Centers, fund raising and distribution—briefly, back to where we were in Montreal." Second, Clarke went on, the AHSA objected to the structural inequality in the nomination procedures for the proposed supra board, since the ASA would have a free hand to select its nominees while at the same time also helping to choose the AHSA representatives. This, he objected, would ensure that "only those AHSA nominees (who must also be members of ASA) would be elected who offered the least obstacle to ASA's interests." Finally, the members of the AHSA executive were suspicious of Curtin for having signed the Emerson-Kilson-Nye-Rotberg letter and would not have negotiated with him if they had been aware of this in advance. "Put in black and white," Clarke concluded, "the whole thing is stacked. White overwhelmingly vote white, black vote oreo. . . . It's a beautiful scheme but blatantly arrogant and insulting! I reject it. . . . For the present, this letter ends all official relationships between our respective organizations" (Cowan and Clarke 1970:2–5). Thus did the AHSA take its leave, forgetful of the Africanist establishment by which it has largely been forgotten.

One immediate result of the rupture was the resignation of Joseph Harris, one of the Jamaica gatherers, as the program chairman for the 1970 ASA meeting (Harris 1970:8–9). The long-term consequences, however, were more important. Although not changing the ASA in any fundamental way, the fallout from Montreal helped to open up the organization and give a greater voice to hitherto disfranchised groups.

Mention has already been made of the abolition of the College of Fellows, a direct result of Montreal that enfranchised all ASA members. Emboldened by the actions of the AHSA activists, a group of white activists formed a "radical caucus," the principal objective of which was to support the AHSA demands. Indeed, it was the Radical Caucus that first seems to have raised the cry of "one-person-one vote" within the ASA. On its formation, the Radical Caucus, which later changed its name to the Pan-Africanist Radical Baraza, was endorsed by over sixty individuals (Resnick 1969b:14–15). The Radical

Caucus later formed teams of "research guerrillas" to expose the "extended family" that controlled African studies (Segal 1970:22). Another group that emerged on the political coattails of the Black Caucus–AHSA was the Women's Caucus, which came into its own at the 1970 Boston ASA meeting, pushing through resolutions committing the organization to oppose, both within its ranks and in the academy generally, discrimination "on the basis of sex, marital status, and parenthood." As part of this commitment the ASA agreed "that day-care facilities for children be established at annual meetings, staffed by both men and women" (Women's Caucus 1970:2–3).

Indeed, 1970 was a year of reflection, retrenchment, and consolidation for the ASA. After Montreal and what came in its wake—the departure of the AHSA, the disillusionment of most of the black scholars who did not join the AHSA, the demoralization of many white Africanists, and a string of resignations by both white and black members—there were numerous predictions of the ASA's imminent death (Cowan 1970b:343–44). The ASA survived, though initially in a reduced form, as evidenced by the number of people who registered for the Boston meeting: 900, little more than half the 1,600 who registered for Montreal. Even though some of those attending the Montreal meeting were Canadian Africanists, this was a considerable decline, reflecting in part the approximately 225 individuals recorded as having *withdrawn* their membership in the year after 1969 (African Studies Association 1970:5). Under the circumstances, the ASA "extended family" conceded the need for reform, hence the relatively painless incorporation of the Radical and Women's Caucuses, which were accorded official recognition in Boston.

In a further concession to those demanding social relevance, the ASA board formed the Committee on Current Issues to deal with "current controversial issues . . . of concern to Africanists," the resolution being presented by Marshal Segall and incoming president Philip Curtin (African Studies Association 1970:9). To many, the Committee on Current Issues appeared clearly to have been a preemptive strike, aimed at taking the sting out of new proposals that encompassed and went beyond the demands made by the ASHA. Even with the AHSA gone and the white insurgents—radicals and women—being incorporated, it seemed that the clouds of another political storm were gaining force. This time, however, the eye of the storm, instead of being out at sea, had already made landfall: the renewed challenge would come from within the ASA board.

The challenge was led by two of the newly elected board members. In an unprecedented move directly related to the post-Montreal realignment, the ASA in 1970 elected three black scholars to the board—Johnetta Cole, Victor Uchendu, and Willard Johnson. Johnson and Cole immediately drafted a resolution on "the dignified survival and liberation of African people, at home and abroad." The resolution called on the ASA board to implement the Montreal accord, giving the AHSA control of half of the board, "if the AHSA so desires." Even more controversial was the resolution's proposal to divide ASA membership dues in halves, one of which would go to an "African Liberation Fund." The fund would be managed by a board consisting equally of ASA members, AHSA representatives ("if that organization so desires"), and the nominees of "continental African members and guests of the ASA" ("Resolution on the . . . Commitment to the Liberation" 1970:3).

The ASA board, apparently in a tactical maneuver aimed at avoiding another Montreal-style showdown, voted to approve the Johnson-Cole resolution. From the discussion that preceded the vote, however, it is clear that many of those who voted for the resolution fully expected that it, like the ill-fated Montreal accord, would be defeated by legal maneuverings as well as a vote of the full membership. Thus L. Gray Cowan, a member of the board by virtue of being the immediate past president, asserted during the discussion of the resolution that it "in effect creates a third organization" (the second presumably being the AHSA), and that he doubted whether a "non-profit bureaucracy could contribute to a liberation fund" like the one envisaged by the Johnson-Cole resolution (African Studies Association 1970:11–12).

As the Johnson-Cole resolution awaited its predestined fate, it became the subject of intense politicking. The AHSA, returning temporarily to the fray, warmly endorsed it as clearing "the air for meaningful dialogue" with the ASA ("Johnson Resolution . . ." 1970:25). Such optimism was highly misplaced. Firing the first symbolic shot, Martin Kilson declared, "For me, at least, the ASA is now certainly dead"; he then indignantly resigned from the board and attacked the "utterly bizarre" behavior of board member Willard Johnson. Momentarily abandoning his first calling as a political scientist and assuming the role of psychoanalyst, Kilson continued: "Clearly a sizeable portion of the ASA's white membership, profoundly sycophantic in its guilt-ridden relationship to the silly political posturing and bizarre intellectual antics of black militants within the ASA, has no intention of retrieving its common sense and returning to the first principles of an academic organization" (Kilson 1970:20–21). Kilson, however, vastly overestimated the state of guilt-riddenness among the ASA's white members.

A petition demanding a vote by the entire membership on the Johnson-Cole resolution, circulated by Ruth Schachter Morgenthau, quickly gained over 400 signatures. When the votes were counted, the resolution had been defeated by a wide margin, 607 to 272. Meanwhile the board had heard from the ASA attorney, who opined that not only was the resolution probably illegal under the law of the State of New York (where the ASA was incorporated), but its adoption would also endanger the organization's tax-exempt status. (The IRS subsequently requested the ASA's 1968 records as part of an investigation of its tax-exempt status [*African Studies Newsletter* 3, nos. 3–4

(May-June 1970): 13].) The foundations underwriting the ASA also weighed in, stating that their support was conditional on the organization's remaining tax exempt. Like the Burke amendment the previous year, the Johnson-Cole resolution was now dead, and with it went the last glimmer of hope for reconciliation between the ASA and the AHSA. Johnson and Cole both immediately resigned from the ASA board (special issue of *African Studies Newsletter* [Feb. 14, 1971]: 3–7).[21] The dominant majority had spoken, and its message betrayed little of the sycophancy Kilson had accused it of harboring.

The Disintegration of the Africanist Enterprise?

Although temporarily destabilized by the activities of black malcontents and rebels at home and abroad, the Africanist enterprise survived largely unchanged through the 1970s. A number of Africanists left the field, and a few more blacks were incorporated into the higher reaches of the ASA, while the new black studies programs were left alone. Particularly significant were those black studies programs, by all accounts a minority, that struggled to bridge the divide between the study of the African continent and that of the diaspora. Where they were most successful, these initiatives resulted in departments, not programs, a status that distinguished them from the Africanist-controlled African studies units.[22] Overall, however, the segregation of the study of continental Africa and that of the diaspora remained in place and was even strengthened in often unintended ways by the creation at major research universities of programs that were largely restricted to the study of African Americans. For all intents and purposes, then, the Africanists maintained their dual roles as "liberal mediators," interpreting continental Africa for the West, and "secular missionaries," offering (mostly unsolicited) advice to African governments.[23]

Far more unsettling for Africanists were signs of the ebbing of federal, state, and private funding. Still, even at the end of the 1980s, surveys of the field remained optimistic about its future. Thus Eddie Bay, executive director of the ASA, concluded in 1991: "African area studies would appear to be strong in the American academy. Having expanded dramatically in the 1960s and suffered contraction along with all other fields after 1970, Africanists nevertheless have continued to be trained and hired over the past 20 years. . . . African studies as a field is for the moment in reasonably good health" (Bay 1991:17, 18). Indeed, membership in the ASA had continued to grow, reaching 2,000 in 1990 (Bay 1991:5).

By the early 1990s, however, Africanists could no longer depict the problems they faced as the inevitable result of a maturing field of academic inquiry. Shades of the past returned: the earlier challenges from continental African scholars and advocates of pan-African perspectives were revived in new forms, as is charted in the introduction and various chapters of this volume. This time around, though, Africanists found themselves confronting a new and even more formidable foe: wavering support on the part of those who wield power and control resources within and without the academy, that is, the very forces that had created and sustained the institutional pillars of the field.

The roots of this transformation can be traced to stagnation in the world economy and the decline of U.S. hegemony. As U.S. economic and political power seemed to wane in the 1980s, longstanding definitions of U.S. global interests and commitments began to fall away. During the 1970s and 1980s continuing wars of national liberation in southern Africa had kept the continent on the priority list of national policymakers. By the early 1990s, however, a whole series of events began to demolish the logic that had underpinned area studies and particularly federal support for Africa and African studies. Most notable were the end of the cold war, the federal government's fiscal crisis, the emergence of new economic rivals in Europe and Asia, and the end of the speculative boom induced by Reagonomics and the military expansion of the 1980s. At the same time it became all too apparent that the models and expectations of "development" for Africa and the now ill-defined "Third World" were little more than illusions (see Arrighi 1989).

Under the weight of these reversals, U.S. strategic interests in Africa were called into question. At the same time the demise of radical socialist states and the emergence of a pro-Western, majority-ruled, and nonnuclear South Africa removed any serious African challenges to U.S. foreign policy. In addition, Africa's economic importance to the United States became even more marginal than it had been, while the World Bank and the International Monetary Fund proved quite effective in disciplining unruly African governments. As the 1980s gave way to the 1990s, it became clear that private and public policymakers were rapidly losing interest in Africa. In common parlance, Africa had "fallen off the policy map" and become an anarchic and unrewarding area, one best left to suffer alone (see, e.g., Chege 1992; Michaels 1993). Crowder's depiction of the situation in Britain, where the collapse of imperial pretensions and Thatcherite cuts came even earlier, mimicked the U.S. situation: "Those who run the government have lost or are losing interest in Africa, a continent which is seen increasingly as one of unending problems which they just wish would go away" (Crowder 1987:110).

How were Africanists to respond? A common reaction was to reassert the importance of African and areas studies to the national interest. Given the continuing decline in federal and even state support in the 1970s and 1980s, the area studies establishment launched a series of studies aimed at bolstering federal support. Not surprisingly, in a move reflecting the financial politics of the Reagan years, these attempts stressed area studies' links to national and military interests. Lambert's major 1984 study proposed, for example, "a central funding and administering body for language and area studies" responsive to the "national interest" and with direct involvement by the Department of Defense (Lambert et al. 1984:279, 186, 278). This was followed by an Association of American Universities (AAU) study[24] that argued for a "first priority, stated at the most elemental level: to preserve and improve the quality of a unique and vital asset, the national resource base in language and area studies dedicated to training the specialists the nation requires to protect our global interests" (Association of American Universities 1986:2).

The AAU's proposal for a national body encompassing all federal funding never materialized. Elements of this proposal, however, were co-opted by Senator David Boren in the early 1990s, leading to the creation of a new program for international exchanges funded from, and located within, the Department of Defense. Financed by the annual income on a $150 million trust fund, the National Security Education Act (NSEA, subsequently NSEP) was attacked both by conservative politicians anxious to cut aid and international commitments and by area studies faculty and organizations that objected to its Pentagon and intelligence connections.[25] Given the small amounts involved, however, even a fully positive response to calls for direct linkages between academicians and "national security" agencies (e.g., Goodman 1992) would hardly supplant existing federal and state funding.

By the mid-1990s area and African studies were confronting even more serious trends: the final collapse of the cold war division of the world into fixed regions and the increasing disdain of both government and business for area studies programs. Most evident was the redefinition of European boundaries in the wake of the demise of the Soviet Union and the definition of new world regions matched to rising economic rivals in Europe and particularly in the Pacific Rim.

Classified surveys of "national needs" surrounding the Boren initiative reveal, moreover, just how much the interests of the federal and business establishments are at odds with existing area studies programs. As a National Endowment for the Humanities study made clear, neither Africanists nor other area studies scholars were to be considered important players in the reordering of international priorities and programs: "In discussions with various language advocates in the higher education community, the suggestion was occasionally made that the individual language teaching associations and the area studies associations be consulted to determine where the needs are. Yet even here the doubters believe that the *parochial* interests of these associations will be difficult to overcome" (National Endowment for the Humanities 1992:5; emphasis added). Advice from the corporate community was solicited, with little result:

Program planners for the NSEA would in theory benefit from the collective wisdom of the business community, who, after all, are the primary players in ensuring the continued "economic strength of the U.S." (in the words of the enabling legislation). Sad to say, however, that business interests do not appear to speak with a common voice (if they speak about foreign languages at all). . . . Small wonder, then, that a recent *Business Week* survey found that only 6% of corporate managers believed that foreign language competency was important for their employees. (National Endowment for the Humanities 1992:6)

The NEH was far clearer as to who had an organized, clear voice on needs in language and area studies: "The intelligence community, through its Foreign Language Committee, has indicated that it stands ready to identify critical languages and countries from the perspective of the DLI [Defense Language Institute], FSI [Foreign Service Institute], NSA [National Security Agency], and CIA." Appended to the NEH report were individual assessments by the CIA, DLI, Defense Intelligence Agency, FBI, NSA, and Departments of State, Army, Air Force, Navy, and U.S. Marine Corps. These studies, however, reveal little in the way of renewed interest in African or area studies beyond the mention of a few strategic locations. Besides the expected assessment of needs related to the Gulf War operations, the primary concern was to rationalize language training across the services and bureaucracies, reducing federal language and area training (particularly among the Army's Military Intelligence linguists) and relying far more on the private sector.[26]

An even more serious threat to the major African studies programs is posed by the frustration with, if not incipient abandonment of, area studies on the part of foundations and university administrations, which in the 1980s had often covered declining federal funding. It is increasingly evident, for example, that existing area studies programs are being judged as enclaves of overspecialization, concentrating scarce resources on isolated and archaic world areas. Area studies programs are thus deemed as inherently incapable of addressing new "threats" to the United States arising from global social, cultural, and economic upheavals. The Mellon Foundation consequently chided area studies for being unable to understand "the diffusion of values associated with contemporary Western culture, the spread of world-wide markets and the profound implications of conflicting developments such as the increasing power of fundamentalism, desecularization and traditionalism in many parts of the world" (in Williams 1994:3). As Williams (1994), Heginbotham (1994), and Heilbrunn (1996), among others, have noted, funders are now more interested in cross-regional, worldwide scholarship— an agenda difficult if not impossible to achieve within the existing conceptual and institutional framework of area studies programs. This view was supported by a Rand Corporation survey, which revealed that the CEOs of both leading research universities and multinational corporations saw current academic programs as unable to prepare students for an increasingly transnational, globalized world (Bikson and Law 1994).

In this context African and international area programs have increasingly become the targets of ongoing waves of academic restructuring and downsizing. In ways unimaginable in the 1960s, 1970s, and even 1980s, Africanists now find themselves called on to justify their existence in the academy. Given the decisions made in the 1950s and 1960s, however, African and area studies are ill equipped to respond. Attempts to ride the "multicultural" wave within the university are undercut, for example, not only by the separation of Africa from the diaspora but also by the lack of degree programs, undergraduate and graduate courses, and faculty appointments.

Placed on the defensive, Africanists now often defend their field by reference to those who control such resources: the disciplines. The recent Bates, Mudimbe, and O'Barr volume makes this line of argument explicit, its editors hoping that "any chair, dean, or provost who doubts the significance of research from Africa will find in this book reason to change" (Bates, Mudimbe, and O'Barr 1993:220). Seeking an "armory" to defend the study of Africa, Bates et al. advance the claim that African studies is to be valued precisely because of its contributions to the disciplines and the latter's search for universal truths: "Fields of knowledge become disciplines in part because they aspire to universal truths; disciplines provide generalized understandings. To emphasize once again: we believe that the study of Africa belongs in the core of the modern university precisely because research in Africa has shaped the disciplines and thereby shaped our convictions as to what may be universally true" (1993:xiii–xiv). There is little evidence, however, that retreating to a defense of the nineteenth-century European division of knowledge into disciplines will have any success in the face of the parochialism of the disciplines and their disdain for comparative and area studies. This is the case even in new fields such as literary and cultural studies. As Christopher Miller argued in his contribution to the Bates et al. volume: "In order to gain legitimacy and tenure, Africanists have had to respond to the requirements of their departments—usually English or French departments—whose very raison d'être has, of course, been Western Literary canons and national literatures. Literary Africanists . . . have tended to be marginal figures. . . . My contention is that Africa has been allowed to contribute almost nothing to the Western academy up to the present moment" (Miller 1993:220). As for work by Africans, Miller continues: "My bleak assessment is supported by Abiola Irele. . . . Irele asserts that 'African scholarship is at best marginal, and at worst nonexistent in the total economy of intellectual endeavor in the world today'" (1993:220–21).

Even in disciplines more deeply engaged in African studies, the future is

hardly bright. As even Bay's upbeat 1991 study showed, few among the relatively large cohort of older African specialists in history and political science,
among other disciplines, expect to be replaced by other Africa specialists.[27]
Indeed, restating African studies' importance to national needs or even
multicultural and gender studies[28] shows equally few signs of success because
of the foundational premises of the enterprise: the call for addressing *transnational* gender and racial processes is subverted by the Africanists' strict
focus on continental Africa. This stance also prevents Africanists from joining any movement aimed at breaching disciplinary boundaries (see
Gulbenkian Commission on the Restructuring of the Social Sciences 1996)—
even if African studies, in an unintended way (Wallerstein 1997:228), challenges disciplinary provincialism through the multidisciplinary study of an
area outside the United States.

Despite Africanists' claim to an international and global perspective, there
thus seems to be little relation between their world and the new global studies programs. New investments addressing "globalization," even when
headed by senior Africanists, have most often been made in international
majors, programs, or centers located outside, if not posed against, area and
African studies. Christopher Lowe—commenting on essays by Robert Bates,
Ron Kassimier, and Pearl Robinson and Priscilla Stone in an *Africa Today*
collection—goes further and explicitly argues that Africanists' welcome of a
global perspective is both deceptive and dangerous. Lowe's very first sentence
is "A new academic globalism is eroding the Area Studies framework," while
"debates among Africa scholars do not yet adequately address the potentially
undesirable consequences of these changes" (1997:297).

Given their attention to locality, recent trends in cultural, postmodern, and
postcolonial studies have attracted some Africanists (see Parpart 1995; Karp
1997). Yet most Africans outside South Africa (Vaughan 1994; Nkosi 1993)
decline to follow the latest Western academic fads, rejecting the parochialism often inherent in U.S. cultural studies in particular (see Karp 1997:290–
91). Furthermore, these new paradigms provide little support for African
studies in relation to the disciplines, lacking as they do either a strong power
base in the academy or a positivist logic to reaffirm the study of Africa and
Africans as isolated cultural or geographical entities.

Reprise

In short, Africanists currently face challenges extending well beyond the most
visible and long-standing discussion of funding constraints. One by one
unexpected developments have heralded a crumbling of the basic pillars of
the enterprise: the dissolution of a world ordered into separate strategic regions related to post–World War II boundaries, the demise of material sup-

port linked to a cold war logic, and the decline of U.S. power worldwide. At the same time the legacy of separating the study of Africa from that of Africans at home and abroad has come back to haunt Africanists.

Africanists are hardly alone in facing an uncertain future. Yet unlike those rooted in either the core disciplines within the academy or in recent national initiatives—tied mainly to globalization or fears of new economic rivals, terrorism, "Islamic fundamentalism," drug cartels, or "rogue" states—Africanists have been unable to seize the opportunities opened by the imposition of structural adjustment within and without higher education. Indeed, African studies proponents largely seem to have pulled into a defensive stance, believing there is no alternative to their control over the study and knowledge of continental Africa. New initiatives to revitalize area studies by the foundations and continuing federal support for Title VI area centers are often grasped as evidence for the wisdom of this stance. Over the long run, however, there seems to be little prospect that African studies will offer federal, state, university, or disciplinary officials the kind of knowledge and training being sought in the coming century. Given these trends, our conclusion is a stark one: there is little prospect that African studies, as we have known it and experienced it, will survive another generation.

Such a conclusion could be seriously contested if a broader vision of the study of Africa were permitted. As the introduction and other chapters of this volume document, a reconfiguration of the study of Africa opens the prospect of a quite different intellectual endeavor, one that would address a wider African world and thus find broader public support. Such an agenda would require not only accepting an infusion of the new intellectual currents charted elsewhere in this volume but jettisoning the Africanist strictures on the constitution of proper scholarship, institutions, and constituencies for the study of Africa.

For some, the hiring of senior African scholars from the continent (even as directors of major African studies centers) heralds just such a change, finally opening the door to the study of Africa by and for Africans (see Taiwo n.d.). In addition, there appears to be greater collaboration between African and Africanist institutions, often due to common financial strictures. Take, for example, the Council for the Development of Economic and Social Research in Africa (CODESRIA), the pivotal research consortium in Dakar. Although CODESRIA has long sought to construct African intellectual networks separate from Africanist influence, it has recently engaged with U.S. Africanists by sharing a major foundation grant, appeared on ASA conference panels chaired by World Bank officials, and constructed web pages in alliance with a U.S. Title VI African studies center.[29]

Far more difficult for Africanists—and even continental scholars, given that their past resistance to Africanist domination was based on accepting a continental divide—is overturning the separation of continental Africa from the larger African world. The great conundrum here is, of course, the division between African and African American studies, one of the bedrocks on which the Africanist enterprise was founded. Only a few scholars, usually junior and untenured, are willing to breach this divide, despite the revival of interest in Africa among African American students, scholars, and communities. Thus despite explicit attempts by both the federal government and major foundations to fund links between the major African studies centers and historically black colleges and universities, little if any progress has been made. Indeed, Africa-related projects at historically black schools funded in the early 1990s as part of the Title VI program have lost this funding in the latest round of grants, with little note or assistance from far wealthier, historically white institutions.

There is no more pitiful illustration of the state of the Africanist enterprise than the gulf between the renaissance of Africa in popular culture and movements on the one hand and, on the other hand, the almost complete inability of the predominantly white Africanist enterprise to envision any relation between continental Africa and North America, to say nothing of the rest of the Americas, Asia, and Europe. The contemporary revival of transcontinental black dialogues and perspectives may have surprised many, but the Africanists' response has hardly moved beyond incorporating as many as possible within their defensive, unreconstructed laager—which, in our view, is likely only to seal the fate of the field. If the study of Africa is to survive, much less flourish, it seems that nothing less than a fundamental revision of current assumptions, alliances, and agendas among scholars of Africa is in order.

Notes

1. In this connection see, especially, the various contributions in *Africa Today* 44, no. 2 (Apr.–June 1997) and *Africa Today* 44, no. 3 (July–Sept. 1997).

2. See Carter 1983:7. In addition to President Melville Herskovits (Northwestern University) and Vice-President Gwendolen Carter (Smith College), the board of trustees consisted of W. O. Brown (Boston University), Father John Considine (Maryknoll Seminary), Walter Goldschmidt (University of California at Los Angeles), E. Franklin Frazier (Howard University), C. W. de Kiewiet (University of Rochester), and Vernon McKay (Johns Hopkins University). Also in attendance were officials from the Rockefeller Brothers Fund, the Ford Foundation, the Social Science Research Council, the Rockefeller Foundation, the Federal Reserve Bank of New York, the Carnegie Endowment for International Peace, the Council on Foreign Relations, and Farrell Lines (Cowan 1957; Noon n.d. [1957?]).

3. Until the elitist College of Fellows was abolished in the wake of the 1969 revolt, reports on membership could easily be misleading. In 1960 the 866 members included 291 fellows, 270 associate fellows, 120 student members, 157 institutional members, 8 sustaining members, and 14 exchange members.

4. The formation of programs and centers in the United States—and to some extent in Europe, the Soviet Union, and Africa—may be followed in the early issues of the *African Studies Bulletin* and the *African Studies Review.* Definitions of what constituted "comprehensive centers" are, of course, highly subjective; the sources here follow the Africanist tradition reflected in Bennett's definition, with major programs by the mid-1960s being equated with university-recognized, multidisciplinary programs with language and area courses and an administrative locus integrating research and instructional activities (see Lambert 1973:14–15). This excludes, it must be noted, such pioneering efforts as those at Howard University (begun by William Leo Hansberry in 1923) or the work by St. Clair Drake and Lorenzo Turner at Roosevelt University.

5. African students in the United States in 1957 numbered 1,515, or 3.5 percent of foreign students; by 1965 this number had more than quadrupled to almost 7,000, representing over 8 percent of foreign students (Institute of International Education 1990:16). Prior to the emergence of African studies programs at historically white universities, a significant proportion of African students were located at Howard and other historically black universities (Harris 1970:20; Institute of International Education 1961).

6. All dollar conversions are based on the U.S. government's Consumer Price Indexes, base year = 1982–84.

7. The U.S. Office of Education's *Bulletin on Education in the USSR* (May 1957) openly made the case for a "national emergency" in language and area studies. See, for example, the account in Axelrod and Bigelow 1962:12. The chief of the Language Development Section of the U.S. Office of Education was equally blunt in describing the Soviet challenge in Africa, writing that "the USSR on its side has not been idle," opening African language schools in three cities and refurbishing an African institute, beaming numerous hours of broadcasts to Africa, and "offering African students generous scholarships." In short, it was "apparent that the big Soviet push to capture tropical Africa" had to be countered (Mildenberger 1960:20–21).

8. Where to locate new courses and faculty to teach African languages proved to be a more difficult problem. Although a separate department under A. C. Jordan was created at Wisconsin, such a development was rare—language was usually relegated to staff in existing departments (e.g., linguistics), leaving African studies programs without the support enjoyed by other area studies programs in European language departments (Spanish, Portuguese, or Russian). Prior to the rise of the new Africanist centers, it should be noted, instruction in African languages resided at Howard and the historically black universities. This allowed Howard University to become the only program that could meet the Title VI requirements in language instruction in 1958—and thus Howard became the first and only Title VI Center in the first year of the operation of the NDEA program.

9. To his great surprise, Hansberry heard of the program's establishment from his students while he was in Liberia—finding on his return to Howard that the grant had been made under "arrangements which excluded [his] courses in African Studies from the program and therefore from any of the benefits accruing from the grant" (in Harris 1974:16–17). E. Franklin Frazier, committed to the separation of continental Africa from the diaspora, led the new program; he was at the time the most accepted and prominent black scholar in the discipline of sociology, having been elected in 1948 to the presidency of the American Sociological Society. However, like Du Bois and others of his cohort, he would never hold a permanent post in a white university (Green and Driver 1978:44–45).

10. Vansina, for example, was tracked down in Rwanda, where "Helen Codère succeeded

on her arrival in July 1959 in enrolling me as a member of the infant African Studies Association in the United States, although I had never been there and had no intention of going!" (Vansina 1994:71). While not exclusively male, as Curtin suggests, Africanists were overwhelmingly male, which was true of the international studies faculty nationwide. We know of no data that could provide a gender or racial breakdown of ASA membership through the years; Lambert's 1973 report estimated that 90 percent of area studies faculty were male (Lambert 1973:43).

11. Foreign recruits, like those from the United States, needed to "fit" the politics of the disciplines, departments, and the academy. Thus in 1968 Curtin and Vansina refused to hire Martin Legassick, a white South African and "fiery populist" who, bedecked in "long hair and earring to flowery shirt," denounced liberal South African historiography. Instead, the job went to Steven Feierman, who arrived on campus in an "impeccable conservative outfit" with a "nineteenth-century romantic, faintly melancholy demeanor" (Vansina 1994:143). There were no problems in hiring white scholars from the Commonwealth and especially South Africa, as the careers of C. W. de Kiewiet and Leonard Thompson indicate. Indeed, as late as 1960 the ASA presidential address was entitled "The Outlook for the White Man in Africa, Particularly as Settler," a group that, according to the address, was "a primary target of the African revolution, and may well be one of its victims" (Brown 1960:3).

12. See, for example, lists of the recipients of Carnegie grants (Murphy 1973: appendix A, 245–58) or the coverage of grants and contacts in the early issues of the *African Studies Bulletin.*

13. The Carnegie Corporation was active in linking British and U.S. activities, holding highly select meetings of academicians, government officials, and foundation staff from both countries (Murphy 1973). Similarly, the Rockefeller Foundation underwrote the creation of the International Institute of African Languages and Cultures in 1926 (changed in 1946 to the International African Institute), with the "main purpose of bringing together scholars, missionaries and administrators of the colonial powers" (Crowder 1987:112). Within a few years the institute had forty-one U.S. members (Crowder 1987:113). Such ties continued through the 1960s, as in Rockefeller's subvention of the founding of the preeminent Africanist history journal, *Journal of African History* (*African Studies Bulletin* 2, no. 4 [Dec. 1959]: 45). Both foundations and federal programs, including the Fulbright Foundation (see Pifer 1953), relied heavily on British connections in the formative years of their African programs, funding European (mainly British) as well as South African and Rhodesian scholars.

14. The definition of world regions and area studies may be traced back to early postwar assessments of wartime programs and needs made by the Committee on World Area Research, which was set up by the Social Science Research Council (Hall 1947) and the Commission on the Implications of Armed Services Education Programs, a creation of the American Council of Education (Fenton 1947). The cold war division of Europe into East and West also paralleled the creation of a new world region, the Soviet Union and Eastern Europe, which included areas such as Bohemia and Hungary that formerly had been considered part of Central Europe. Given this new region's prominence in policy concerns, area studies institutions dedicated to it were funded at much higher levels than were African programs, a phenomenon exemplified by Carnegie's grant of $740,00 (over $4 million in 1994 dollars) to Harvard alone in 1948 for the creation of its Russian Research Center, the largest endowment of this kind at that time. Africanists, by contrast,

had to settle for smaller sums, as in the Carnegie grants to the Apter team in 1956 ($100,000, or $540,000 in 1994 dollars), and to Curtin's Wisconsin's program in 1961 ($215,000, or over a $1 million in 1994 dollars) (Murphy 1973:85, 260).

15. During the conference out of which this volume emerged, a past editor of the *Journal of African History* noted his frustration at being unable to carry forward an initiative to obtain submissions by Africans; he was informed by African conference participants that scholars on the continent had agreed to boycott the journal after having found its European editorial board unwilling to countenance scholarship by Africans.

16. According to John Henrik Clarke, the caucus was called by P. Chike Onwuachi, director of the African-Caribbean Studies Center at Fisk University, and included Michael Searles, Nicholas Onyewu, Leonard Jeffries, John Henrik Clarke, Nell Painter, Jan Douglass, and Shelby Faye Lewis (Clarke 1969:7).

17. The other members of the committee were John Henrik Clarke, Adelaide Hill, Shirley K. Fischer, Simon Ottenberg, and William Schwab, the latter two also being ASA board members. Leonard Jeffries and Marcia Wright served as consultants at one of the committee's meetings.

18. The members of the committee were Ihieukwumere A. Anozie, John Henrik Clarke, Leonard Jeffries, Maina Kagombe, Joseph O. Kofa, Shelby Lewis, Samuel T. Massaguoc, J. K. Obatala, P. Chike Onwuachi, Nell Painter, Michael Searles, Ronald Taylor, and Harold Weaver (*Pan-African Journal* 1968).

19. The word *Heritage*, added to *African Studies Association*, was apparently derived from an antipoverty program, the Heritage Teaching Program, of which John Henrik Clarke served as director.

20. Besides Hill, Challenor, Onweyu, Onwuachi, and Vilakazi, those attending the meeting included Samuel Allen, Keith Baird, Johnetta B. Cole, James L. Gibbs, Roy Glasgow, Joseph Harris, Leonard Jeffries, Hollis Lynch, Mlacheni Njisane, William Shack, and Elliott P. Skinner. Martin Kilson and Davidson Nicol were invited but did not attend.

21. The black insurgents were probably not amused by the cover of the special issue of the *African Studies Newsletter* that bore all this bad news. Above a bouquet of flowers inside a heart, it implored, "Be our Valentine."

22. These divergent approaches explain the sharp contrast between Nathan Huggins's 1985 *Report to the Ford Foundation on Afro-American Studies* and Molefi Asante's response, which stresses not only that black studies must encompass America and Africa but also that "an interdepartmental program, if one can be found to work, might provide a series of courses about black people but cannot and will never advance the intellectual direction of the discipline [of Afro-American Studies]" (Asante 1986:259). As noted previously, Africanists' early commitments to existing disciplines, and thus the creation of programs rather than departments, left them vulnerable to the whims of the disciplines and doomed the prospect of a strong transdisciplinary project. See also McWhorter and Bailey 1984a, 1984b.

23. The terms "liberal mediators" and "secular missionaries" are borrowed from Immanuel Wallerstein 1983.

24. This study was funded, it must be noted, by the Department of Defense, contract No. MDA904-85-C-4151. Nor was this a new phenomenon: Lambert et al.'s 1984 study was funded jointly by the Department of Defense (contract No. DAMD17-83-C-3093) and the National Endowment for the Humanities (grant OP 20159-83).

25. Although progressive Africanists, particularly those associated with the Association

of Concerned Africa Scholars (see Association of Concerned Africa Scholars 1994, 1997, and coverage in the *ACAS Bulletin*), led opposition to the Boren Bill, it should be noted that Africanists had little to lose. Exchanges with Africa, always a small percentage of international and study abroad activities, were quite marginal by this time. As the needs assessment study by National Endowment for the Humanities for the Pentagon reported, of the over fifty thousand students engaged in study abroad programs, only slightly over 1 percent was going to Africa by the late 1980s, with half of these going to Kenya alone (calculated from figures supplied in [1] National Endowment for the Humanities 1992: tables 1 and 2, a report prepared for the Pentagon in order to implement NSEA and using statistics supplied by the Department of Education's Institute of International Education, apparently the primary source for these figures, and [2] a Modern Language Association report dated Mar. 16, 1992). Even if one excludes Western European countries from these calculations, Africa's percentage rises to only five percent. On NSEP and related points, see also the chapter by Horace Campbell in this volume.

26. The CIA is experimenting with "immersion programs conducted in U.S. cities with large ethnic communities and abroad," thereby allowing "students to . . . gain fluency and confidence in an authentic environment that both fosters language growth and increases cultural awareness" (National Endowment for the Humanities 1992:n.p.) (as noted by the National Security Agency as well and "enthusiastically" endorsed by the interagency summary); the FBI has come to rely on outside agencies, including FSI, Berlitz, and Middlebury College, to meet its training needs; and the Army turned to outside sources in response to needs for Arabic linguists during the Gulf War, drafting linguists from National Guard battalions, who were added to some 600 Kuwaiti students recruited through the Kuwaiti Embassy in Washington.

27. As Bay details, by 1990 both history and political science had disproportionately high numbers of Africanist faculty in the over-forty-nine-years-old cohort. History departments experienced a significant falloff in the production of African-related Ph.D.s in the 1980s (fewer than twenty per year in the mid- to late 1980s versus well over thirty in the mid-1970s), matching the small number of student members of the ASA affiliated with history departments. Trends in political science converged with those in history for a more disquieting reason: the increasing pressure on scholars to concentrate on more "comparative/theoretical" study. Overall, 17 percent of ASA members over the age of fifty-five did not expect to be replaced upon their retirement (Bay 1991:18).

28. See the essays in the special issue of *ISSUE* (Winter-Spring 1995) on the restructuring of African studies.

29. The $425,000 grant is from the Ford Foundation to CODESRIA and Northwestern University's Program in African Studies; the web pages appear on a University of Illinois server: http://wsi.cso.uiuc.edu/CAS/codesria/codesria.htm; and the panel listing in the 1997 ASA conference program was entitled "Sorcery, State, and Society in Contemporary Africa," the panel being chaired by Cyprian Fisiy of the World Bank with Achille Mbembé of CODESRIA as discussant.

References Cited

"African Heritage Studies Association." 1968. *Pan-African Journal* 1, no. 4 (Fall): 161–62.
African Studies Association. 1958. "Genesis of the Association." *African Studies Bulletin* 1, no. 2 (Nov.): 13.

————. 1959. "Training and Career Opportunities for the American Specialist on Africa." *African Studies Bulletin* 2, no. 4 (Dec.): 13–26.

————. 1960. "Minutes, Third Annual Business Meeting: Report of the Executive Secretary." *African Studies Bulletin* 3, no. 3 (Oct.): 6.

————. 1966. Research Liaison Committee. *Summary Report of the Conference on the Position and Problems of the African Scholar.* New York: African Studies Association.

————. 1969. "The 1969 Annual Meeting." *African Studies Newsletter* 2, nos. 6–7 (Nov.–Dec.): 1–3.

————. 1970. "Minutes: ASA Board Meeting, Oct. 21, 1970." *African Studies Newsletter* 3, no. 7 (Nov.–Dec.): 5–9.

Africa Research Group. 1970. *Africa Retort: A Tribal Analysis of U.S. Africanists: Who They Are, Why to Fight Them.* Cambridge, Mass.: Africa Research Group.

Arrighi, Giovanni. 1989. "The Developmentalist Illusion." In *Semiperipheral States in the World-Economy,* ed. William G. Martin, 11–42. Westport, Conn.: Greenwood.

Asante, Molefi. 1986. "A Note on Nathan Huggins' Report to the Ford Foundation." *Journal of Black Studies* 17, no. 2:255–62.

Association of American Universities. 1986. *To Strengthen the Nation's Investment in Foreign Languages and International Studies: A Legislative Proposal to Create a National Foundation for Foreign Languages and International Studies: A Draft.* Washington, D.C.: Association of American Universities.

Association of Concerned Africa Scholars. 1994. *Open Scholarship or Covert Agendas? The Case against NSEP Funding for the Study of Africa.* Leaflet.

————. 1997. *The Case against DOD and CIA Involvement in Funding the Study of Africa.* Leaflet.

Axelrod, Joseph, and Donald N. Bigelow. 1962. *Resources for Language and Area Studies.* Washington, D.C.: American Council on Education.

Bates, Robert, V. Y. Mudimbe, and Jean O'Barr, eds. 1993. *Africa and the Disciplines: The Contributions of Research in Africa to the Social Sciences and Humanities.* Chicago: University of Chicago Press.

Baum, Robert D. 1965. "Government-sponsored Research in Africa." *African Studies Bulletin* 8, no. 1 (Apr.): 42–47.

Bay, Edna. 1991. "African Studies." In *Prospects for Faculty in Area Studies,* ed. National Council of Area Studies Associations, 1–18. Stanford, Calif.: American Association for the Advancement of Slavic Studies.

Berman, Edward H. 1982. "The Extension of Ideology: Foundation Support for Intermediate Organizations and Forums." *Comparative Education Review* (Feb.): 48–68.

Bikson, T. K., and S. A. Law. 1994. *Global Preparedness and Human Resources: College and Corporate Perspectives.* Santa Monica, Calif.: Rand Corporation.

Bretton, Henry L. 1969. Letter about Montreal. *African Studies Newsletter* 2, nos. 6–7 (Nov.–Dec.): 19–20.

Brown, William O. 1960. "The Outlook for the White Man in Africa, Particularly as Settler." Presidential address, Third Annual Meeting, African Studies Association. *African Studies Bulletin* 3, no. 3 (Oct.): 1–11.

Burke, Fred G. 1969. *Africa Report* (Dec.): 25.

Carter, Gwendolen. 1983. "The Founding of the African Studies Association." *African Studies Review* 26, nos. 3–4 (Sept.–Dec.): 5–19.

Chege, Michael. 1992. "Remembering Africa." *Foreign Affairs* 71, no. 1:146–63.

Clarke, John Henrik. 1969. "Confrontation at Montreal." *African Studies Newsletter* 2, nos. 6–7 (Nov.–Dec.): 7–13.

Cowan, L. Gray. 1957. Minutes, Ad Hoc Committee for the African Studies Association Meeting, Feb. 8. Howard University, Moorland-Spingarn Research Center, E. F. Frazier papers, Box 131–19, Folder 8.

———. n.d. (ca. 1969). "A Summary History of the African Studies Association, 1957–1969." Mimeograph.

———. 1969. "Ten Years of African Studies." *African Studies Bulletin* 12, no. 1 (Apr.): 1–7.

———. 1970a. "ASHA and ASA Representatives Meet for Discussion." *African Studies Newsletter* 3, no. 1 (Feb.–Mar.): 2.

———. 1970b. "President's Report." *African Studies Review* 13, no. 3 (Dec.): 343–52.

———. 1972. "Report of the Committee on Change in Intellectual Perspectives." *ISSUE* 2, no. 4 (Winter): 1–5.

Cowan, L. Gray, and John Henrik Clarke. 1970. "Exchange of Letters between L. Gray Cowan and John Henrik Clarke." 1970. *African Studies Newsletter* 3, nos. 3–4 (May–June): 2–5.

Crowder, Michael. 1987. "'Us' and 'Them': The International African Institute and the Current Crisis of Identity in African Studies." *Africa* 57, no. 1:109–22.

Curtin, Philip D. 1971. "African Studies: A Personal Statement." *African Studies Review* 14, no. 3 (Dec.): 357–68.

de Kiewiet, C. W. 1971. *The Emergent African University: An Interpretation.* Washington, D.C.: American Council on Education.

Drake, St. Clair. 1990 [1987]. *Black Folk Here and There: An Essay in History and Anthropology.* Los Angeles: Center for Afro-American Studies, University of California, Los Angeles.

Duffy, James. 1970. "Report on Response to ASA Questionnaire." *African Studies Newsletter* 3, no. 1 (Feb.–Mar.): 2–4.

Emerson, Rupert, Martin Kilson, Joseph S. Nye, and Robert I Rotberg. 1969. Letter about Montreal. *African Studies Newsletter* 2, nos. 6–7 (Nov.–Dec.): 21–33.

Fenton, W. N. 1947. *Area Studies in American Universities: For the Commission on Implications of Armed Forces Educational Programs.* Washington, D.C.: American Council on Education.

"Ford Foundation Grant." 1961. *African Studies Bulletin* 4, no. 1 (Mar.): 50.

Fraser, C. Gerald. 1969. "Black Caucus Deliberations at Montreal: Who Should Control African Studies and for What End?" *Africa Report* (Dec.): 20–21.

Goggin, Jacqueline Anne. 1993. *Carter G. Woodson: A Life in Black History.* Baton Rouge: Louisiana State University Press.

Goodman, Paul. 1992. "The CIA and the Universities: The Prospects for Improved Relations Have Never Been Better." *Chronicle of Higher Education,* Nov. 25, p. B1–2.

Green, Dan, and Edwin Driver. 1978. "Introduction." In *W. E. B. Du Bois on Sociology and the Black Community,* ed. Dan Green and Edwin Driver, 1–48. Chicago: University of Chicago Press.

Gulbenkian Commission on the Restructuring of the Social Sciences. 1996. *Open the Social Sciences: Report of the Gulbenkian Commission on the Restructuring of the Social Sciences.* Stanford, Calif.: Stanford University Press.

Guthrie, Robert V. 1976. *Even the Rat Was White: A Historical View of Psychology.* New York: Harper and Row.

Hall, R. B. 1947. *Area Studies: With Special Reference to Their Implications for Research in the Social Sciences.* Washington, D.C.: Committee on World Area Research.

Hance, William A., and Philip Curtin. 1966. "African Studies in America and the American Scholar." *African Studies Bulletin* 9, no. 1 (Apr.): 24–32.

Harris, Joseph E. 1970. "Letter from Joseph E. Harris." *African Studies Newsletter* 3, nos. 3–4 (May–June): 8–9.

———. 1974. "Profile of a Pioneer Africanist." In *Pillars in Ethiopian History: The William Leo Hansberry African History Notebook,* ed. Joseph E. Harris, 3–30. Washington D.C.: Howard University Press.

Haynes, Jane Banfield. 1969. "ASA Meeting Disrupted by Racial Crisis: Black Militants Challenge the Association and Question the Moral Bases of African Studies." *Africa Report,* Dec., pp. 16–17.

Heginbotham, Stanley. 1994. "Rethinking International Scholarship." *Items* 48, nos. 2–3:33–40.

Heilbrunn, Jacob. 1996. "The News from Everywhere." *Lingua Franca* 6, no. 6:48–56.

Herskovits, Melville J. 1930. *The Anthropometry of the American Negro.* New York: Columbia University Press.

———. 1958a [1941]. *The Myth of the Negro Past.* Boston: Beacon.

———. 1958b. "Some Thoughts on American Research in Africa." Presidential address, First Annual Meeting, African Studies Association, Evanston, Ill., Sept. 8, 1958. *African Studies Bulletin* 1, no. 2 (Nov): 1–11.

———. 1958c. Letter to the Hon. Allen W. Dulles, Feb. 20, 1958. Herskovits Papers, Northwestern University, Box 75/5.

———. 1986 [1925]. "The Negro's Americanism." In *The New Negro,* ed. Alain Locke, 353–60. New York: Atheneum.

Hill, Adelaide Cromwell. 1970. "Report on the Dialogue on Black Scholars and African Studies." *African Studies Newsletter* 3, nos. 3–4 (May–June): 5–8.

Institute of International Education. 1961. *IIE Survey of the African Student: His Achievements and Problems.* New York: Institute of International Education.

———. 1990. *Open Doors 1989–90.* New York: Institute of International Education.

Janken, Kenneth Robert. 1993. *Rayford W. Logan and the Dilemma of the African-American Intellectual.* Amherst: University of Massachusetts Press.

Johnson, Thomas A. 1969. "Blacks Interrupt Parley on Africa." *New York Times,* Oct. 19.

"Johnson Resolution Is the Subject of a Task Force Panel: 'New Directions in African Studies.'" 1970. *African Studies Newsletter* 3, no. 7 (Nov.–Dec.): 25.

Karp, Ivan. 1997. "Does Theory Travel? Area Studies and Cultural Studies." *Africa Today* 44, no. 3:281–96.

Keppel-Jones, Arthur. 1969. Letter about Montreal. *African Studies Newsletter* 2, nos. 6–7 (Nov.–Dec.): 27–28.

Kilson, Martin. 1970. Letter. *African Studies Newsletter* 3, no. 7 (Nov.–Dec.): 20–21.

Ladner, Joyce A. 1973. *The Death of White Sociology.* New York: Random House.

Lambert, Richard D. 1973. *Language and Area Studies Review.* Philadelphia: American Academy of Political and Social Science.

Lambert, Richard D., with Elinor G. Barber, Eleanor Jordan, Margaret B. Merrill, and Leon I. Twarog. 1984. *Beyond Growth: The Next Stage in Language and Area Studies.* Washington D.C.: Association of American Universities.

Letters from Members. 1970. *African Studies Newsletter* 3, nos. 3–4 (May–June): 9–12.

Lowe, Christopher. 1997. "Unexamined Consequences of Academic Globalism in African Studies." *Africa Today* 44, no. 3:297–308.

Matthews, Z. K. 1952. Letter to C. P. Dent, University of Fort Hare, July 20. University of Cape Town Archives, BC 706, Z. K. Matthews Autobiography, File B1.1-B41.1.

McCracken, John. 1993. "African History in British Universities: Past, Present, and Future." *African Affairs* 92, no. 367:239–353.

McWhorter, Gerald A., and Ronald Bailey. 1984a. "Black Studies Curriculum Development in the 1980s: Its Patterns and History." *The Black Scholar* 15, no. 2 (Mar.–Apr.): 18–31.

———. 1984b. "An Addendum to Black Studies Curriculum Development in the 1980s: Its Patterns and History." *The Black Scholar* 15, no. 6 (Nov.–Dec.): 56–58.

Meier, August, and Elliott Rudwick. 1986. *Black History and the Historical Profession, 1915–1980*. Urbana: University of Illinois Press.

Michaels, Marguerite. 1993. "Retreat from Africa." *Foreign Policy* 72, no. 1:93–108.

Mildenburger, Kenneth W. 1960. "African Studies and the National Defense Education Act." *African Studies Bulletin* 3, no. 4 (Dec.): 16–23.

Miller, Christopher. 1993. "Literary Studies and African Literature: The Challenge of Intercultural Literary." In *Africa and the Disciplines*, ed. Bates, Mudimbe, and O'Barr, 213–31.

Murphy, E. Jefferson. 1973. *Creative Philanthropy: Carnegie Corporation and Africa, 1953–1973*. New York: Teachers College Press.

National Endowment for the Humanities. 1992. *National Security Education Program.* Report submitted to the Pentagon, Mar. 16. Washington, D.C.: National Endowment for the Humanities.

Nkosi, Lewis. 1993. "US Diary." *Southern Africa Review of Books,* July–Aug., p. 24.

Noon, John A. N.d. "African Studies Association News Release." Howard University, Moorland-Spingarn Research Center, E. F. Frazier papers, Box 131–19, Folder 18.

Obichere, Boniface I. 1976. "The Contribution of African Scholars and Teachers to African Studies, 1955–1975." *ISSUE* 6, nos. 2–3:27–32.

Palat, Ravi. 1996. "Fragmented Visions: Excavating the Future of Area Studies in a Post-American World." *Review* 19, no. 3:269–315.

Parpart, Jane L. 1995. "Is Africa a Postmodern Invention?" *ISSUE,* 23 no. 1:16–18.

Payne, William Alfred. 1970. *African Studies Newsletter* 3, no. 7 (Nov.–Dec.): 22.

Phelps-Stokes Fund. 1949. *A Survey of African Students Studying in the United States.* New York: Phelps-Stokes Fund.

Pifer, Alan. 1953. *Forecasts of the Fulbright Program in British Africa.* London: United States Educational Commission in the United Kingdom.

Ray, Edna, William Schaap, Karl Van Meter, and Louis Wolf. 1979. *Dirty Work 2: The CIA in Africa.* Secaucus, N.J.: Lyle Stuart.

Resnick, Idrian N. 1969a. "Report of the Radical Caucus." *African Studies Newsletter* 2, nos. 6–7 (Nov.–Dec.): 14–15.

———. 1969b. "Dialog: The Future of African Studies after Montreal." *Africa Report,* Dec., pp. 22–23.

"Resolution on the African Studies Association's Commitment to the Liberation and Dignified Survival of African People." 1970. *African Studies Newsletter* 3, no. 7 (Nov.–Dec.): 3.

Rowe, Cyprian Lamar. 1970. "Crisis in African Studies: The Birth of the African Heritage Studies Association." *Black Academy Review* 1, no. 3:3–10.

Schecter, Daniel. 1976. "From a Closed Filing Cabinet: The Life and Times of the Africa Research Group." *ISSUE* 6, nos. 2–3:41–8.

Segal, Aaron. 1970. "ASA Weighs Its Future: Boston Meeting Seeks New Directions." *Africa Report,* Dec., p. 22.

Shepperson, George. 1974. "The Afro-American Contribution to African Studies." *Journal of American Studies* 8, no. 3:281–301.

Smith, Anne. 1970. "Race and African Studies." *Africa Report,* Apr., p. 42.

Staniland, Martin. 1983. "Who Needs African Studies?" *African Studies Review* 26, nos. 3–4 (Sept.–Dec.): 77–97.

———. 1983–84."Africa, the American Intelligentsia, and the Shadow of Vietnam." *Political Science Quarterly* 98 (Winter): 595–616.

Sutton, Francis X. 1977. "American Foundations and Public Management in Developing Countries." In *Education and Training for Public Sector Management in the Developing Countries,* ed. Laurence D. Stifel, James S. Coleman, and Joseph E. Black, 117–33. New York: Rockefeller Foundation.

Sutton, Francis X., and David R. Smock. 1976. "The Ford Foundation and African Studies." *ISSUE* 6, nos. 2–3:68–72.

Taiwo, Olufemi. N.d. "International Dimensions of Knowledge Production in African Studies." Unpublished paper.

United States Department of State. 1958. Office of Intelligence Research and Analysis. Bureau of Intelligence and Research. "African Studies Association: The First Annual Meeting." External Research Report no. ER-5, Oct. 17. Howard University, Moorland-Spingarn Research Center, E. F. Frazier papers, Box 131–19, Folder 19.

van Essen, Marcel. 1960. "The United States Department of State and Africa." *Journal of Human Relations* 8, nos. 3–4:844–53.

Vansina, Jan. 1994. *Living with Africa.* Madison: University of Wisconsin Press.

Vaughan, Megan. 1994. "Colonial Discourse Theory and African History; or, Has Postmodernism Passed Us By?" *Social Dynamics* 29, no. 2:1–23.

Wade-Lewis, Margaret. 1992. "The Impact of the Turner-Herskovits Connection on Anthropology and Linguistics." *Dialectical Anthropology* 17, no. 4:391–412.

Wallerstein, Immanuel. 1983. "The Evolving Role of the Africa Scholar in African Studies." *Canadian Journal of African Studies/Revue Canadienne des Études Africaines* 17, no. 1:9–16.

———. 1997. "The Unintended Consequences of Cold War Area Studies." In Noam Chomsky et al., *The Cold War and the University: Toward an Intellectual History of the Postwar Years,* 195–231. New York: New Press.

Williams, Cynthia. 1994. "Funders Rethink Priorities: New Era Requires Innovative Approaches to Area and International Studies." *Communiqué* 4, no. 2 (Nov.–Dec.): 1–3.

Women's Caucus. 1970. "Resolutions on the Status of Women." *African Studies Newsletter* 3, no. 7 (Nov.–Dec.): 2–3.

Woodard, Maurice C., ed. 1977. *Blacks and Political Science.* Washington: American Political Science Association.

5 Low-Intensity Warfare and the Study of Africans at Home and Abroad

Horace Campbell

World War II was a political and military turning point in Europe. The Gulf War marked a similar realignment for the United States of America. One of the more profound aspects of these transitions was the fact that the existing modes of organizing social life, institutions, and ideas had exhausted their historical effectiveness. The United States emerged from World War II as a major force in global politics, with its leaders taking the moral high road in opposing the old form of nineteenth-century colonialism in Africa. By 1990, however, the United States had become the dominant imperial power proclaiming a "new world order."

In the half-century since the end of World War II, the United States has attempted to police the globe and crush aspirations for self-determination. During the period of the cold war, when the United States led the "free world," there were supposedly two competing models of social organization: the Soviet and the Western schemes. In reality both these models of economic planning were based on the same Fordist system of production and differed only as to who should own the means of production. The centrality of armaments production for the reproduction of the system indicated the similarities between the competing models, with both of them legitimized by an educational infrastructure.

In the United States the implications of this mode of knowledge production had severe implications for the study of Africa. Inside the academy the principal institutions devoted to studying other societies were integrated into a branch of investigation called "area studies." These programs and centers were in turn linked directly to the foundations and research fronts of the armaments industry. Centers with better access to foundation support and those professors whose former students staffed the governmental bureaucracy dealing with international education dominated area studies.

Although the resources of the government and foundations went to area and African studies in order to contain and direct the anticolonial thrust in Africa, it was the massive rebellion of African American youth in the 1960s that formally brought African American studies into the academy. This is not to say, however, that the study of Africa by Africans had no prior history, as the previous chapter in this volume shows. Over eighty years ago—when African Americans faced lynching, rape, and segregation—Carter G. Woodson organized the Association for the Study of Negro Life and History. This organization, now called the Association for the Study of Afro-American Life and History, sought to carry on the tradition of African American intellectual interest in Africa by focusing public attention on the achievements of Africans and their contributions to world civilizations. Nonetheless, today's scholars face challenges as formidable as those faced by Woodson and W. E. B. Du Bois, his contemporary, during and after World War I.

Indeed, in some senses the challenges today are even greater, since those who hold power are perfecting a system of low-intensity warfare by, among other things, harnessing the resources of the academy to spread destruction without formally declaring war and mobilizing troops. Psychological warfare, disinformation, and the doublespeak of "peacekeeping" and "conflict resolution" are now important elements of an educational system geared to justify deepening divisions at the global and national levels. Thus while decrying investment in public education in both Africa and in the inner cities of the United States, the ideologues of warfare drafted the National Security Education Act (NSEA). The NSEA mobilized $150 million from the defense and intelligence budget of the United States, in the words of the legislation, "to lead in developing the national capacity to educate citizens to understand foreign cultures . . . and enhance international cooperation," both in areas such as Africa, historically underrepresented in existing programs, and among underrepresented student populations.

The future of pan-African studies (i.e., the study of Africa, Africans in the Americas, and dispersed Africans everywhere) now stands at a turning point: it can either be part of the new narrative meant to silence those demanding fundamental changes in the orientation of African studies, or it can be part of the search to transcend the deeply rooted paradigms that have justified and covered up colonialism, militarism, and underdevelopment (Rodney 1972). Given this choice, the objective of this chapter is to chart the impact of low-intensity warfare on the study of Africa in order to challenge the dominant conceptions of "civilizing" and "modernizing" the African. It is in this context that the new strategies for studying the pan-African world should be understood. To decisively break the divisions between African Americans, native peoples, and other oppressed nationalities, there needs to be a critical appraisal of the future of pan-African studies as it is linked to pan-African politics domestically and internationally.

If deliberate efforts are not made to rise above the system of geopolitical expansionism and the forceful spreading of so-called democracy, then pan-African studies as represented by the current divisions between African studies and African American studies could become just another vehicle for legitimating African oppression—as is already evident in scholarship on Cuba. The alliance between the universities, the corporations, and the military is driving African American studies away from its roots in the black liberation struggle. One of the present tasks in the study of the pan-African world is thus to take up the challenge posed in the 1940s by scholars such as Du Bois and others in the Council on African Affairs who sought to end alienation in the academy by linking the study of Africa to both the decolonization process and the struggle for civil rights in the United States.

The rest of this chapter, which is devoted to a discussion of the previously mentioned issues, is divided into five sections. The first section focuses on the Council on African Affairs and the cold war's impact on African studies. The second and third sections show how low-intensity warfare became a central aspect of African studies in Britain and the United States. Section 4 analyzes the relationship between African studies and African American studies in the context of the black liberation movement in the United States, and the fifth section offers a critical assessment of Afrocentrism as an emerging trend in the study of Africa. By way of conclusion, the chapter touches on the questions of intellectual freedom, accountability, and the democratization of information and knowledge production. It draws on the Kampala Declaration on Academic Freedom to seek ways in which the present community of African scholars could be held accountable both to students and to the wider community.

The Council on African Affairs

In this century intellectuals who addressed the alienation and exploitation of the African faced the distortion and falsification of human history, which also meant that some of them internalized the racism of Western culture. Those who opposed the educational system made major contributions to the advancement of our understanding of human transformations. Individual pan-Africanists such as Du Bois, Marcus Garvey, C. L. R. James, George Padmore, Cheikh Anta Diop, Walter Rodney, and Samir Amin took up the challenge of correcting the distortions, but this was not a task for individuals, however great their contribution to an emancipatory intellectual culture. Meeting this challenge also required the political liberation of the continent and the organized activity of social forces most able to support these intellectual projects. In addition, none of these pan-Africanists was sufficiently concerned with confronting the deformities of patriarchy.

In the 1940s one group that was committed to the study of Africa for the purposes of emancipation was the Council on African Affairs. Described by many historians as the most outstanding formation in the United States working for political independence in Africa between 1937 and 1955, this organization carried forward the democratic components of the Garvey program, such as providing information and educating Americans on the conditions in Africa. The scholarly experience of Du Bois, William Hunton, and Max Yergan, combined with Paul Robeson's advocacy role, ensured that though its membership was small, the council's influence was projected through newsletters, conferences, and various pamphlets and papers documenting the anticolonial thrust.

The significant point brought out in biographies of the leading activists of the council is the organic link between this work on Africa and the African American community, especially in Harlem. This link, along with the council's radical pan-Africanism, partly explains the demise of an African American approach in the study of Africa that went back to the nineteenth century. Two works detail how the U.S. government harassed and persecuted the principal members of the council: Hollis Lynch's *Black American Radicals and "The Liberation of Africa": The Council of African Affairs, 1937–1955* (1978) and Penny von Eschen's *Race against Empire: Black Americans and Anticolonialism, 1937–1957* (1997).

Lynch's study has many implications for the unraveling of the modern origins of the African Studies Association, despite the fact that Lynch did not have access to the correspondence between the leading scholars in African studies who, for example, wanted to starve Du Bois and others of funds to do research on Africa. The decision to dissolve the council in 1955 took place in the McCarthyite period as the Subversive Activities Control Board and other agencies of the government campaigned intensely against the organization.

McCarthyism as a form of cultural repression affected institutions in the United States and beyond. Indeed, as a celebration of militarism in the arts and the academy, McCarthyism followed a long tradition in Europe that had ensured self-censorship among scholars in order to glorify monarchs, colonialism, racism, and patriarchy. As John M. MacKenzie (1986) shows in his study of the manipulation of British public opinion, the dominant institutions of ideological reproduction—the cinema, the music hall, the publishing industry, and the school system—all conveyed the messages of colonial adventure and white superiority.

African Studies in Britain

The ideas underlying propaganda and imperial domination were most influential in the development of African studies in the United Kingdom. Whether it was in the celebration of "explorers" such as Stanley or Livingstone, the entrepreneurial spirit of Cecil Rhodes, the indirect rule and massacres of Lord Lugard, or guided decolonization, the British university at the end of World War II established a tradition of African studies that sought to ensure foreign control over Africa. Former colonial officials were the major professors teaching about Africa (Fage 1989). The experience of Sir Andrew Cohen as the brain behind peaceful decolonization was to find expression in institutes of development studies and aid agencies. In societies where Africans resorted to armed struggle, the resources of the British intellectual community were organized (with the assistance of American foundations) to support the low-intensity operations of the British.

Thus from the outset of the struggle of the Land and Freedom Army in Kenya (Mau Mau), British anthropologists and historians organized research on all aspects of African culture that could explain how, as the investigators saw it, Africans could have turned from the civilizing mission of the colonial enterprise to the barbarism of waging war against Britain. The research for the army was subsequently given academic legitimacy and published as the *Historical Survey of the Origins and Growth of the Mau Mau* (Corfield 1960). Although crude in its formulations, the study used a format that was to inform the sectoral analysis of African societies that later became prominent in the country studies of the International Bank for Reconstruction and Development (IBRD) and the U.S. Department of Defense.

Prior to the outbreak of armed struggles, the militant opposition of African workers in Ghana, Nigeria, and Uganda had led to conferences on Africa at Cambridge in 1948, at the height of the activity of the Council on African Affairs. These meetings sought to initiate an agenda that could contain and control the decolonization process, as revealed by the contrast between the Council on African Affairs' campaigns against colonial atrocities and the major studies of former security officials such as Frank Kitson, who became the principal theoretician on low-intensity operations (Kitson 1971). Kitson drew heavily from the military, intellectual, and cultural agenda of the war against the Kenyan producers to initiate a trajectory in the study of Africa that was to have a lasting effect on all areas where Africans took up arms. His 1960 book, *Gangs and Counter-gangs,* would later inform the creation of the Mozambique National Resistance (MNR), as well as UNITA (National Union for the Total Independence of Angola) in Angola and Inkatha's armed wing in South Africa.

This concern with pacification and creating divisions among Africans was also a factor in the massive output on ethnicity and ethnic groups. For a long period every African student who journeyed to Britain was encouraged to do research on his or her ethnic group—and with rich irony, it was this same racist environment that exposed some students to pan-African ideals. In the British African studies community, the London School of Oriental and African Studies stands as a monument to the tradition of subversion through the academy. One former African student from this center commented in a recent article that even after forty years of formal political independence in some parts of Africa, "the School has failed to initiate a clearly defined policy on racism and political intolerance. At a time when the West has suddenly discovered the use of the word 'democracy' to beat the heads of undemocratic African countries (governments that SOAS has helped to influence and guide), the classes and seminars deliberately exclude African analyses. It would appear that Africans will perpetually remain objects of focus rather than participants in their reconceptualisation" (Houghton 1992).

The conception of Africans as objects of analysis was to take even deeper root in the United States when the established institutions for the study of Africa attempted to exclude African Americans. The overt racism of the former colonial officers had inspired a section of the British left to break with the intellectual orientation of modernization and "tribal" studies. Although this leftist segment (heavily dominated by white South African exiles) developed journals and other alternative reference points for the study of Africa, the elitism and arrogance among many of them nevertheless sustained an element of paternalism toward Africans, including intolerance and hostility to independent African thinkers (especially Walter Rodney). Students from the left wing of British African studies, moreover, came to dominate international nongovernmental agencies in Africa. British liberalism was tame, however, when compared to the far more nefarious links between low-intensity operations and the university that were refined in the United States during the cold war.

African Studies and the Ideas of Low-Intensity Warfare in the U.S. Academy

Insofar as wars are fought over popular conceptions and ideologies, the university's role in reproducing the ideas of militarism is an important component of warfare. The extent of the relationship between the structures of industry, scientific research, the war-making capabilities of the Pentagon, and the university establishment has received some attention among peace activists in North America (e.g., Diamond 1992) and, more recently, scholars of the early cold war period (Chomsky et al. 1997). There has been, however, very little work on the explicit relationship between the studies and research on Africa (and Africans) and the low-intensity strategies that have been perfected by the national security establishment in the United States.

The use of the term "low-intensity conflict" (LIC) came into the academy in the 1980s after the Joint Low Intensity Project presented a clearly articulated set of doctrines to the U.S. Joint Chiefs of Staff. The report, presented in 1985 after years of research, reports, and conferences with academicians, argued that "low intensity conflict is a limited politico military struggle to achieve social, economic or psychological objectives. It is often protracted and ranges from diplomatic, economic and psycho-social pressures through terrorism and insurgency. Low intensity conflict is generally confined to a geographic area and is often characterized by constraints on weaponry, tactics, and level of violence" (in Klare and Kornbluh 1987:53).[1] This definition lets us better understand the wars in Southern Africa and the arming of insurgents in Angola, South Africa, and Mozambique despite peace accords.

The Pentagon study focused on the military objectives of LIC and obscured the importance of academicians in formulating the strategies of low-intensity conflict. Yet social scientists have been engaged at all levels in the formulation of the tactics and strategies of low-intensity warfare through workshops, conferences, and contract research. Many of these scholars fail to connect theoretical assumptions about order, communism, stability, and strategic interests to the actual violence and carnage wreaked in other societies. The NSEA, however, makes explicit the intelligence community's control over research grants and student fellowship as part of the imperative to increase knowledge of other cultures and languages of critical areas outside Western Europe. This thrust had been made clear earlier by the consultants to the Joint Chiefs' project, who observed: "The biggest 'battalions' and most sophisticated weaponry do not necessarily lead to 'success.' Rather, the effectiveness of US involvement is most often dependent upon the quality of personnel on the ground, and their knowledge of the conflict as it is shaped by a foreign culture and indigenous politics" (Sarkesian 1988:13).

This position has become so deeply rooted that even many critics of NSEA opposed only the bill's form, not its content, thus reinforcing the domination of the national security apparatus over the study of other cultures, including Africa. Those in the African Studies Association (ASA) who opposed the bill took pains to discuss the narrow question of whether the funds should be disbursed by the Department of Education rather than the Department of Defense, with no effort to develop a generalized debate and public critique on the real intentions behind this legislation. Many universities did not even go so far as to oppose the form of the legislation but proceeded to lobby for the money for their institutions and students—and continued to do so when new legislation required student fellowship holders to work for federal agencies with "national security responsibilities" (Rubin 1996, 1997).

Indeed, the very process of issuing press releases against the Boren Bill, as the proposed NSEA legislation was called, involved a deepening of the contacts and informal relationships between area studies specialists and the security infrastructure. In the specific case of African studies, this has led to close relationships, as indicated in the title of an article by Bowman (1990): "Government Officials, Academics, and the Process of Formulating U.S. National Security Policy toward Africa." This study highlighted the four main security organs of the U.S. government and the forms of their interaction with Africanist scholars:

1. the State Department, specifically though the Bureau of Intelligence and Research (INR), the Foreign Service Institute (FSI) and the United States Information Agency;
2. the Department of Defense, through the Defense Intelligence Agency (DIA) and the Defense Academic Research Support Program (DARSP);
3. the Central Intelligence Agency (CIA) through academic consultancies, workshops and conferences; and
4. the National Security Council.[2]

From time to time the intelligence newssheets and newsletters (such as *Africa Confidential*) have carried detailed listings on who is consulting for which security agencies, depending on the region of Africa and how the "crisis" is to be represented in the media.

Although the computation of the various forms of interaction between the security apparatus and academia is revealing, there has been little attempt to connect the destruction in southern Africa and the research work sponsored by the CIA or DIA; initial work on the 1960s and 1970s (e.g., Ray et al. 1979) has not been continued. This is not to deny that a significant number of scholars (especially those from the Association of Concerned Africa Scholars) actively resist the universities' integration into the reshaping of the agenda for unconventional conflicts. Some scholars and even military strategists are aware of the destruction wreaked by low-intensity warfare, and this is reflected in the debates within the U.S. military (Drew 1988:2). These scholars, however, are not the ones who have influence over research funds within the foundations and the Department of Education Title VI grants for studying Africa.

The current funding squeeze for university-based research on Africa has made scholars even more susceptible to the growing institutionalization of contacts between Africanists and the national security establishment. Junior scholars and graduate students are most vulnerable in the context of competition for scarce research funds, and for many of these intellectuals, with little experience in Africa, the boundaries between the applied research of senior scholars and the agenda of the Department of Defense and low-intensity planners are not always clear.

The DIA's direct approach in the early 1980s to harness the intellectual energies of African studies was thus a bold effort to strengthen the information base of the Pentagon with respect to Africa.[3] This effort, along with the ambivalent relationship between military intelligence and the universities (see Watson and Dunn 1984),[4] deserves more scrutiny, if only to enhance the integrity of those scholars not associated with the project of "national security policies toward Africa."

Collaboration between the universities and the military and intelligence establishment has a long history, rooted in the old colonial centers. When the United States found that the decolonization process had long-term implications for its competition with Western Europe, the Pentagon began to finance the kind of applied research that had been initiated by the French university system (Luckham 1982). During the 1960s, after the intellectual leaders of the Council on African Affairs had been hounded out of the university and ultimately out of the United States, the Pentagon began producing historical background studies of Algeria and Kenya.

An "appeal" by the Defense Science Board and the National Academy of Sciences in the early 1960s was most explicit in its call for applied research to serve the needs of the intelligence community:

> In recent years the Department of Defense (DOD) has been confronted with many problems which require support from the behavioral and social sciences. . . . The armed forces are no longer solely engaged in warfare. . . . Their missions now include pacification, assistance, "the battle of ideas," etc. All these missions require an understanding of the urban and rural populations with which our military personnel come in contact—in the new "peace-fare" activities or in combat. For many countries throughout the world, we need more knowledge about their beliefs, values, and motivations; their political, religious, and economic organizations; and the impact of various changes or innovations upon their socio-cultural patterns. . . . We believe that DOD has been singularly successful in enlisting the interest and services of an eminent group of behavioral scientists in most of the areas relevant to it. . . . The behavioral science community must be made to accept responsibility for recruiting DOD research managers. The following items are elements that merit consideration as factors. . . . Collaborate with other programs in the U.S. and abroad that will provide continuing access of Department of Defense personnel to the academic and intellectual resources of the free world. . . . (in Africa Research Group 1970:90)

These sentiments helped to shape the principal questions for social science research on Africa in the 1960s, with the main object being to "learn the lessons for other potential conflicts." Initiated by the Pentagon, research was coordinated among the major foundations, the State Department, and the universities, especially the programs of African studies (Berman 1979). This episode has received little documentation and should be the raw material for future doctoral studies on the origins of African studies in the United States.

The relationship of Africanists with security agencies, including the ways in which Title VI grants and foundation support have gone to a select group of universities, journals, and scholars, is an old yet constant refrain. The presidential address at the African Studies Association's 1986 annual conference summed up the contradictions of the links with the intelligence community in this way:

> As scholars dedicated to the study of Africa, we face both old and new challenges today. Government-funded scholars are being harassed when they exercise their constitutional rights in Africa. Officers of our association are included on so called "enemies" lists, and there is a growing and dangerous trend of reduced private foundation support of African scholarship. Accompanying the Reagan administration's cold war perspective has been a shift in funding of scholarship on Africa from the Department of Education to Defense and civilian intelligence agencies. Ten years ago few members of this association would have considered it appropriate for the DIA or the CIA to fund, or perhaps more, to set the research priorities for individual or institutional scholarship on Africa. . . . Today, however, we see prominent scholars and African Studies Centers prepared to accept funding from intelligence agencies. The Rockefeller Foundation's decision to drop its support of international studies will probably encourage more of this type of research support, which will compromise and jeopardize the credibility and integrity of university-based scholarship on Africa. (Bender 1988:6–7)

This speech underscores the doublespeak of those who were working as consultants for the State Department during its policy of constructive engagement with minority-ruled South Africa and the problems endemic to links with the intelligence agencies, including their ability to set priorities and research agenda in linguistics, anthropology, economics, geography, and politics. That the DIA continues to have long-term influence in this area is manifest in the funds it now spends on language training and bibliographies, as in the allocation of $290,000 to the African bibliography project at the University of California at Los Angeles. Library and bibliographic information remains part of the concentration and centralization of resources, which privileges certain scholars. Too many of the libraries and resources on Africa are reserved for the exclusive use of a few.

The experience of Angola illustrates all too well how peacekeeping and negotiations are now elements of low-intensity warfare. After laying out the conditions for international support for UNITA in its war against the Angolan people, former assistant secretary of state for African affairs Chester Crocker wrote a book explaining how to keep peace in Africa (Crocker 1993). Similarly, how can one understand recent U.S. efforts to orchestrate peace in Somalia after years of arming the Siad Barre regime? To extend the discussion beyond the sanitized version of academic discourse, it is necessary to see that military assistance (which was justified by low-intensity scholarship) has had devastating effects in Africa.

Research on war and peace in Africa has focused on the output of "conflict resolution" organizations, such as the various centers for strategic studies that have a vested interest in war. The tragic degeneration of Angola forces progressive men and women to reconsider dominant narratives with respect to the bases of "civil wars" and "black on black" violence. Jacques Depelchin (1993) poses the question as follows: how do those who long for peace but reap war conceptualize these experiences when the most accessible modes of expression and communication are imposed by forces that are directly or indirectly responsible for their situation?

This question is now often posed in the debates in and on postmodernism and postcolonialism in the advanced capitalist countries, where there are both conscious and unconscious attempts to erase discussion on the continuing effects of colonial plunder and pacification campaigns. The whole output of literature on "civil wars" in Africa is part of a long-standing effort to delegitimize the struggles for national liberation on the African continent. Cruder experts abandon the sophisticated language of markets and democracy entirely and call for the outright recolonization of Africa (e.g., Johnson 1993).

The theoretical challenge in the study of the African producers is thus to show how silenced narratives can provide alternative conceptualizations for understanding the effects of war and peace on societies that social scientists have rationalized as naturally suited for war. Low-intensity warfare studies, the current cover for militarists, involve the creation of new "terrorists" to replace the freedom fighters who had previously been labeled as "communist" insurgents (Herman and O'Sullivan 1989). War makers—in part to keep the order books for weapons open in the aftermath of the disintegration of the Soviet Union—now conjure images of narcoterrorists and religious fundamentalists who threaten the new world order. With such terms new narratives are created to bind citizens in the North to lopsided expenditures on warmaking institutions.

It is in this context that the challenge for the unity of African studies and African American studies becomes meaningful. Those centers that have opted for the formation of Africana or pan-African studies in the United States are faced with the task of ensuring that scholarly work aims at uplifting and advancing all people. This requires linking the study of Africans to African scholars' struggles to democratize knowledge production. One of the urgent requirements in this process is to make a decisive break with past and present links to the coercive apparatus of the U.S. government.

The struggle for democracy in Africa has taken new directions as working people have created new political bases in their efforts to oppose commandism, militarism, and one-party dictatorships. African scholars have joined in this new mode of politics and are struggling for academic freedom. These struggles have united African scholars and brought to the fore a new cadre of scholars seeking to break the domination of the centers of low-intensity scholarship. The platform for this new direction can be seen in the pages of the *CODESRIA Bulletin* from Dakar and *Southern Africa Political and Economic Monthly* (*SAPEM*) from Harare. The Kampala Declaration on Academic Freedom in 1990 was a bold attempt by a group of African scholars who believed that "the academy remains without any doubt central to the production and reproduction of ideas, knowledge and action necessary for the social transformation of our continent, for liberation from ignorance, disease, and poverty; for economic and technological progress, and the expansion and deepening of the spiritual and cultural contents of the lives of our peoples" ("African Freedom Revisited" 1993:1).

African scholars have thus begun to clarify the break with white overlordship in the reproduction of ideas and the linkage of ideas to action. This development is taking place at a time when African American scholarship's response to low-intensity African studies has been to develop a brand of Afrocentrism to counter the racist content of education in the United States.

African American Studies and the Black Liberation Struggle in the United States

Unlike the modern variant of African studies in the United States, which was conceived during the period of decolonization and the cold war, African American studies—or black studies, in its modern incarnation—was initiated in the 1960s as an expression of the Black Power movement and the radical traditions of Africans in the Americas. Racial segregation in the United States had dictated the emergence, from the end of the Civil War, of black colleges and universities to cater to the African American middle strata of teachers, preachers, lawyers, and doctors. Most of these historically black colleges taught some African history, and those tied to religious institutions developed missionary links with Africa.

The fact that the recent evolution of African American studies began in the context of rebellions meant that the programs' contents were influenced by the dynamism of the civil rights and Black Power movements. As Alkalimat (1992) has suggested, this movement was linked to the radical black tradition of Woodson, Du Bois, Langston Hughes, and Ida B. Wells and had five aspects: pan-Africanism, liberation theology, nationalism, feminism, and socialism. Despite the radical traditions of African American studies, the development of this interdisciplinary inquiry faced obstacles set by the demands of academic activism and the state's need to control the African population following World War II.

The expansion of the U.S. economy at this time required the training of a new layer of African Americans. Thus, the pressures of urban rebellion and the need for a new cadre of administrators opened opportunities for African Americans to attend formerly all-white institutions. The ferment of the civil rights movement affected virtually every institution in the United States, including the university. Many African American youth, influenced by both Martin Luther King and Malcolm X, rose beyond the idea that the young should be subservient and pull themselves up by their bootstraps. The interest in Malcolm X in particular proved to be so enduring that research on his life and work has continued to grow over the past thirty years, eliciting attempts by the ruling class to present sanitized versions of the man—in films, black history celebrations, and other forums—that are shorn of radical pan-African demands for African liberation. Efforts to bring to the forefront the relations between Malcolm X and revolutionary Cuba (Mealy 1993) or the plots against Malcolm X (Evanz 1992) have been overtaken, for example, by the hype surrounding the Spike Lee film.

Against this backdrop it is possible to take stock of the thirty-year-old contribution of scholarship in black studies, especially as it relates to the clarification of the tasks of emancipation in the United States. It is now time to assess the number of scholars trained, the journals supported, and the research agenda delimited by the founders of black studies. The important point to note is that while the State Department and the foundations were sponsoring seminars on ways to groom Mobutu and modernize African armies, the content of black studies was being influenced by organizations such as the Black Panther Party, the Student Nonviolent Coordinating Committee (SNCC), the Nation of Islam, the black church, the Congress of African People, and the black student unions that became an important base in the call for African American studies (Norfolk 1992).

It is important to recall that SNCC and the Black Panthers became role models for students of a generation that opposed militarism, a stance that found expression in the massive antiwar consciousness consequent on the bombing of Vietnamese villagers. It was in the context of this general ideological climate that African Americans confronted the direction of African studies in the United States and broke away from the African Studies Association to form the African Heritage Studies Association (AHSA). Unfortunately, as the AHSA became embroiled in the domestic debate over Afrocentrism, its capacity to develop meaningful links with African scholars on the continent was undermined.

Attempts to unite African studies and African American studies continue
to be marked by major ideological rifts among African American scholars.
Initially the intervention of scholars such as Walter Rodney and Amilcar
Cabral had ensured that the false dichotomy between Marxism and nationalism did not dominate the discussion of African American studies (Rodney
1990:81–122; Cabral 1972). Yet rugged individualism had always been an important aspect of the philosophical traditions in the United States, and African Americans did not escape these idealistic conceptions of ruling-class
ideology. The deep hostility to a class analysis of society, along with the historical vacillation of the white left (especially the Communist Party), made
many African American radicals wary of Marxist and socialist ideas.

This ideological divide, which had been manipulated by the U.S. government to undermine the Council on African Affairs, exploded two decades
later in the aftermath of major African Liberation Day rallies, which mobilized grassroots interest in Africa through the church and local community
groups. As part of this movement, the African Liberation Support Committee (ALSC) had promised to be an important united front for African studies, but sharp divisions and individualism shook this organization and led
to its demise. The differences came to the forefront over the question of
Angola in 1975, as nationalists sought to distance themselves from their
"Marxist" counterparts in black studies.

The divisions in the ALSC were reproduced in the conferences of the leading exponents of black studies. One small group took seriously the ASA
walkout in Montreal (see Martin and West's chapter in this volume) and
attempted to link the study of the African continent to the study of Africans
in the diaspora. Universities and foundations, however, took pains to promote those scholars who were considered "neutral" and whose intellectual
work focused on poverty, the black underclass, and those categories of social science research that did not challenge capitalism at home or imperialism and militarism abroad. During the 1980s the Ford Foundation, for example, commissioned no fewer than five studies to keep up to date with the
direction of black studies in the United States (Fierce 1991).

The present state of black studies needs careful investigation in the light
of the demands of the twenty-first century, the transition from Fordism to
just-in-time production, and the decline of U.S. economic hegemony, which
has affected the social stock of the inner cities and the quality of life in the
African American community. This decline has affected the university and
the entire content of education as well. These changes in the economy pose
the question of whether universities will end up promoting "savage inequality," as suggested by ideologues such as William Bennett, or whether they will
become part of the democratization process, reversing the lobotomization
and marginalization of peoples of color.

In the era of the "new world order," far-sighted elements in the ruling class have tapped some African American centers to participate in the recolonization of Africa. This can be seen most vividly in the series of conferences in the Ivory Coast and Gabon between luminaries of the African American community and repressive leaders of Africa. Thus, with bold claims about "African Americans saving Africa," more than 800 African American leaders gathered in Gabon in 1993 to participate in the second African American summit.[5]

The structure of the meeting and the content of the discussion indicated how cut off African American studies had become from the struggles in Africa. African American students, happy to be able to journey to Africa, participated in these meetings when African students were being persecuted by the military and security elements in Gabon and the Ivory Coast. This lack of substantive links between African scholars on the continent and those in the United States is compounded by present U.S. efforts to compromise historically black colleges and universities. The CIA's targeting of historically black colleges has already resulted in the dispensation of funds from the intelligence budget for the establishment of the Critical Language Consortium.

CIA efforts to lobby certain African Americans for subversion is not new. Employing anticommunist hype, the pro-Savimbi lobby, with support from the Bush administration, launched a major public relations campaign to obtain African American support for the destabilization of Angola. Under the name of "Black Americans for a Free Angola (BAFAFA)," a campaign was initiated to promote Savimbi's cause among African Americans, providing unwitting support for the cause of apartheid and destruction across southern Africa. In 1987, at the grave of Martin Luther King in Atlanta, this group changed its name to Black Americans for Peace and Democracy in Angola. But while "praying for peace, it was promoting the military aid that enabled Savimbi to continue the war" (Windrich 1992:57–58). Such support exposes how the concepts of peace and democracy were manipulated by cold war warriors.

The U.S. government's use of African Americans on the continent of Africa in various capacities has also led to stereotypes of African Americans, masking the struggle for dignity and social justice in the United States. This has reinforced the artificial distinction between the study of Africans in Africa and in the diaspora, serving those committed to careerism while undermining efforts to raise the general knowledge of Africa in the broader society. Idealism with respect to past kingdoms and a romanticized version of Africa, which is promoted by some African American studies centers, further plays into the hands of the low-intensity planners.

The interventions of the national security apparatus in the African American arena emerged after a period of ideological retreat and the so-called professionalization of black studies. The divide between nationalists and Marxists, which arose in the mid-1970s, proved to be permanent and led to widespread hostility to Marxist interpretations of social reality in the United States. This became evident in the deliberations of the National Council of Black Studies (NCBS) and in the *Journal of Black Studies*.

As both the AHSA and the NCBS moved into the mainstream of American academia in the 1980s, they were affected by the intellectual poverty of the United States. And as more radical elements in African American studies were silenced through the tenure process, it became increasingly difficult to maintain a continuity with the tradition of the 1960s. Filling this void was the emergence of Afrocentrism as a principal ideology of black studies in the United States.

Afrocentrism and the Study of Africa

Afrocentrism, which claims to be in the vanguard of African American studies and the study of Africa, was popularized in the 1980s though a number of scholars and universities. Afrocentrism was a direct response to the deepening racist culture of education, yet it is primarily concerned with the study of African empires and kingdoms. Although such a focus on African kingdoms had been a liberating experience during the colonial period, in the era of political independence this concentration has obscured the realities of structural adjustment and economic hardships in Africa. The preoccupation with great empires and leaders has, moreover, allowed the intellectual giants of the Afrocentric movement to hold meetings in Africa in complete disregard to African-based scholars' calls for academic freedom and accountability.

Afrocentrism does raise fundamental issues with respect to knowledge and power. This is especially the case in the context of struggles over the curriculum and the place of Western civilization relative to other cultures. Although posing a challenge to the center of power in the U.S. educational system, however, in its current form Afrocentrism remains the other side of Eurocentrism (Amin 1988). Insofar as Afrocentrism does not challenge the culture of capitalism, it survives and thrives in the university and among public school teachers and is popularized by the youth, especially rap artists.

Afrocentrism similarly fails to address the relationship between Africans in the United States and those elsewhere in the Americas and between Africans and other oppressed nationalities. In the first place, the present-day tragedies in Haiti, Rwanda, Burundi, Cuba, Somalia, Angola, Liberia, and Sierra Leone demonstrate the failure of Afrocentric thought and action: there has been a noticeable reluctance on the part of those in the Afrocentric movement to intervene politically on the side of the suffering masses of Africans. Thus, despite the active work of Haitian refugees during the period of

Aristide's exile, the main exponents of Afrocentrism demonstrated little public support for the democratic struggles of the Haitian people. This is not new, for in the past the Black Power and pan-African movements refused to intervene to support African liberation in Haiti even while the ALSC was at its height. The Duvaliers' dictatorship had postured as the guardian of black authenticity, and the fact that this was a black-led government silenced those who claimed to champion the cause of African liberation.

Then there is the issue of Afrocentrism's conception of multiethnic societies such as the United States. The exponents of Afrocentrism must recognize that Native Americans were almost made extinct by the genocidal activities of U.S. expansionism. The fact that these Americans have been relegated to reservations does not mean that they should be invisible to those making claims for dignity and equal rights. This issue is linked to further questions concerning the relationships between African Americans and the other oppressed nationalities who form a large section of the working class. A clear position on the relations between African Americans and Latino/a peoples, for example, is required to define a progressive, anticapitalist agenda for the coming decades. Furthermore, Afrocentrism in its present manifestation cannot provide intellectual leadership for the multinational and multilingual alliance that is necessary to challenge the melting-pot theories of the ruling class—despite the presence in the Afrocentric movement of some scholars who view Afrocentric education as one aspect of a broad effort to overcome economic and educational marginality.

One emerging group of African Americans —the black feminists—offers a clear critique of the capitalist order that challenges not only white cultural superiority but the sexual oppression of women in all parts of the globe. Its goals include critiquing the present construction of society, expanding the scope for the self-definition of men and women, and opening new horizons with respect to activism and self-determination. In particular, black feminist thought has posed a fundamental challenge to the ideas, power relationships, and the politics of empowering African American women (Collins 1990).

Black feminists in the United States have been at the forefront of conceptualizing race, class, gender, and the structures of oppression of all peoples. This development has not only challenged the dominant discourse of mainstream feminism but led directly to an engagement with African women on the continent as they struggle with the exercise of male power in all places, including the university. The plethora of struggles that African women confront on a daily basis has ensured the development of an elementary solidarity between African women at home and abroad. In the words of one of the leading theoreticians of black feminist thought: "The unshackling of women, the producers and reproducers of labour power, must become the priority of Pan-Africanist organisers because it makes sense. How can women be expected to play an effective role in the wider movements needing their talents and energies when they are hemmed in by life itself, when they are constrained by multiple social oppressions which are not the chief concerns of pan movements? Imagine a Pan-Africanism vibrant with social truth and activated by free women!" (Harris 1993–94:54). Eusi Kwayana is even clearer as to the place of African scholars in the struggles of the twenty-first century. Afrocentric and pan-African scholarship will be relevant, he says, only if "it relieves itself of a sense of mission in relation to the African continent where informed and concerned activists are legion; if it grapples concretely with the concrete problems posed by present day society—the full emancipation of women and the consequent humanization of the male, harmonious conditions for the growth of the youth and a concerted assault on poverty . . . and insistence on conditions of empowerment and equal opportunity for the oppressed of all ethnic groups" (Kwayana 1993–94: 50). These challenges are, moreover, being confronted across the continent, as became evident at the Seventh Pan African Congress held in Kampala in April 1994 (see the essays presented at the congress, compiled in Abdul-Raheem 1996).

There Are No Clear Paradigms, Only Explorations

Through all the preceding remarks runs a constant theme: the present crisis in education in the United States is part of the larger crisis of a society in the midst of a major transition and the globalization of capital. It is significant that in this transition the leading intellectuals are not to be found in the academy. Rather, the rebellious spirit of the Black Power era and the call for the reorganization of social life in the United States is now conveyed through music, dance, art, theater, film, and new forms of religious identification.

The major challenge for those who teach subjects involving Africans in the Americas rests in democratizing the processes of knowledge production, which is linked to the wider task of democratizing society. Africans and other oppressed nationalities in the United States have a vested interest in the restructuring of the university and the teaching about humanity—either the appetite of youth for self-expression and creativity can be supported, or the education system will become an arena for marginalization as part of the process of pacifying social elements capable of challenging the present system. The war on drugs is only one salvo in this new battle.

To meet this challenge pan-African scholarship must devise a coherent strategy capable of breaking decisively with the culture of capital. African scholars who have emerged from two decades of repression have launched new areas of research geared to providing Africa with opportunities to break from the bottom of the international division of labor. These scholars, with African women in the forefront, have raised new questions with respect to the logic and meaning of democracy.

The meaning of democracy is most hotly contested in South Africa, where the African majority is calling for thorough democratization. In response international capital, along with the principal research institutions and universities, has attempted to formulate an agenda for democracy that would Africanize the structures of governance without fundamentally changing the division of the social product. South African universities cannot escape a continuation of the struggles over the study of South Africa and the much wider world.

For those in established centers of African studies, the present discourse on democracy in Africa is only one more example of doublespeak and the poverty of their work. Those who were once in the forefront of low-intensity research are now belatedly on the bandwagon of the democracy debate—well after the African producers moved decisively against dictators who were heralded as bearers of modernity. Scholars who speak of liberalization and suggest that capitalism is equivalent to democracy and that the market is the only rational choice now dominate the circuit of African studies in the United States.[6] They are becoming increasingly irrelevant in Africa, however, where African scholars have begun to make concrete links with those militants who are creating new sites of politics (Wamba-dia-Wamba 1992).

The struggle beyond elite politics carries with it the call for renewal and reconstruction for Africans in Africa and overseas. These explorations exist not only at the level of ideas but at the level of organization as well. The call for self-reliance and a break with the low-intensity scholarship of African studies in the United States has been heeded all over the continent. In calling for revolutionary commitment on the part of the African scholar, Archie Mafeje remarked: "For the social scientists, artists and philosophers, the intellectual task of identifying, evaluating and synthesising popular cultural notions, various progressive nationalist and socialist pre-conceptions and demands is Herculean but not impossible. A beginning has been made. . . . However, so far no clear paradigms have emerged but only explorations" (Majefe 1992:27). African intellectuals have been energized both by the deformities of colonial and neocolonial education and by the repression of intellectuals and intellectual freedom. The articles of the Kampala Declaration on Academic Freedom properly identified the intellectual's responsibility to guard intellectual freedom. The emphasis on social responsibility and accountability is even more urgent in the period of the NSEA. As the Kampala declaration admonishes: "Members of the intellectual community are obliged to discharge their roles and functions with competence, integrity and to the best of their abilities. They should perform their duties in accordance with ethical and the highest scientific standards. Members of the intellectual community have a responsibility to promote the spirit of tolerance towards different views and positions and enhance democratic debate and discussion" ("Academic Freedom Revisited" 1993:2). This resolution has a direct bearing on whether the turning point in African studies is a movement away from the traditions of British African studies and the imperatives of the cold war. Actions such as monitoring the arrest and detention of African scholars would be concrete steps in developing contacts and relations between African scholars at home and abroad. In the face of the NSEA, those concerned about academic integrity should take seriously the call from Africa that they work for freedom in a variety of respects: "No member of the intellectual community shall participate in or be a party to any endeavour which may work to the detriment of the people or the intellectual community or compromise scientific, ethical and professional standards and principles" ("Academic Freedom Revisited" 1993:2).

Notes

1. For a critique of the principles behind the Joint Low Intensity Project, see Klare and Kornbluh 1987.

2. Under the Bush administration the impetus for low-intensity planning was streamlined to the point where there was a full-time director for Africa on the National Security Council staff.

3. For details of the approach and the exchange between the African studies centers and the Defense Academic Research Support Program, see Wiley 1983–84 and Carlsson 1982.

4. For an account of this relationship, see Trumpbour 1989, esp. "Federal Government, Universities and the Rise of Area Studies" (52–57).

5. For details of those attending the meetings and the agenda, see *African World* 1, no. 1 (Nov.–Dec. 1993).

6. For a critique of this position on the market, see Amin 1990.

References Cited

Abdul-Raheem, Tajudeen. 1996. *Pan Africanism: Politics, Economy, and Social Change in the Twenty-first Century.* New York: New York University Press.

"Academic Freedom Revisited: Three Years after the Kampala Declaration." 1993. *CODESRIA Bulletin* 3:1–2.

Africa Research Group. 1970. *Africa Retort: A Tribal Analysis of U.S. Africanists: Who They Are, Why to Fight Them.* Boston: Africa Research Group.

Alkalimat, Abdul. 1992. "Black Power in U.S. Education: Ideology, Academic Activism and the Politics of Black Liberation." *Africa World Review,* May–Oct., pp. 9–10.

Amin, Samir. 1988. *Eurocentrism.* New York: Monthly Review Press.

———. 1990. *The Future of Socialism.* Harare: SAPES Books.

Bender, Gerald. 1988. "Ideology and Ignorance: American Attitudes toward Africa." *African Studies Review* 31, no. 1:1–7.

Berman, Edward H. 1979. "Foundations, United States Foreign Policy, and African Education, 1945–1975." *Harvard Educational Review* 49, no. 2:145–76.

Bowman, Larry. 1990. "Government Officials, Academics, and the Process of Formulating U.S. National Security Policy toward Africa." *ISSUE* 19, no. 1:5–20.

Cabral, Amilcar. 1972. *Return to the Source.* New York: Monthly Review Press.

Carlsson, Bert. 1982. "U.S. Counter-Insurgency Research in the Social Sciences in Africa." *ACAS Bulletin* 7:2–16.

Chomsky, Noam, et al. 1997. *The Cold War and the University: Toward an Intellectual History of the Postwar Years*. New York: New Press.

Collins, Patricia Hill. 1990. *Black Feminist Thought*. New York: Routledge.

Corfield, F. D. 1960. *The Historical Survey of the Origins and Growth of the Mau Mau*. London: HMSO.

Crocker, Chester. 1993. *High Noon in Southern Africa: Keeping Peace in a Rough Neighborhood*. New York: Norton.

Depelchin, Jacques. 1993. "Warfare and Peace in Southern Africa (1880–1993): Between Popular and Institutional Memories/Histories/Silences." Unpublished paper.

Diamond, Sigmund. 1992. *Compromised Campus: The Collaboration of the Universities with the Intelligence Community 1945–1955*. New York: Oxford University Press.

Drew, Dennis M. 1988. *Insurgency and Counter Insurgency: American Military Dilemmas and Doctrinal Proposals*. Maxwell Airforce Base: Air University Press.

Evanz, Karl. 1992. *The Judas Factor: The Plot to Kill Malcolm X*. New York: Thundermouth.

Fage, J. D. 1989. "British African Studies since the Second World War: A Personal Account." *African Affairs* 88, no. 352:397–413.

Fierce, Milfred C. 1991. *Africana Studies outside the United States: Africa, Brazil and the Caribbean*. Cornell University, Africana Studies and Research Center, Monograph Series, no. 7. Ithaca, N.Y.: Africana Studies and Research Center.

Harris, Bonita. 1993–94. "Combatting Women's Overrepresentation among the Poor in the Caribbean." *Southern Africa Political and Economic Monthly* 7, no. 3:51–56.

Herman, Edward, and Gerry O'Sullivan, eds. 1989. *The Terrorism Industry: Experts and Institutions That Shape Our View of Terror*. New York: Pantheon.

Houghton, Irungu. 1992. "SOAS and Imperialism," *Africa World Review*, May-Oct., pp. 12–14.

Johnson, Paul. 1993. "Colonialism's Back—and Not a Moment Too Soon." *New York Times*, Apr. 18, pp. 22, 43.

"Kampala Declaration on Academic Freedom in Africa." 1993. *CODESRIA Bulletin* 3:5–7.

Kitson, Frank. 1960. *Gangs and Counter-gangs*. London: Barrie and Rockliff.

———. 1971. *Low Intensity Operations: Subversion, Insurgency, Peacekeeping*. London: Faber and Faber.

Klare, Michael, and Peter Kornbluh, eds. 1987. *Low Intensity Warfare: CounterInsurgency, ProInsurgency, and Antiterrorism in the Eighties*. New York: Pantheon.

Kwayana, Eusi. 1993–94. "The Caribbean Pan-African Record." *Southern Africa Political and Economic Monthly* 7, no. 3:49–50.

Luckham, Robin. 1982. "French Militarism in Africa." *Review of African Political Economy* 24:55–84.

Lynch, Hollis. 1978. *Black American Radicals and the Liberation of Africa: The Council on African Affairs 1937–1955*. Ithaca, N.Y.: Cornell University, Africana Studies and Research Center.

MacKenzie, John M. 1986. *Propaganda and Empire: The Manipulation of British Public Opinion, 1880–1960*. Manchester: Manchester University Press.

Mafeje, Archie. 1992. *In Search of An Alternative*. Harare: SAPES Books.

Mealy, Rosemari. 1993. *Malcolm and Fidel*. Melbourne: Ocean.

Norfolk, Robert. 1992. "The Black Studies Revolt and the Radical Black Student Unions, 1967–1972." Pan African Research and Documentation Project, Discussion Paper 2, May.

Ray, Ellen, William Schaap, Karl van Meter, and Louis Wolf, eds. 1979. *Dirty Work 2: The CIA in Africa*. Secaucus, N.J.: Lyle Stuart.

Rodney, Walter. 1972. *How Europe Underdeveloped Africa.* Dar es Salaam: Tanzania Publishing House.

———. 1990. *Walter Rodney Speaks: The Making of an African Intellectual.* Trenton, N.J.: Africa World Press.

Rubin, Amy Magaro. 1996. "National Security Education Program Alters Service Requirement." *Chronicle of Higher Education,* Oct. 4, p. A50.

———. 1997. "Service Requirement Broadened for Federal Foreign-Study Program." *Chronicle of Higher Education,* Oct. 27, p. A61.

Sarkesian, Sam C. 1988. "The Myth of US Capability in Unconventional Conflicts." *Military Review,* Sept., pp. 2–17.

Trumpbour, John. 1989. "Harvard, the Cold War, and the National Security State." In *How Harvard Rules,* ed. John Trumpbour, 51–128. Boston: South End.

Von Eschen, Penny. 1997. *Race against empire: Black Americans and Anticolonialism, 1937–1957.* Ithaca, N.Y.: Cornell University Press.

Wamba-dia-Wamba, Ernest. 1992. "Beyond Elite Politics of Democracy in Africa." *Quest* 1, no. 1 (University of Zambia).

Watson, Bruce W., and Peter M. Dunn, eds. 1984. *Military Intelligence and the Universities: A Study of an Ambivalent Relationship.* Boulder, Colo.: Westview.

Wiley, David. 1983–84. "Action on Relations of Scholars with U.S. Defense and Intelligence Agencies." *ACAS Bulletin* 10–11:10.

Windrich, Elaine. 1992. *The Cold War Guerrilla: Jonas Savimbi, the U.S. Media, and the Angolan War.* New York: Greenwood.

6   From Euphoria to Gloom? Navigating the Murky Waters of African Academic Institutions

Zenebeworke Tadesse

Confronted daily with triumphalism abroad, surrounded by Afro-pessimism at home, and beset by ever-diminishing material resources, Africa's emergent scholarly community faces seemingly herculean challenges. In its heyday developmentalism pushed us to catch up with the "West." Today, we are told, the task of Africa is to catch up with the newly industrialized countries.

The first step we must take, however, is to escape these traps. We need to draw the primary lesson from the pitfalls of over thirty years of "development," "nation building," and "bridging gaps": abandon the search for illusory shortcuts based on imitative knowledge acquisition.

The gap in transcontinental power and resources in the production of knowledge can be conceived as enormous. To lament this gap—or worse, to be overwhelmed by it—is the fastest route to a debilitating paralysis. A much more fruitful and difficult choice is to reconceptualize and revalorize our options. Here I am presumptuously referring to "knowledge" and "resources" in Africa.[1] As a contribution to beginning this process, I outline in this brief chapter the historical trajectory of the institutionalized production of social scientific knowledge by African scholars. The outline focuses on universities. Although universities are now beleaguered institutions, they undoubtedly remain the primary arenas for the generation of written knowledge in Africa and, especially, the suppliers of future generations of scholars.

Phase One: The Formative Years

The initial phase of the establishment and development of higher education and research institutes in Africa roughly spans the years 1945 to 1960. The exceptions, however, are important to note: Fourah Bay College in Sierra

Leone was already functioning in the late 1870s, and Fort Hare in South Africa, Makerere College in Uganda, Achimota in the Gold Coast, and Yaba in Nigeria all offered postsecondary education by 1935 (Hinchliffe 1987). Still, most of the first African institutions of higher education were built in the turbulent post–World War II years. Thus colleges were formed in Ibadan in 1949, Legon in 1949, and Sierra Leone in 1960; the University of Dakar was established in 1957–58. The institution-building aspects of this period are well known and need not be belabored here (see, e.g., Ashby 1964).

Several broader and rarely noticed aspects of this phase, however, do need to be drawn out and emphasized. First, it is noteworthy that these initial institutions of higher education were *subregional* in outreach. Second, three interrelated resistance movements in the world at large had a direct bearing on these European-dominated universities. These were pan-Africanism, the emergent notion of the "Third World" following the 1955 Bandung Conference, and concomitantly, the African nationalist movements struggling for independence and aspiring toward "nation building."[2] Focused as it is on the institutional structure, the widely available literature does not provide us with sufficient information on these major elements in the construction of Africa's universities, much less the intellectual history of the early graduates.

A third characteristic of this phase that needs greater attention and emphasis is the location of and material comfort provided to universities, particularly in English-speaking Africa. Premised on the notion that effective education required isolating students from their cultural roots, universities were developed as detached and self-sufficient communities located at some distance from urban centers. Such locations necessitated roads, clinics, schools, and transport service. As a result, "municipal services unrelated to the direct process of higher education often consumed half of the available budget of the university" (Court 1991:331–32). These "golden days" of privilege, with significant flows of resources that set the academic community apart from civil society, lasted until the late 1970s, well beyond the initial phase of African university construction.

In addition to those who attended these universities, a growing number of students were awarded scholarships to study in Europe and the United States. It was also during this period that professional societies and journals began to be published, including *Transactions of the Historical Society of Ghana, Sierra Leone Studies, Ghana Notes and Queries, La Voix du congloais, La Voix de l'Afrique noire,* and so on.

Phase Two: University Building

The second phase of the establishment of African universities and research institutions can be roughly demarcated as covering the years from 1960 to 1974. Numerous universities and research institutes were established during this period, and previously established colleges received full university status. Independence and "nation building" implied the dissolution of regional institutions[3] and the creation of national universities in every country. This period also witnessed the universities' ever-increasing subordination to state control. In country after country the head of state became the university's chancellor and thus appointed the senior administration and in some cases even the governing council and members of the staff appointments board. Higher education consequently came to be tied to the development of the state.

The predominant imperative of this phase was "Africanization," a series of institutional transformations ranging from curriculum reform to academic and administrative control of higher education institutions. The process was often highly conflictual, generating many debates. As Washington Okumu and Thomas Odhiambo argued in 1964, "Europeans who now run our [university] affairs for us cannot undertake any major reforms because they are prisoners of their own irrelevant and out-of-date prejudices" (in Southall 1974:ix). This phase witnessed both a phenomenal increase in enrollment at institutes of higher education and a corresponding increase in the number of faculties and departments. At the same time research institutions proliferated. Reflective of the hegemonic spread of developmentalist ideology, almost every university had an "Institute of Development Studies." Perhaps nothing portrays the "imported" nature of universities better than the numerous research institutions devoted to what was known as African studies, as illustrated by the 1974 meeting of West African Studies Institutes (Seminar on African Studies 1974).

It would be misleading, however, to focus only on these imported influences. Indeed, in outlining the highlights of this phase, three major events in the history of the formation of the African social science community need to be stressed. First, nascent schools of thought, most notably in historical studies, emerged in Ibadan, Tanzania, and Senegal.[4] In addition to these new intellectual approaches and the various debates they engendered, provocative works by Samir Amin (1974a, 1974b), Amilcar Cabral (1969), Walter Rodney (1970, 1972), Archie Mafeje (1971), Issa Shivji (1976), and Mahmood Mamdani (1976) sparked the fire of the emerging African social science community. Third, regional professional associations and research centers began to emerge. These included the Association of African Historians, with its journal *Zamani*; the African Association of Political Science; the Association of African Universities; and the Council for the Development of Economic and Social Research in Africa (CODESRIA) and its journal *Africa Development*. In addition almost all universities launched both discipline-specific and intradisciplinary journals and newspapers. Most of these publications, alas, were short-lived.

Although the initial impetus behind the historical schools was the rising tide of nationalism, other voices arose in the wake of the decolonization project's apparent failure.[5] Dependency theory was on the rise, and its un-critical use in the analysis of African reality put a brake on the search for al-ternative explanatory frameworks. Undue generalizations and unjustified comparisons with Latin America tended to limit our understanding of what could be historically specific to Africa. More important, there was the dis-appointing outcome of the Algerian War of Independence and the promise of better alternatives in the Portuguese colonies of Angola, Guinea-Bissau, and Mozambique. The period from the mid-1960s to the mid-1970s was in-deed a euphoric one, seemingly full of intellectual promise. Nonetheless, a *tradition* of research and publishing was not institutionalized.

Phase Three: Toward a Politics of Inclusion, Exit, and Democratization?

The third phase covers roughly the years from 1974 to 1990. This phase in-cluded the emergence of new, previously silenced groups of scholars. Fore-most among these was the Association of African Women for Research and Development (AAWORD; subsequently housed in CODESRIA); this orga-nization, formed in 1977 by a group of women, brought together women scholars, who were few in number at institutions of higher learning and ab-sent from existing research networks. Since then a number of similar "women and development" units have sprung up. Although male scholars have be-gun to pay lip service to its importance, the conceptualization of gender re-lations has for the most part been left to women. The few courses on this topic offered, for example, are left on the margins of the discipline-based seminars, and the related issues are usually ignored in the team-taught, interdiscipli-nary, thematic courses.

In the years after the mid-1970s authoritarianism spread across the Afri-can landscape with varying degrees of intensity. In almost all countries of Africa, the state tightened its grip on the university, banned critical work, and began to intimidate or arrest critical scholars and students. It was during this period that relatively large numbers of well-known academicians began to emigrate. Such was the case with a significant number of Zairian, Ethiopian, Ugandan, Guinean, and Ghanaian academicians, many of whom relocated to other African universities. Not all stayed in academia, however.

As the economic and political crisis deepened and living standards plum-meted, this exodus of teaching personnel picked up speed, with many scholars moving to African countries that offered better salaries and fringe benefits, including Kenya, Zimbabwe, Botswana, Lesotho, Swaziland, and the so-called homelands of South Africa (see Zeleza 1990). The well-published senior aca-demicians migrated to Europe or, more often, to the United States. No one to my knowledge has explored the obvious critical question of whether and to what degree these migrants can maintain intellectual and other links to

their homelands as well as in their new places of residence. Even more intriguing would be a comparative study of the new intellectual migrants in
relation to their predecessors in the diaspora.

As the 1970s gave way to the 1980s, a deepening socioeconomic and political malaise ensued. Shorn of the possibilities of previous generations of
scholars, a new social group—the educated unemployed—became a disturbing indicator of a volatile future. The emerging independent research centers addressed these conditions at least in part. Up to this point, almost all
social science research centers had been part of the university structure. New
groups subsequently moved to set up institutions that were independent of
the national universities and beyond the control of the state. Two examples
of such nonuniversity-based research centers with strong but voluntary intellectual links to universities are the Southern Africa Political Economy Trust
(SAPES) in Harare and the Centre for Basic Research in Kampala.[6]

SAPES publishes the widely circulated periodical *Southern Africa Political and Economic Monthly* and has launched a burgeoning book series. From
its base in Harare, SAPES has sought to establish links throughout southern
Africa, organizing a monthly public forum on critical issues of social transformation that has attracted growing public participation. SAPES also or-
ganizes academic conferences in various southern African cities. The Centre for Basic Research is, by contrast, locally focused even while it maintains
strong links to subregional and regional research organizations. In a relatively
short time, the center has produced an impressive set of monographs. It also
has a library, an essential but increasingly scarce research tool at many African universities.

The questions that beg for further consideration are straightforward: Are
such independent research centers likely to grow in number and forge a culture of critical inquiry and cumulative knowledge base? How autonomous—
that is, nondonor driven—are they likely to remain?

As the 1980s came to a close, all these developments were marked by the
undeniable emergence of democratization. Given the nature of authoritar-
ian rule, democratic forces gained a substantive number of victories. Chief
among these are fundamental rights such as the freedom of assembly and the
freedom of expression, essential rights long sequestered in most of Africa. In
short order the deafening silence of the past has been replaced by a democratic public sphere in which a polyphony of voices, expressing a broad spec-
trum of interests, can be heard. The creation of such a public sphere has
unleashed energetic, angry, fearful, and hopeful debates in universities and
civil society across the continent.

Ironically, this current wave of democratization marks the end of the
university community as a major political actor engaged in reproducing,
resisting, and transforming existing power relations and the distribution of
resources. As a result, contemporary debates are conducted off campuses, in

a manner that is more or less disorganized, enthusiastic, and partial. One must therefore look off university campuses for intellectual vitality and alternative social projects.

Looking to an Uncertain Future

For African scholars and students today, almost all the major aspects of their existence are undergoing fundamental transformations, from the organization of university life and the amenities they enjoy to the career implications of the courses they choose. For most university staff and students, the emergent landscape looks uniformly bleak. Throughout the last decade, we have witnessed a contested process through which lecturers have become deskilled and disempowered.[7] Like other workers, university lecturers are being transformed economically, becoming less advantaged, more vulnerable to increased workloads, and forced to pursue applied fields while more critical themes remain underfunded. The key unanswered question we must begin to address is clear: what are the long-term implications of these transformations for the reproduction of a scholarly community?

Some initial observations may be directly made. It is evident that the significant deterioration of teachers' salaries in real terms has increased the need for additional sources of income, implying less time for teaching and the preparation of lectures. This often leads to oversimplification and dogma at the expense of scholarship and research. We should not be surprised, therefore, that faculty are unable to enrich their teaching, inspire and stimulate students, and provide a dynamic atmosphere for learning. Dilapidated library sources together with a weak research tradition can similarly lead to a paralysis of new ways of generating knowledge. Yet as we move away from the "conventional mode" of teaching, mostly through force majeure, it is possible to perceive, however dimly, the emergence of innovative pedagogies.

Taken together, all these changes signal the end of an era that triggered the "explosion of aspirations" and the myths of "meritocracy," national "development," and progress in imitation of purported patterns in the West. Despite all the negative factors previously charted, moreover, education remains the most contested arena of public policies, with signs of renewal emerging as opportunities are seized consequent on the collapse of old ideological and institutional structures.

The Entrepreneurial University

The transformation, if not end, of the state's dominance in providing and financing higher education reveals contradictory processes at work. Henceforth universities will likely assume greater responsibility for raising funds to support instruction. In 1992, for example, President Museveni of Uganda announced plans to relinquish his position as the chancellor of Makerere University. "Autonomous" institutions such as the National Council for Higher Education in Uganda will now coordinate national and donor investments in the educational subsector. In the meantime, new private universities are being launched. To avoid controversies, efforts will be made to develop "a consensus" for reform acceptable to all parties, such as university administrators, professors, students, and public and private employers. As has been noted in the case of Kenya, among others, the political will required to implement cost-sharing measures is not insignificant. Such measures will include admitting students as day scholars, streamlining student housing and dining operations, and abolishing allowances.

From all indications, the next cost-cutting measures will be the rediscovery of "centers of excellence," viable mega-universities to serve students from whole subregions or cooperative programs in specialized areas. In this context, South African universities are likely to play a significant role. Before this happens, however, the most likely measure will be the painful phasing out of faculties and programs and the targeting of other areas to cut. Resources will then be redirected to areas deemed to have greater potential.

The focus on efficiency, cost cutting, and centralization with an emphasis on stronger management is not simply a fiscal affair, for it redefines the goals of research and the development of knowledge—and links the latter to the production of "marketable products" rather than social knowledge. Accountability can all too easily entail responsibility only to the organization funding the project.

By Way of Conclusion: The End of a Preferred "Subject"

By the mid-1980s the African state, that omnipresent and veritable bulwark of our life and research focus, appeared to be an endangered species. Today a depressing number of countries or "states" are on the verge of collapse, while the post–cold war period has triggered numerous wars in Africa. There appears to be no alternative model to the unbridled "free market" and the "new world order," with the International Monetary Fund and the World Bank firmly installed in the driver's seat moving to an as-yet unknown destination.

All these developments threaten the requisite material conditions needed for reflection and "intellectual revival" in the near future. Yet as I have tried to illustrate, the disappearance of almost all verities of the post–World War II era have impelled an exercise in retrospection. It is thus heartening to come across "pockets of resistance" filled with groups of scholars, students, and others who, against all odds, continue to document the evolving realities of the African continent. The unfolding drama in South Africa can only push

this process forward, ushering in a new round of old debates, including hitherto taboo subjects such as ethnicity, which are forcing themselves onto the
research agenda.

Finally, we need to recall one major emphasis: the magnitude, diversity,
and vibrancy of associational life can no longer be subsumed within state-
centric, developmentalist methodologies. As generalizations about the "Third
World" cease to hold sway, African researchers are being forced to reexam-
ine the theoretical terrain, free, at last, of the illusions of imitating foreign
intellectual trends—and in the process, one hopes, creating a richer African
social science tradition.

Notes

1. I owe this insight to two colleagues whose work I hold in great respect. Each one of
them would have conveyed the message more eloquently. See Hountondji 1997 and
Mkandawire 1990.

2. To get a glimpse of the intellectual ferment of this period and its similarity to the
contemporary period, see Mudimbe 1992. In the words of Alioune Diop, the founder of
Présence africaine, the longest-surviving and most widely read journal of the pan-African movement, the idea of the journal "goes back to 1942–43. We, a certain number of
students from overseas, were in Paris in the very middle of the suffering of a Europe that
was questioning itself on its essence and the authenticity of its values; we gathered together
to study the situation and the characteristics that defined us, too. Neither White, Yellow,
nor Black, unable to return completely to our original tradition nor to assimilate to Europe, we had the feeling that we were a new race, mentally cross-bred, but one that had
not been taught to know its originality and that had barely become aware of it" (in
Mouralis 1992:96).

3. Eisemon and Salmi (1993:159) point out that "most major donor agencies reacted to
the dissolution of the University of East Africa by diminishing their support."

4. For the texture of this development and the debates they generated see Kapteijns 1977;
Mbodj and Diouf 1986; Ranger 1968.

5. The critics of Flag Independence are too many to cite. For example, all the previously
mentioned authors engage in a succinct critique. At the first meeting of African universities, G. C. Mutiso said that the second generation of academicians generally "matured
intellectually in the mid- and late 1960s, when the euphoria of Independence was wear-
ing off. They are basically cynics, as reflected in the literary writings of the mid-1960s. They
are the children of despair. They recognize that juridical independence led to neo-colonialism and the indirect control of all critical institutions of the society" (Mutiso 1973:153).

6. Note the historical irony. In the colonial period we had the East African Institute of
Social Research in Uganda and the Rhodes-Livingstone Institute in what was then Northern Rhodesia.

7. The passionate debate at the Symposium on Academic Freedom, Research, and the
Social Responsibility of the Intellectual in Africa, which took place in Kampala during
November 26–29, 1990, anticipated this process of deskilling and loss of autonomy. See
the papers in Diouf and Mamdani 1994.

References Cited

Amin, Samir. 1974a. *Neo-Colonialism in West Africa*. Harmondsworth: Penguin.
———. 1974b. "Accumulation and Development: A Theoretical Model." *Review of African Political Economy* 1:9–26.
Ashby, Eric. 1964. *African Universities and Western Tradition*. London: Oxford University Press.
Cabral, Amilcar. 1969. *Revolutions in Guinea*. New York: Monthly Review Press.
Court, David. 1991. "The Development of University Education in Sub-Saharan Africa." In *International Higher Education: An Encyclopedia*, ed. Philip G. Altbach, 329–47. New York: Garland.
Diouf, Mamadou, and Mahmood Mamdani, eds. 1994. *Academic Freedom in Africa*. Dakar: CODESRIA.
Eisemon, Thomas O., and Jamil Salmi. 1993. "African Universities and the State: Prospects for Reform in Senegal and Uganda." *Higher Education* 25:151–68.
Hinchliffe, Keith. 1987. *Higher Education in Sub-Saharan Africa*. London: Croom Helm, 1987.
Hountondji, Paulin J., ed. 1997. *Endogenous Knowledge*. Dakar: CODESRIA.
Kapteijns, Lidwien. 1977. *African Historiography Written by Africans, 1955–1973: The Nigerian Case*. Leiden: Africa-Studiecentrum.
Mafeje, Archie. 1971. "Ideology of Tribalism." *Journal of Modern African Studies* 9, no. 2:353–61.
Mamdani, Mahmood. 1976. *Politics and Class Formation in Uganda*. New York: Monthly Review Press.
Mbodj, Mohamed, and Mamadou Diouf. 1986. "Senegalese Historiography, Present Practices and Future Perspectives." In *African Historiographies: What History for Which Africa*, ed. Bogumil Jewsiewicki and David Newbury, 207–14. Beverly Hills, Calif.: Sage Publications.
Mkandawire, Thandika. 1990. "Problems and Prospects of Social Sciences in Africa." *International Social Science Journal* 45, no. 1 (Feb.): 129–36.
Mouralis, Bernard. 1992. "*Présence Africaine*: Geography of an 'Ideology.'" In *The Surreptitious Speech*, ed. V. Y. Mudimbe, 3–13.
Mudimbe, V. Y., ed. 1992. *The Surreptitious Speech: "Présence Africaine" and the Politics of Otherness, 1947–1987*. Chicago: University of Chicago Press.
Mutiso, G. C. M. 1973. "The Future University: Towards a Multi-disciplinary Research and Teaching Approach." In *Creating the African Universities: Emerging Issues of the 1970s*, ed. Tijani M. Yesufu, 149–58. Ibadan: Association of African Universities.
Ranger, Terence O., ed. 1968. *Emerging Themes of African History: Proceedings of the International Congress of African Historians Held at University College, Dar es Salaam, October 1965*. Nairobi: East African Publishing House.
Rodney, Walter. 1970. *A History of the Upper Guinea Coast, 1545–1800*. Oxford: Clarendon.
———. 1972. *How Europe Underdeveloped Africa*. Dar es Salaam: Tanzania Publishing House.
Seminar on African Studies. University of Liberia. 1974. *Final Report of the Seminar on African Studies, July 18–19, 1974*. Monrovia: University of Liberia.
Shivji, Issa G. 1976. *Class Struggles in Tanzania*. London: Heinemann.

Southall, Roger. 1974. "Introduction." *Federalism and Higher Education in East Africa,* ix–xii. Nairobi: East African Publishing House.

Zeleza, Tiyambe. 1990. "The Intelligentsia and Academic Freedom: The Question of Expatriate African Scholars in African Universities." Paper presented at the Symposium on Academic Freedom and the Social Responsibility of the Intellectual, Kampala, Nov. 26–29.

PART 3

Breaking Paradigms and Silences

7   Braudel and African History: Dismantling or Reproducing the Colonial/Capital Paradigm?

Jacques Depelchin

Writing in *Le Monde diplomatique* in August 1993, Ricardo Petrella, a former European commissioner turned professor at the University of Louvain-la-Neuve (Belgium), passionately called for global economic disarmament. Denouncing the collective blindness that is leading the world into financial globalization and fragmenting communities that value solidarity, he urged a complete rethinking of the whole United Nations system—a process that would require multilateral negotiations. Another step would involve the UN Security Council's approving a memorandum on world economic security to be presented at the UN Conference on Social Issues. Petrella also called for a campaign to "devalue the high price put on competition and all other indicators which constitute the ABC of current economic thought" (Petrella 1993:32).

For Petrella, the madness of the current global system became apparent only recently, its origins going back no more than the last twenty-five years. Almost twenty-five years before Petrella issued his call, however, Eduardo Galeano's *Open Veins of Latin America* (1973)—among a host of other works—had eloquently shown that the dehumanizing nature of the global system had much deeper roots.[1] Ignoring the groans and denunciations of hundreds of millions of people from the slave ships of the sixteenth century to the homeless of Harlem today, capitalism has gone from triumph to triumph, consolidating itself and acquiring such a formidable armor that no existing counterweapon seems capable of disabling it, let alone destroying it.

This essay is written from the premise that history holds together and that purported ruptures, although appearing as such to those who are close to them, are more like fissures or cracks when seen from a distance. Capitalism has always been lethal, yet most of its written history, as well as the rules specifying how history should be written or recognized, has been the handi-work of those who did not see it as deadly. In this respect the growth of capi-talism bears an uncanny resemblance to the growth of Nazism in Germany. Just as the latter emerged legally, so too did capitalism. Only now, when the inhumanity of the system is beginning to be felt inside the core, from where it all started, are the "well-thinking heads" beginning to recognize its destruc-tive nature. The processes that are currently attributed to the 1980s, such as globalization and privatization, have a much longer history going back at least to Atlantic slavery and the destruction of Arawaks and other Native Ameri-cans. One can be certain that to the descendants of those who were nearly wiped out in that long history, the arrival of Hitler was no aberration. Alter-native attempts at building socialism by borrowing from the same arsenal of thought (out-competing capitalism in the production of commodities) could not but fail.

Indeed, the *Lebensraum* for which Hitler went to war is now being claimed by a system. The language and the words may differ, but the principles are the same; the well-being of millions of people is being sacrificed on the altar of one idea: a coalition of owners and managers of capital struggling to gain more space (called "markets") for corporations. We need to ask whether the current worship of an economic system, regardless of the patent destruction it has caused and continues to cause, differs from the worship of one man and one race that overtook Germany.

It is this understanding of the relationship between various strands of histories that has informed my choice of Fernand Braudel through which to offer a critique of Africanist history and, implicitly, of the so-called major histories—particularly of Western Europe and the United States. I will ar-gue that African history is usually approached with a series of preconceptions derived from the historiography of Western Europe and North America. By the time most historians in Europe and the United States begin to specialize on Africa, they have been immersed in their own national histories. In the first few years after colonial rule, moreover, this generalization also applied to most African historians.

Although changes in the practice of history are currently under way, they are not proceeding as quickly as one may think—in part because those who established the paradigms, along with their students, still control positions of power at research and teaching institutions as well as the editorial boards of the most important journals. The relationship between Western national histories (be they Western European or North American) and those of Af-rica is thus dealt with in a cursory manner, if at all. It is thus not surprising that with such a distorting mirror in hand, few historians dare look at At-lantic slavery as an integral and at times crucial factor in the prosperity of the West.

The choice of Braudel as a representative of such a historical practice may appear to some as excessively polemical.[2] I hope that the rest of the text will demonstrate the contrary. Braudel's ideological slants do not appear until he ventures into geographical and historical areas outside his area of specialization, France and Western Europe. The excuse that Braudel was writing on matters about which he knew little only sidesteps the nature of the problem, which is how power relations are reproduced, generation after generation, through the production and reproduction of historical knowledge.

Michel Morineau's 1988 critique of Braudel anticipated some of the points I will raise, as well as some of the criticisms made by the Africanist historian Steven Feierman (1993), whose analysis fails to identify the reasons historians change the way they reproduce historical knowledge. Put in a succinct and possibly exaggerated way, Feierman seems to operate from the same perspective as Christopher Columbus: just as Columbus did not discover what he claims to have discovered, so too one can say that historians do not produce history. It is already there, but given their profession—discoverers of history?—they cannot but continue to propagate the notion that it is they who are the first producers of histories.

This perspective is one side of the abolitionist coin. The other is the syndrome of discovery: that is, the reproduction of power relations mediated through and by economic and political clout, so that historians associated with that power circle can claim that what has been written was unknown until they wrote about it.[3] Morineau's and Feierman's critical texts are an unmistakable sign that we are about to witness a radical change in the kind of uncritical awe that initially overcame many readers of Braudel's work.

What Is the Purpose of a Grammar of Civilizations?

In 1987 Braudel's *Grammaire des civilisations* was republished. It was first published in 1963 as a text for sixteen- to eighteen-year-old students in the final years of the *lycée;* when Braudel wrote it, he had not yet reached the reputation he would enjoy in 1987. Without claiming to know how Braudel himself ordered the importance of his own work, it is clear that he ranked *Grammaire* very high—high enough for him to write about it (in 1983) in one of his columns for the Italian newspaper *Corriere della sera* (Braudel 1987:5).

When *Grammaire* first appeared, it was seen as a promotional exercise to popularize the historical vision of the most celebrated academic historian in France. Maurice Aymard's introduction to the text helps the reader to understand what is described as Braudel's visionary conception of history. A critical approach to the text, however, will also show how limiting, limited, and at times retrograde this visionary conception can be, which can be seen when it is dissected from the perspective of those who have refused to be silenced because their language does not fall under the grammatical rules that are being imposed.

Braudel's project was to produce a text that would give students an idea of the modern world, not just simply on the basis of contemporary observations, but above all on the basis of a historical understanding of the ways in which the past had shaped the present. Nonetheless, it would have been more informative if Braudel, who stressed that one always starts from the present, had elaborated the present causes that made him see the urgency for producing such a work.

The Context and Conundrum: From Colonial Confrontation to Postcolonial Universality; or, Multiculturalism in the Making

Braudel does not analyze the difficulty he faced in terms of the transition France was experiencing: an imperial power on the decline, but one still trying to impose its views. France was then responding to a difficult and traumatic challenge from colonial subjects from Indochina to Algeria. The emerging historical context, it must be recalled, differed from the one prevailing at the time of territorial occupation. Territorial conquest had been pursued and achieved through brutal violence. There was no need then to be liked or to be loved by the colonized peoples. The primary objective was subjugation through terror and fear (see Mannoni 1956).

Once decolonization was perceived as inevitable, however, the colonizers changed their attitude regarding the use of force and violence, at least at the level of official discourse, and began preparing for a "kinder and gentler" postcolonial era. The resulting "friendship" treaties allowed France to maintain its old colonial control by other means. The realization that changes had to take place did not prevent the French from seeking to ensure that such changes would occur according to their wishes: in the wake of the humiliating defeat at Dien Bien Phu, France had to fight another bloody war, this one in Algeria from 1954 to 1962.

Although fear and violence were never far from the post–World War II transition, the colonial states sought to present themselves as altruistically interested in the welfare and well-being of their subjects. Universality, therefore, was not so much a statement of fact as the expression of the departing colonial powers' desire, wish, and hope that their former subjects would be interested in sharing an idea of a future in which they would be not subjects but equal partners. *Grammaire des civilisations* can be seen as Braudel's translation of the desire of the French to continue to be seen as selfless civilizers.

The expression of such a desire was predicated on the conviction that the colonized would understand their future interests to lie in sharing the colonialists' desire for universal brotherhood—a desire that, needless to add, went hand in hand with an automatic erasure of a past steeped in murderous terror and violence. It was the desire to be embraced, to be loved against all evidence pointing in the opposite direction, that led to the production of a world history that everyone, including bitter recent foes, could be encouraged to share.

Moving from a monocultural to a multicultural history of the world is indeed a difficult exercise, one that calls for something akin to a rupture. In practice, however—at least in the case of Braudel—what we get is merely an appearance of a rupture, which nevertheless reaffirms colonial ideology regarding the nonexistence of African history. Instead of a real rupture, there is a confrontation between the ideological negation of history and the reality of historically existing newly independent states; the denial is still maintained since history is seen as emerging from decolonization instead of as having always been there, although suppressed.

Braudel articulates well many of the problems inherent in introducing French youth, accustomed to a Eurocentric history, to a multicentric (multicultural) history of the world: "And it seems to me essential that at the age of eighteen, on the brink of preparing for whatever career, our young people be initiated into the problems of society and the economy today, the great cultural conflicts in the world, and the multiplicity of its civilizations" (Braudel 1994:xxxiii). The problem has less to do with young people than with Braudel's conviction that a multicultural world should still be defined, ordered, ruled, and studied from Europe and for Europeans. It is surely not a coincidence that Braudel highlights cultural rather than economic conflicts, for is this not a means of asserting that cultural differences should be tolerated as long as they do not interfere with different conceptions of the economy? Or could it be argued that the proclamation of cultural diversity as a worthwhile objective is possible only in a context where the superiority of the colonial powers' economic system can no longer be in doubt and where the parameters of a multicultural world are imposed by those who control the economic destinies of the majority of the population?

The one central question Braudel never directly entertains is the role of those who were subjugated in posing the parameters of history. When it is entertained, it is not in economic terms but in terms of warfare in the history of nationalism. Braudel did pose these questions in an article for an Italian audience, although it was disingenuous for him to wonder whether Italians would be interested in such matters. Given their own colonial past, the Italians have views about the past and the future similar to those of the French. The same rhetorical question would be much more difficult if it were posed to any African, Palestinian, or Haitian refugee or to any other person whose history has long been presented from a subjugated or oppressed position.

Braudel's answer to these queries is revealing because it fails to come to terms with the silences that have been generated beyond the borders of the national histories of European states: "Who can deny the violence that has stemmed from history? Of course, historians have no business fabricating dubious national myths—or even pursuing only humanism, which I myself prefer. But history is a vital element in national self-awareness. And without such self-awareness there can be no original culture, no genuine civilization, in France or anywhere else" (1994:xxxiv). But the ingredients that have gone into making the French—or, say, Italian—national conscience include, among others, histories of slavery and colonial exploitation. Braudel would probably not have subscribed to the notion that Africa had no history, yet his way of defining the relationship between civilization and history in the case of France and Italy echoes the familiar denial.

Is Western Europe the Birthplace of Civilization?

In spelling out the rules of his "grammar," Braudel reiterates a European definition of civilization: "The word 'civilization'—a neologism—emerged late in France, and unobtrusively, in eighteenth-century France" (Braudel 1994:3). When he elaborates on the definition and how and when it began to be used, it is not clear whether Braudel is aware of the built-in bias. He points out that around 1732, civilization referred to a jurisprudential notion that designated an act of justice or a judgment that turned a criminal trial into "civil" proceedings (1994:3). But he does not see that such a definition also opens up the opposite possibility: turning criminal a civilizing process. As if to cut short further discussion, Braudel states abruptly that "at all events the word appears because it was needed" (1994:4).

It is symptomatic that in a book that seeks to move away from a culturally biased definition of civilization, no attempt is made to deal with the possible definitions that certainly exist in non-European languages. Not surprisingly, then, the recognition that the notion of civilization in the singular discriminates against other civilizations is described as yet another sign of the superiority of Western European civilization. Thus, "In the twentieth century, in fact, the plural of the word predominates and is closest to our personal experience" (1994:7).

Clearly, at least in Braudel's mind, the twentieth century is personified by a Western European. Braudel is deliberately vague when it comes to explaining how the original eighteenth-century meaning of *civilization* came to be displaced; he sees it merely as a fortunate development attributable to the twentieth century: "The twentieth century, happily, has abandoned a certain number of such value-judgements, and would be hard put to decide—and on what criteria—which civilization is best" (1994:7).

If it is not the twentieth century that is presented as the active subject defining the meaning of the word, then it is a sort of universal phenomenon "to feel somewhat uneasy about using the word *civilization* in its old sense, connoting human excellence or superiority" (1994:7). The singular use of the word now has universal reference. Nonetheless, it would be wrong to see this universalizing process as a kind of natural evolution. The speed of modern communications, which is cited as one of the reasons for this process, is only a by-product of the much more violent economic, social, and political relations of domination. Braudel is aware of this but prefers to downplay it: "The history of civilizations, in fact, is the history of continual mutual borrowings over many centuries, despite which each civilization has kept its own original character" (1994:8).

It is in this blatant contradiction between trying to combat hierarchical definitions of civilizations and defining civilizations in Western European terms that one can see the greatest value of Braudel's book: it illustrates the choices faced by dominant societies when they realize that, for the sake of their own survival, they have to do away with domination. Braudel's own work precludes him—almost by definition—from breaking with the paradigms on which he conceptualized and then built the history of capitalism's superiority.

The notion of superiority dies hard in the hands of those who, like Braudel, pass the sentence but are unable to carry it out. As he sees it, each civilization proceeds through a sieving process during which, very slowly but irremediably, some things are rejected and others are incorporated, with the culmination of this process identified as having occurred during the twentieth century. Braudel's clearest reproduction of a hierarchical conception of civilizations is read through a reconstruction of the current technological superiority of Western Europe, which in turn mirrors economic superiority. Aware of the sharp inequalities generated by the growth of capitalism since the sixteenth century, Braudel does warn that unless these inequities are addressed, civilization—or civilizations—risks being annihilated (1994:21).

But Braudel is too good a chronicler to reduce the transition of civilizations or their contacts to peaceful episodes. Quite the contrary: the relationships between civilizations were usually violent confrontations, often tragic, and frequently ended in failure, as demonstrated by "colonialism," which "may have triumphed in the past . . . but today is an obvious fiasco" (1994:33). Yet the question has to be asked: a fiasco for whom? Braudel seems to argue that since the vanquished eventually outlive their temporary submission, one can take pride in the fact that colonization—that is, "the submergence of one civilization by another"—has more often than not been a failure (1994:33). From the remarks on civilization as economies, however, it is clear that the victors are indeed the powers that distinguished themselves in building colonial empires and in the process shaped and fashioned capitalism as we know it today.

In the end, Braudel pictures the confrontation between Western Europe and Africa in rather idealistic terms. He does not deny the devastation caused by Atlantic slavery, but for him the balance sheet, particularly the demographic aspects, is ultimately positive (1994:132). For someone who looks at history as long processes that cannot be compartmentalized, this presentation of the historical relationship between Africa and Western Europe in the form of a balance sheet is startling. Even in accounting terms, assets and liability are treated not as separate inventory items but rather as reflections of each other.

By the time Europe took possession of colonial territories in Africa, they were no longer two separate entities. By then European economic wealth and political power were, at least in part, the result of Europe's exploitation of the African continent. This is quite different from the depiction given by Braudel:

> One is not defending such things by admitting that the shock of colonization was often decisive and even at length beneficial for the social, economic, and cultural development of the colonized black peoples themselves. . . . It was a developed and demanding industrial society [Europe], with modern means of action and communication, which met and invaded black Africa. And Africa itself was receptive, more flexible than ethnographers even recently believed: it was able to seize the objects and practices offered by the West, and *reinterpret* them, giving them new meaning, and matching them whenever possible to the needs of its *traditional* culture. (1994:133; emphasis added)

In short, one finds in Braudel's text just those conceptions that provided the foundation of anthropology. As stated earlier, Braudel the historian could not go along with one of the tenets of colonial ideology, that Africa had no history. In addition to affirming this history, however, he also writes, adopting the denial typical of anthropologists and political scientists trained in the 1950s, that most of Africa,

> in recent years, has achieved independence. "Negritude" or the search for indigenous roots, which has been called "a form of humanism in the making," has begun to articulate specifically African values and possibilities. Africans are eagerly seeking their own history, which has to be pieced together and almost invented. All this gives black Africa one great advantage: it is a cultural world in full and rapid evolution. To the outside observer it offers every conceivable pattern of life, from the most archaic to the most modern and urban. It also embodies every stage of culture-contact. (1994:136)

A Comforting Past for an Even More Comforting Future

The supposed universality of Western civilization rests on its current apparent economic triumph. The latter, in turn, is presented as the result of humankind's universal desire to improve its well-being. Although the past may be blemished by certain events and processes, it is argued that humanity is—overall—better off now than it was, say, one or two centuries ago. In a world increasingly dominated and driven by technological innovations, the future looks brighter than anything known in the past. The corollary is, of course, that one should look more to the future and less to the past.

Braudel's text is interesting in this regard because it was produced at the point of transition from a colonizing view of Africa to one that seeks to erase a shameful history by simply pretending that the history never existed; instead, Braudel offers a vision in which everyone will be able to dream about a bright future. Braudel represents the transition from a history that refuses to see itself as it was to one based on wishes for a harmonious future for all peoples. Thus colonial history as a purely altruistic adventure is reproduced by a quotation from a Czech national, working in Guinea under Sékou Touré, who became so exasperated that he asked himself how France and England could possibly have tied themselves down with such dead weights (Braudel 1994:147–48).

Braudel: A Pioneer in Multiculturalist Studies?

In their criticisms, Morineau and especially Feierman reject Braudel's vision of world history as outdated primarily because of the greater accumulation of knowledge over the last generation. Feierman, however, is unable or unwilling to see the relationship between Africanist knowledge and Braudel's unquestioned hierarchy of civilizations and cultures. What can be observed in Braudel's *Grammaire* is one of the early bases on which multiculturalism—as understood and practiced in the major U.S. academic institutions in the 1990s—has been built. It is a sort of apartheidization of history whereby the horrors of the system are kept out of sight, dealt with by the so-called marginal histories (African history, African American history, women's history, Native American history, ethnic studies, etc.). The dominant history is then presented as a history to which all can go and celebrate because it is the triumph of the human spirit.[4]

Slavery and the slave trade as central historical themes are thus relegated to Africa. They are mentioned only in passing in the histories of Western Europe and the Americas, as if the process of conquest and enslavement was peripheral to the socioeconomic growth of Europe and America. This Manichean view of world history can be seen at work again when Braudel spells out what he considers the defining characteristics of Europe: Christianity, humanism, and scientific thought (Braudel 1994:338–39). As in the case of his defining the word *civilization,* Braudel proceeds to define humanism as a fundamental aspect of Western (i.e., European) thought: "It is a learned expression, coined by German historians in the nineteenth century" (1994: 339).

Even when he acknowledges that the meaning of the word has changed beyond its original scholarly conception, however, it is unambiguously clear that the term *Western Europe* defines the arena for discussion: "In historical studies, we find references to the humanism of the twelfth century (under-lying scholasticism), to that of the Renaissance or the Reformation, to the humanism of the French Revolution (by which is often meant its originality and many-sidedness) and even to the humanism of Karl Marx or of Maxim Gorky" (Braudel 1994:339).

In a discussion on Africa today and tomorrow, Braudel seems to use in-terchangeably the terms *humanization, modernization,* and *westernization.* Braudel is much more than a Eurocentric historian, however, for his concep-tualization of history is more a by-product of the expansion of capitalism. Thus, just as its contact with Africa valorized Europe economically, so too Africa can valorize itself only by adapting itself to the West. The production of historical knowledge must therefore be approached as a valorization ex-ercise, in the same manner that France's mission in the nineteenth and twen-tieth centuries was characterized as *"la mise en valeur."*

Prior to westernization Africa's history has only use value, which in Braudel's world is tantamount to uselessness. Metaphoric terms such as the "awakening of Africa" obscure the real historical language Braudel uses, lan-guage that replicates the real processes of capitalist expansion. Capitalism is perceived as a deus ex machina: only through its magic touch can anything gain value. Describing the tasks awaiting tomorrow's Africa as it moves from tribal society to modernization and industrialization, he concludes, "Every-thing has to be created—even the right mentality" (1994:137).

Even in the purely cultural arenas—that is, in the arenas where one would think even Braudel might have second thoughts about using the concept of valorization—one sees no hesitation. African literature gains in value, appre-ciates (as in commodities), and is appreciated as it westernizes itself: "Their Western style alone denotes a literature 'uprooted from the communities of which it continues to dream.' There is a parallel here with the first Latin writers in Gaul" (Braudel 1994:149).

Feierman would probably agree with John Thornton that Braudel did not take Africa seriously, but on the key question of the impact of slavery, Feierman's more thorough and yet more cautious assessment indicates that disagreement with a Braudelian approach may indeed produce drastically different results—depending, in this case, on whether one is convinced that the method is fundamentally sound. Feierman's strongest argument against Braudel's view of world history is that the accumulated knowledge on Afri-can history would probably force even someone like Braudel to revise his views. Yet Thornton has shown that, for a disciple, changing the view does not necessarily mean changing the power relations that determine whose questions and whose histories are given more weight. The late Nathan Huggins, reacting to those who, like Feierman, celebrate the amount of newly accumulated knowledge, warned that what is at issue can no longer be contained by questions related to more precise statistical data on the profitability of slavery, its demographic impact, shipments, and so on. In Huggins's view, one ought not be satisfied that slave narratives demonstrate their authors and their descendants to have had their own histories. Rather, he argued, the accumulation and content of the narratives had reached a point where a qualitative change had to be made: the relationship between so-called marginal (i.e., slavery) history and the center had to be transformed; historical questions should now be framed from the perspective of those who, while marginalized in all aspects of life, were at the very core of the economic system and without whom the whole history of the United States as a nation would have been different (Huggins 1990:xi–xvi).

Applied to Africa, this approach would show that a world history is indeed possible and that such projects should be encouraged; however, the perspectives and parameters defining them would have to be established by those who have resisted the onslaught of the homogenizing and hegemonizing processes of a system that continues to dehumanize not only those who resist it but also, paradoxically, those who profit from it. In a way one could look at Riccardo Petrella's call for economic disarmament and the dismantling of the current liberal economic orthodoxies as a distant echo of the abolitionists, who realized that slavery had to end because it did not reflect well on slave owners.

Thus although today's multiculturalism, of which Braudel can be seen as a pioneer, has put hegemonic cultures on the defensive, it has also become a device whose effects are similar to the old imperial motto of "divide and rule." Early in his essay Feierman wonders, given the previous exclusions, "which populations, and which domains of human experience, they [historians] themselves are excluding today" (Feierman 1993:169). The question as formulated reflects a restrictive understanding of history, for it implies that only historians produce historical knowledge. A more interesting question would have been to ask what accounts for Western-trained historians' propensity systematically to avoid certain kinds of questions. In his 1993 work *Culture and Imperialism* Edward Said points out that the central problem in dealing with the decolonization of histories is that imperialism created and consolidated the acceptance of various norms, standards, and habits of thinking that do not need demonstrations since they are axiomatic.[5] With regard to history, there are paradigms that continue to be reproduced without being questioned. They cannot be questioned because doing so would be so out of place,

and so eccentric, as to relegate the questioner to the margins of the profession—as happened to the Senegalese scholar Cheikh Anta Diop, whom
Feierman seems happy to keep there.[6]

The current vogue of multiculturalism nevertheless indicates changing
patterns of power relations, but the relative consensus regarding the necessity to change begins to disappear as soon as challenges are raised to embedded interests, established concepts, and the norms and standards of power
relations, recognition, and rewards. Ironically, most challengers stop short
of radical change as soon as the power system rewards them through some
sort of recognition, often sadly transforming advancing battle trenches into
stagnating intellectual ghettos. This form of multiculturalism is to the
postcolonial era what assimilation was to colonial rule.

Braudel and Africanist History

In his book *Africa and Africans in the Making of the Atlantic World, 1400–1680*
(1992), John Thornton provides an excellent illustration of the impact of
Braudel's schemata on African history. Thornton details how he was
influenced by Braudel's work and how, after noting that "Braudel did not take
Africa . . . seriously enough," he decided that he "would write a work along
at least some of the lines opened by Braudel, but one that would not neglect
Africa" (Thornton 1992:vii). Thornton wanted to do for the Atlantic what
Braudel had done in *La Méditerranée et le monde méditerranéen dans les temps
de Philippe II* (The Mediterranean and the Mediterranean world in the age
of Philip II) (1949; rev. ed. 1966).

The adoption of the model is so complete that it overwhelms from the start
the specificity of African history as compared to European history. The Atlantic is described as the scene of "major intercontinental migrations."
"Thousands of European settlers moved from their homes to the Americas,
and joining them was a still larger group of Africans" (Thornton 1992:1).
Although *migration* may be the correct term for the European movement, it
is a distortion of what happened to the Africans, who did not migrate of their
own volition but were shipped across the ocean under the worst conditions
imaginable (Inikori 1982, 1992; Huggins 1990). Thornton thus reproduces
Braudel's efforts to sanitize the history of Atlantic slavery. For Braudel, "Black
slave-trading was not a diabolical invention from Europe"; rather, the main
culprit was Islam, which "first practised the black slave trade on a large scale"
(Braudel 1994:130). More important for Braudel is the fact that against the
obviously negative impact there is also the positive side, such as the abolitionist movement.

Thornton writes that his "book seeks to resolve a number of these contradictory positions." He then proceeds to list the questions that he sought
to answer:

Is it correct to see Africa as being on a lower level of development than Europe and this imbalance as being the cause for the slave trade? Were the African slaves in the Americas too brutalized to express themselves culturally and socially, and thus, to what degree was their specifically African background important in shaping Afro-American culture? On the whole, the conclusions of the research on which this book is based support the idea that Africans were active participants in the Atlantic world, both in African trade with Europe (including the slave trade) and as slaves in the New World. (1992:7)

Thornton echoes Braudel's argument against the demonization of Europe's expansion by stating that although slave raids may have taken place, most of the trade was conducted amicably because the Europeans, though dominant at sea, could not impose themselves on the coast (1992:39–42). Thornton's efforts on the Atlantic world are similar to Braudel's attempt at a world history. The disciple's challenge to historians such as Walter Rodney (1972) rests on pushing the African initiative argument to its most extreme limits by positing that "the African role in the development of the Atlantic would not simply be a secondary one, on either side of the Atlantic. In Africa, it was they who would determine their commercial role, and in America they were often the most important group among the early colonists" (Thornton 1992: 42).

In his attempt to give Africans greater initiative in the shaping of the Atlantic world, Thornton challenges the notion of the "'impact' brought in from outside. . . . Instead, it [the slave trade and Atlantic trade in general] grew out of and was rationalized by the African societies who participated in it and had complete control over it until the slaves were loaded onto European ships for transfer to Atlantic societies" (1992:74). Later on he concludes "that African participation in the slave trade was voluntary and under the control of African decision makers. This was not just at the surface level of daily exchange but even at deeper levels. Europeans possessed no means, either economic or military, to compel African leaders to sell slaves" (1992:125).

Walter Rodney never denied that Africans were directly involved in profiting from the slave trade and slavery, but to go from there and generalize, as Thornton does, comes dangerously close to saying that the slaves themselves actively promoted what happened to them. In this Atlantic world, the Africans who are described as active agents of their own history never include the slaves themselves. The active agents, when they are specified, are either political rulers or merchants. Since Thornton is writing from the simplified and simplistic perspective of Eurocentric versus Afrocentric history, however, it becomes easier to show that the expansion of capitalism was a process in which "Africans" did participate.

In his counterdemonization of the European impact on African societies, Thornton argues perniciously that the survival of African cultures across the Atlantic shows that slavery was not as bad as it sounds after all:

It is clear that no matter how exploitative the institution of slavery was, or how traumatic the middle Passage and subsequent enslavement were, the condition itself was unlikely to result in a permanent state of psychological shock. Furthermore, even in the most brutal of slave systems, slave communities formed, children were raised, and culture was maintained, altered, and transmitted. Clearly, the condition of slavery, by itself, did not necessarily prevent the development of an African-oriented culture. (1992:182)

One of the pitfalls of this kind of approach is that it relies heavily on measurable evidence, such as rates of profits; number of slaves shipped; evidence of slave owners who took care of their slaves; or evidence of a Jesuit (later canonized) who "greeted every slave, embraced them, and welcomed them to the New World, while constantly assuring them that the Spanish intended to make Christians of them and not oil" (Thornton 1992:161). Thornton admits that such a reception may not have done much to alleviate what the Spaniards eventually did to the slaves, but he goes on to point out that although "never forgotten," these harsh experiences "do not seem on the whole to have been more than temporarily debilitating." And as if to clinch his case, he admits that "we cannot really penetrate the slave psychology on the bases of such limited sources and theoretical statements about psychological trauma. In the end, the real measure of the effects of the slave trade on slaves must be seen in their subsequent situation and behavior in the Americas" (1992:162).

Following this line of reasoning, should one assess the impact of Hitler's rule using the fact that "Jews on the whole are doing well"? Should the impact of the atomic bombs on Hiroshima and Nagasaki be counterbalanced by Japan's having become a powerful nation? It squarely raises the issue of what constitutes evidence in historical narrative. As in the case of the historian who admitted that it was difficult to know what was going on in the mind of the South African slave, Thornton dismisses the evidence that could be based on psychological analysis.[7] On an individual level it might be compared to the dominant rationalization concerning the rapist and the rape victim: her or his survival shows that the rape was not that bad. The victim's silence—"silence means consent"—further confirms the rapist's conviction that the victim consented.

One wishes that Thornton had read other sources that might have modified his perspective, such as Nathan Huggins's *Black Odyssey* (1990). He might have reconsidered his attempt to place the African slave trade and African slavery on the same level as the Atlantic slave trade and Atlantic slavery, for as Huggins put it, "the transatlantic slave trade was something radically new and unimaginable. In a process that could only be related to a witch's spell, one was transformed from person to thing" (1990:26).

In a universal approach to a world history, it is tempting to argue that the evil was indeed universal. Huggins, on the contrary, sought to convey how drastically different Atlantic slavery was from all previous forms of servitude. Atlantic slavery was different, as Braudel should have argued—but did not— by virtue of the way it almost literally stamped the capitalist system on the slaves: "Like a ritual of renaming, a rite of new identity, he and the others, each in turn, were forced to kneel, and a mark or letter was burned into their flesh with a branding iron. . . . Name mattered not, family mattered not, ancestral glories mattered not. He was what the mark on his shoulder said he was, a thing belonging to a company, no more no less" (Huggins 1990:33–34). Finally, the issue of the most evil participants in the slave trade and Atlantic slavery cannot be settled in comparative terms. Atlantic slavery was different because it became part of the history of the expansion of, and submission to, one specific socioeconomic system. But Thornton seems to want to argue that slaves were not so badly off: they managed to rebuild themselves; as the colonizers were to argue later, they were happy. The history of Atlantic slavery is not to be compartmentalized on the basis of the common feelings the participants might have felt. The pain and suffering of the slaves nurtured the happiness of their owners. But Thornton would use the happiness of the slave owners to seek to read back into the lives of the slaves signs of happiness—and of course he would find it. To quote from Huggins again on this very idea: "They were now captives and unfree, in alien hands. From their sale in American markets, they and their seed for two hundred years into the future were to learn the meaning of slavery, a resource by which others could pursue their own happiness" (1990:56).

Conclusion

Some may argue that by focusing on *Grammaire des civilisations*, I may have distorted the substance of Braudel's scholarship. As pointed out by his admirer Thornton, Braudel did not take Africa seriously. If one turns to the three volumes of *Civilisation matérielle, économie et capitalisme, XVᵉ–XVIIIᵉ siècle*, one finds an explicit denial of the role of the slave trade and slavery in the modernization of Europe. In Braudel's view, such a simplistic determinism could be inverted, for "was it not the growth of Europe which, with its passion for sugar, led to the expansion of the sugar and coffee industries?" (Braudel 1979: vol. 2, p. 163) Braudel's caution (note the question form) in denying the relationship is contradicted later on when, writing on Jamaica, he clearly spells out the relationship between the plantations and the growth of financial fortunes in London and Bordeaux: "There is nothing surprising in [the wealthy families'] operating from their base in London; managing their estates from afar, they invest mostly in England, not only in trading, but also in cutting-edge agriculture and other industries. As with the Pellets, these plantation owners have understood that the best way to make money from the colonies is to operate from the metropole" (Braudel 1979: vol. 2, p. 243; author's translation).

It is striking that Braudel, a self-described humanist willing to admit that early twentieth-century certainties of capitalism's superiority have been replaced by doubt, never raises the possibility that such doubts could have existed in the minds of those who, through the centuries, lived under capitalism in conditions that convinced them that the system was irrationally inhuman. Toward the end of his third volume, Braudel reaffirms the guiding principle of his researches on the origins of capitalist mentalities: "to go and look at the Italian cities of the Middle Ages" (1979: vol. 3, p. 517; author's translation).

Braudel argues against the idea of trying to reconstruct the history of the world, especially if it is in the name of an objective or an explanation. But surely, for someone who wrote so eloquently on the *longue durée,* it might be reasonable to reconstruct a history that is articulated around the irrationality and destructiveness of the system. Such a reconstruction would treat devastation with the same seriousness as Braudel uses when he describes the inventiveness of the merchants and financiers. Nor would it take the Holocaust to justify beginning to doubt the superiority and rationality of capitalism. Such a reconstruction would also show the linkages between the mentality of the slave merchants and the way in which the economic and financial experts of the global economy today make their decisions. Again, in the perspective of the *longue durée,* should one be surprised that the enslavement of an entire continent should have been followed by an attempt to wipe out the Jews in gas chambers? Should one be surprised—for it is still the same system—that in the ancestral continent of the slaves, millions of people will die of hunger and war because political and economic rationality so dictates? In such a historical perspective, it is not surprising to hear that capitalism has become more efficient. The rationality and the logic of capitalism are such that it no longer needs external coercion: market forces in Africa today achieve the same effect as did the gas chambers of World War II. Braudel thinks it is useless to ask hypothetical questions about the history of capitalism, such as what if capitalism had first developed in the East. But it is not useless to ask once again questions that were asked and answered but ignored because they were asked and answered by those who had to be silenced for the sake of maintaining capitalism. If they were true humanists, Braudel and his admirers should have been interested in such hypothetical and counterfactual questions.

It is doubtful that historians such as Braudel and Feierman would acknowledge that, despite the almost two centuries separating them, figures such as Toussaint L'Ouverture and Patrice Lumumba had in fact posed similar questions concerning the histories of their peoples. If Toussaint had been taken seriously by historians of the French Revolution, they would have called for his rehabilitation—pantheonization—at the bicentenary celebrations. Did he not, better than Condorcet and Diderot, carry out the ideals of freedom, liberty and equality (see Sala-Molins 1992:193)? As Sala-Molins speculates, perhaps this will transpire in 2089.

Notes

1. One could also include here slave narratives, Bartolomé de Las Casas's (bishop of Chiapas, 1545–47) denunciations of the Spaniards' extermination of the native population (Las Casas 1646), Eric Williams 1944, C. L. R. James 1938, E. D. Morel 1906, Mark Twain 1905, and not least, Frantz Fanon 1991 (esp. the conclusion).

2. Braudel's popularity beyond academic circles (in the United States) is attested by the number of citations and articles in magazines and publications aimed at the larger public, from *History Today* 36 (Jan. 1986) to reviews of his work in *The Economist,* Nov. 10, 1984, and *Business History Review* 58 (Autumn 1984) and 61 (Autumn 1987). See also "A Chat with F. Braudel" in *Forbes* 129 (June 21, 1982).

3. Wamba-dia-Wamba has discussed an aspect of this problem in his 1984 and 1986 essays.

4. Another example of such rewriting were the posters announcing the release (in December 1993) of the film *Geronimo.* The subtitle read: "An American Legend."

5. See in particular *Culture and Imperialism,* 10–17. Said himself is not totally immune to the problem he so lucidly describes, as can be seen in his questionable understanding and treatment of the work of scholars such as Terence Ranger and Valentin Mudimbe in the transformation of Africanist paradigms.

6. As Martin Bernal shows in *Black Athena* (1987:435), one does not need to agree entirely with all of Cheikh Anta Diop's work to recognize his seminal contribution in raising unsettling questions about African history.

7. For a similar kind of reasoning, see John Mason 1990 (425–26, 431).

References Cited

Bernal, Martin. 1987. *Black Athena: The Afroasiatic Roots of Classical Civilization.* Vol. 1., *The Fabrication of Ancient Greece 1785–1985.* New Brunswick, N.J.: Rutgers University Press.

Braudel, Fernand. 1949 (rev. ed. 1966). *La Méditerranée et le monde méditerranéen dans les temps de Philippe II.* Paris: Colin.

———. 1979. *Civilisation matérielle, économie et capitalisme, XVᵉ–XVIIIᵉ siècle.* 3 vols. Paris: Armand Colin.

———. 1987. *Grammaire des civilisations.* Paris: Arthaud-Flammarion.

———. 1994. *A History of civilizations.* (Translation of Braudel 1987.) New York: A. Lane.

Fanon, Frantz. 1991. *The Wretched of the Earth.* Trans. Constance Farrington. New York: Grove Weidenfeld (French original, Paris: Présence Africaine, 1963).

Feierman. Steven. 1993. "African Histories and the Dissolution of World History." In *Africa and the Disciplines: The Contributions of Research in Africa to the Social Sciences and Humanities,* ed. Robert Bates, V. Y. Mudimbe, and Jean O'Barr, 167–212. Chicago: University of Chicago Press.

Galeano, Eduardo. 1973. *Open Veins of Latin America: Five Centuries of the Pillage of a Continent.* New York: Monthly Review Press.

———. 1985. *Memory of Fire.* 3 vols. (*Genesis, Faces and Masks,* and *Century of the Wind*). New York: Random House.

Huggins, Nathan. 1990. *Black Odyssey.* Rev. ed. New York: Pantheon.

Inikori, Joseph, ed. 1982. *Forced Migration: The Impact of the Export Slave Trade on African Societies.* London: Hutchinson University Library.

———. 1992. *The Chaining of a Continent: Export Demand for Captives and the History of Africa South of the Sahara, 1450–1870.* Kingston: Institute of Social and Economic Research, University of the West Indies.

James, C. L. R. 1938. *Black Jacobins.* New York: Dial.

Lacouture, Jean. 1986. *de Gaulle.* Paris: Seuil.

Las Casas, Bartolomé de. 1646. *Brevissima relación de la destrvyción de las Indias; y otros tratados.* Barcelona: Antonio Lacavelleria.

Mannoni, Octave. 1956. *Prospero and Caliban: The Psychology of Colonization.* London: Methuen.

Mason, John. 1990. "Hendrick Albertus and His Ex-Slave Mey: A Drama in Three Acts." *Journal of African History* 31:423–45.

Morel, Edmund D. 1906. *Red Rubber! The Story of the Rubber Slave Trade Flourishing on the Congo in the Year of Grace 1906.* Liverpool: J. Richardson.

Morineau, Michel. 1988. "Un Grand Dessein: civilisation matérielle, économie et capitalisme (XV\ :sup:`e`–XVIII\ :sup:`e` siècle)." In Maurice Aymard et al., *Lire Braudel,* 25–57. Paris: La Decouverte.

Petrella, Riccardo. 1993. "Pour un désarmement économique." *Le Monde diplomatique,* août 1993, p. 32.

Rodney, Walter. 1982. *How Europe Underdeveloped Africa.* Washington, D.C.: Howard University Press (1st ed., Dar es Salaam: Tanzania Publishing House, 1972; London: Bogle-L'Ouverture, 1972).

Said, Edward. 1993. *Culture and Imperialism.* New York: Random House.

Sala-Molins, Louis. 1992. *Les Misères des lumières: sous la raison l'outrage—.* Paris: R. Laffont.

Temu, Arnold, and Bonaventure Swai. 1981. *Historians and Africanist History: A Critique: Post-colonial Historiography Examined.* London: Zed.

Thornton, John. 1992. *Africa and the Africans in the Making of the Atlantic World, 1400–1680.* New York: Cambridge University Press.

Twain, Mark. 1905. *King Leopold's Soliloquy.* Boston: P. R. Warren.

Wamba-dia-Wamba, Ernest. 1984. "Histoire, oui, mais quelle histoire?" *Canadian Journal of African Studies* 18, no. 1:61–65.

———. 1986. "How Is Historical Knowledge Recognized?" *History in Africa* 13:331–44.

Williams, Eric. 1944. *Capitalism and Slavery.* Chapel Hill: University of North Carolina Press.

8 The Challenge of the Africa-Centered Paradigm in the Construction of African Historical Knowledge

C. Tsehloane Keto

A central intellectual challenge of the twenty-first century is to find ways of creating a canon for a multicentered human science that addresses the social complexities of a multicultural world. This is a worldwide issue. As Dr. Federico Mayor, the director general of the United Nations Educational, Scientific, and Cultural Organization, has recently advocated, the United Nations needs to shift from a policy based on reactive peacekeeping to a focus on proactive peacemaking. This can be achieved, he argues, only by a global education program that thrives on the tolerance of diversity and by wealthy nations' commitment to assist efforts to improve materially the lives of ordinary people in less wealthy nations. This is a noble goal. For it to succeed, however, there has to be a corollary development in the intellectual sphere of knowledge creation. In the case of global Africa, the challenge becomes one of applying an Africa-centered paradigm, thereby leveling the playing field for the creation of knowledge about the history of people of African descent.

Definitions

Briefly and simply, knowledge can be defined as information acquired through study or personal experience. Experiential knowledge derives from particular and specific encounters, although it can be and has been "generalized" to group experience. Knowledge through study is mediated information. Such information can be characterized as "truth," according to V. Gordon Childe (1956:106), for whom truth is the "correspondence of the conceptual reproduction of reality with the external reality it should reproduce." Knowledge, according to this model, can be regarded as "a system of propositions which would be true insofar as they correspond with the external world" (Childe 1956:107). Knowledge remains a collective enterprise, however, because it "is not a prerogative of my head or yours; only the many heads of society comprehend it, and it is Society that expresses it in a system of propositions" (Childe 1956:107). Habermas has similarly focused on the power context of knowledge creation, arguing that knowledge always operates in a social context because "knowledge-constitutive interests take form in the medium of work, language and power" (in Masolo 1994:208). Knowledge thus becomes a "paradigm of discourse and representation" (Masolo 1994:192).

Paraphrasing the philosopher Kwasi Wiredu, Masolo points out that "what humans know they know according to given circumstances within which the knowing process takes place and actualizes itself" (Masolo 1994:208). This sentiment is confirmed by Molefi Kete Asante when he asserts that "all knowledge results from an occasion of encounter in place" (Asante 1990:5). Knowledge can thus be defined as "a common product of the dialogue between the scholar, the cultural practitioners or experts, and the social actors of everyday life" (Masolo 1994:186).

Martin Bernal seems to agree with the collective nature of knowledge creation when he describes paradigms as "generalized models or patterns of thought applied to many or all aspects of 'reality' as seen by an individual or community" (Bernal 1987:3). Paradigms emerge from models, argues Bernal, and a model is "a reduced and simplified scheme of a complex reality." The special utility of such intellectual paradigms, according to Jan Vansina (1965: xiv), is that they "are integrated to other forms of knowledge to form a coherent conception of the world and of true reality beyond simple appearances." Mudimbe and Appiah provide us with a concrete, historically based example of paradigms' explanatory power. They point out that what organized "the nineteenth century episteme in anthropology" was "fundamentally a Western paradigm of knowledge" whereby "Western experience . . . [actualized] . . . history, reason, and civilization" (Mudimbe and Appiah 1993:118). Masolo contends that in "the humanities and the social sciences . . . African intellectuals continue to define their world on the basis of Western epistemological standards," although knowledge continues to be "the inseparable joint creation of subjective activity and external reality moving through history" (Masolo 1994:178, 194).

Knowledge about Africa has come down to us historically wrapped in paradigms based on three "centers" that have influenced the process of information creation itself. Although there are extensive areas of convergence and connection in the knowledge created through these three paradigms, especially in the intermixture of geography, demographics, and culture, there are important areas of difference that need to be discussed and understood.

The Africa-Centered Paradigm

The Africa-centered paradigm is the original paradigm that Africans used to create knowledge about themselves, for themselves, and about the physical and social milieus in which they lived. This paradigm dominated African discourse about Africans from the time of ancient Kemet 5,000 years ago until the autonomy of African communities was snuffed out like so many extinguished candles. Although the range of knowledge about other Africans may have been based on the narrowly construed dynamics of local foci—depending on the specific historical experience of such groups as the Yoruba, Akan, Nuer, Berber, and so on—it was still Africa-centered. The distinguishing characteristic of this paradigm was the location of the most central, sacred, and revered part of the world of Africans in Africa itself, whether that part was political, religious, or cultural.

I refer to this as the Africa-centered paradigm because the center of knowledge creation was based on the experiences of continent-based African communities and communicated through African symbols of expression and recording. Medu Neter of ancient Kemet, Ethiopic script, and the Dinka symbols are examples of African recording systems. In opposing totalizing conceptualizations, some scholars argue in favor of highly particularistic designations—such as "Akan-centered," "Harlem-centered," "Yoruba-centered," and "Sotho-centered"—to capture the rich flavor of localized manifestations of the Africa-centered paradigm. In my view, however, we can follow an Africa-centered course of action only if we insist on an overarching frame of reference grounded on the Africans' own experience as the deciding focus of research and discussion.

We witness such an Africa-centered paradigm in the vivid language of *Sundiata: The Epic of Old Mali* (Niane 1965), in the impassioned desciptions in *The Ethiopian Royal Chronicles* (Pankhurst 1967), and in the graphic recollections of *Lithoko Tsa Marena a Basotho* (Mangoaela 1971). All these are African classics that employed an African-centered paradigm of the creation and delivery of knowledge.

Following the enslavement of some Africans and the colonization of others, a major distortion of knowledge about Africans took place, in part through the change of the primary language and the imposition of the enslavers' or the colonizers' language. Consider, albeit in another context, the expression by the Orange Free State Afrikaner leader J. B. M. Hertzog. In his fight to preserve his own language, Afrikaans, against the spread of English among South Africa's Afrikaners, he declared that an oppressor's language on the tongue of the oppressed could only be the language of a slave—an expression that African youth turned against the state in 1976 during their fight against the use of Afrikaans as a medium of instruction in the African township schools.

Since the end of enslavement, colonialism, and segregation, the process of relocating knowledge about Africa and Africans to its proper center has been the central task of certain scholars who employ an Africa-centered paradigm to create and relocate knowledge about Africans. This "new" proactive paradigm is being used to construct knowledge about Africans on the ruins of the knowledge creations of the hegemonic Europe-centered paradigm. Steven Feierman (1993) has characterized this paradigm collapse in history as the "dissolution of world history." In fact, it is a reassessment of world history.

The Asia-Centered Paradigm

The Asia-centered paradigm entered knowledge creation about Africa through a number of social carriers; military conquest, religion, exploration, and trade were among the most prominent. The conquest of North Africa, the Nile Valley, and East Africa since the time of the Hyksos, the Persians, and the Assyrians affected knowledge about Africa. Conquerors from Asia reformulated knowledge about Africa to reflect their own perspective about Africa's place in the world. Although they incorporated knowledge they received from the Africans, they recast it in an Asia-centered paradigm, a very natural development.

Consider the following example with respect to religion. Judaism originated in Asia before the Hebrews' sojourn in ancient Kemet. Despite the incorporation of Kemetic ethics and religious principles, knowledge about Africans portrayed in the Hebrew Bible reflected an Asia-centered paradigm that downplayed African influences. Christianity was the next to apply this paradigm to Africa. By shifting the sacred land to Asia, the centrality of Africa in the origins of the religion was obscured. The preservation of that centrality in a modified form in Christianity was retained by the Coptic church of Ethiopia.

The Asia-centered paradigm made further major inroads into Africa after the advent of Islam in the seventh century of the Common Era. A large body of knowledge about North, West, and East Africa was created in terms of Africa's relation to Islam, whose origin and religious center remained in Asia. The Asia-centered paradigm finds support in Ali Mazrui's view that Africa has a triple heritage, emphasizing as it does the importance of the Asian connection through Islam and Christianity. Finally, one must note the role of explorers and traders from Asia, who began to create and accumulate knowledge about Africa in the third and fourth centuries of the Common Era. Whether they came from Oman, India, China, or Japan, they expressed and preserved knowledge about Africa in terms of their center and the observations they made based on it.

The Europe-Centered Paradigm

Knowledge about Africa based on the Europe-centered paradigm has dominated the global understanding of African people for the last two centuries. This paradigm, which is legitimate on its own terms, became linked with imperialism and the economic expansion of Europe. As the paradigm of the conquerors, it transformed itself into the global paradigm of choice in understanding Africa and constructing knowledge about Africa to be transmitted to generations yet unborn. The fact that this chapter is written in English is itself a testament to the profound impact of the Europe-centered paradigm. The principal vehicles for the propagation of this paradigm were military conquest, colonization, colonialism, religion, trade, and exploration.

The expanding European control of the globe since the fifteenth century c.e. was established and consolidated through military conquest. The Portuguese occupied the islands off the west coast of Africa and the coastal and interior regions of West and East Africa, while the French were active in North, West, and Central Africa, and the British occupied parts of West Africa, the Nile Valley, East Africa, and southern Africa. Through this control the Europeans could then dictate how Africans created new knowledge about themselves and the rest of the world.

The European travels and voyages of exploration before and after military conquest also brought Europe-centered knowledge about Africa to Africa, Europe, Asia, and the Americas. From Mungo Park to David Livingstone, explorers created information about Africa that still colors the way the rest of the world views it.

European colonization greatly affected Europe-centered knowledge formation in three regions. From the arrival of the Dutch in the seventeenth century, information pools dominated by the Europe-centered paradigm began to develop in South Africa. This development was later augmented by the advent of the British in the late eighteenth and early nineteenth centuries. The French settled in what is now Algeria during the early nineteenth century, and the British undertook a colonization scheme in the highlands of Kenya in the early years of the twentieth century. Information from the pens of these European colonists and their descendants has influenced knowledge about Africans up to the present time.

As colonial rule was imposed in the last three decades of the nineteenth century, the creation and transmission of Europe-centered knowledge about Africa deepened, especially with the outpouring of missionary energy from Europe and the United States. Missionaries not only changed African religious beliefs but sincerely thought that the transformation of Africans into imitation Europeans was a blessing to the Africans. The mission schools as-

saulted African culture and inculcated a Europe-centered paradigm among
Africans and all other groups in the colonial societies. The Christianity that
Africans received was a Europeanized one, and in fact Africans were often
told that Western civilization was a handmaiden of Christianity.

Evaluative Criteria

How, then, can we determine whether a specific form of knowledge about
Africa is Africa-centered, Asia-centered, or Europe-centered? There are basically two criteria.

The first criterion is that of language and the medium of symbolic communication. An Asian, European, or African language provides strong prima
facie evidence that the paradigm is associated with the language's original
area. This is not, however, sufficient proof that the knowledge we are about
to consume is centered in one region or another. Ngugi wa Thiong'o, for
example, has struggled with his own creative production and the language
of expression that should convey it. The dilemma and paradoxes that he has
faced demonstrate the endemic problems of using a European language to
express quintessentially African thoughts. Chinua Achebe, on the other hand,
has changed English modalities to accommodate African expressions. The
Sea Islanders off the coast of South Carolina, among African Americans, have
done the same, as confirmed by the linguist Lorenzo Turner, among others.

The second criterion is one of references, focus, and center. The fact that
a work is produced in an African language is no guarantee that it is Africa-
centered. Indeed, there is a great deal of literature about Africa written under missionary and European auspices that is not only Europe-centered but
positively anti-African in its values. This second criterion is crucial in terms
of what an Africa-centered paradigm seeks to advance through critical study,
research, and analysis. African-centered studies can be continental or
diasporan in orientation. Works that reflect mere reaction to hegemonic
Europe-centered claims, without addressing the issue of "center transformation," are simply examples of descriptive "oppression studies."

There is a critical difference between knowledge generated by descriptive
oppression studies in isolation and knowledge generated through the application of an Africa-centered paradigm. Analyses that use an Africa-centered
paradigm are positive knowledge building, extending beyond the recitation
of wrongs done to Africans. Such knowledge corrects distortion by providing alternative interpretations of events and developments, interpretations
that are lucid, insightful, and consistent. These alternative interpretations
provide the foundation for proactive initiatives in policy formulations. Oppression studies projects often concentrate unduly on the negative aspects
of the hegemonic Europe-centered paradigm without throwing light on the

positive side. Since the emphasis is usually on the "bad" things that Europeans did to Africans, it becomes a sort of "victim interpretation" devoid of African agency. The result of this approach is to make the African invisible as an actor in history. This victimization is usually explained in terms of class, race, or gender. Oppression studies concentrate on explicating ways in which oppression was done and so do not necessarily imply the use of an Africa-centered paradigm. In many cases oppression studies can be anti-African, anti-European, and anarchist. What oppression studies do well is to document the face of oppression. We still need to know the center on which "critical" analysis is based, however, since critical analysis involves a value judgment of what is unacceptable about the object of the critique.

Embedded Paradigms and Selected Historical Sources

Tracing sources of information about Africa provides examples that concretely document the three paradigms. Uncritical reliance on sources by empiricists often leads to distorted information because the phenomenon called the "tyranny of sources" colors knowledge creation, obscuring paradigms embedded in the sources. This development is common where a social group or class monopolizes the creation of evidence that is used by later generations of scholars to reconstruct historical knowledge of a particular period or particular events. Examples are to be found in the colonial experience in Africa, where missionary records, imperial records, and private memoirs of European officials are used to re-create African historical reality. A similar phenomenon exists in the Americas, where the plantation records of the Europe-centered planter classes distort the reconstruction of the historical experience of enslaved Africans. In both cases the Europe-centered paradigm embedded in the sources themselves is often treated as inconsequential to the reconstruction project.

Types of Sources

Sources of knowledge about Africa can be internal or external to the continent or African communities outside Africa. Internal sources of knowledge may be written or unwritten. Africa has some of the oldest written sources in the world, ranging across petroglyphs and rock paintings to Medu Netcher, the Meroitic Script, the Kebra Negast in Ge'ez from Ethiopia, and in later periods, texts in different Arabic scripts as well as writings by Africans in African languages over the past two centuries. Indeed, more written documentation exists for the ancient Nile Valley than for any other 4,000-year-old cultural complex in the world. There is now little doubt that ancient Kemet was the creation of Africans. Yet the issues associated with the Nile

Valley and ancient Kemet are unlike the issues associated with other ancient cultural complexes. Discussions surrounding the skin color of the Africans of the Nile Valley, for example, reflect the conceptually based social problems of another age and another place.

In this respect it is interesting to note that there were six early civilizations or cultural complexes that demonstrated what Western scholars would later characterize as "high cultures." Two of the six were located in the Americas (the Maya and Aztec of Mexico and the Inca of the Peruvian highlands); three were located in Asia (the Indus Valley, the Yangtze Valley, and the valley of the Tigris-Euphrates). Only one was located in Africa's Nile Valley. The debate over the racial composition of progenitors is the unique good fortune of the culture found in Africa, a debate vehemently pushed by scholars operating out of a bewildered Europe-centered paradigm.

Another body of internal information comes from oral texts that have been preserved and later committed to writing, as in the case of *Sundiata*. The same may be said of praise poetry or heroic poetry, which is found in many parts of the continent. What is crucial about these productions is that the audience was primarily African, and their mode of expression implied an understanding of an African idiomatic expression that reflected the codes as well as what some psychologists call the "deep structure" of African culture. Cheikh Anta Diop, Janheinz Jahn, and Jacques Maquet exemplify scholars who sought to document historical "Africanity."

Nonwritten sources constitute yet another group of internal sources about African knowledge. Among these sources, the first group consists of texts that are orally transmitted from one part of a geographic region to another and from one generation to another. These kinds of sources, described in Jan Vansina's *Oral Tradition as History* (1986), are primarily geared toward communication. Other nonwritten sources provide information of the past indirectly because they are not geared toward communication. Still, we can and do interrogate and receive valuable information from them. These sources provide evidence that comes from the African earth itself through paleontological and archaeological interpretations; from the social institutions of the Africans, which give us knowledge about Africans through historical linguistics and glottochronology; and from the biology of the African, which acts as a living document establishing the individual African's connection to other Africans through genetics, blood types, and so on.

These nonwritten sources of evidence are easily contaminated by the imposition of Europe-centered or Asia-centered paradigms as well as by other constructs of explanation that emerge from those paradigms. Through interpretation, this evidence can thus be used to distort African reality. Nevertheless, nonwritten sources provide a rich mine of information if we are sensitive to possible "construct" and "reconstruction" problems associated with them.

External Sources

The creation of historical knowledge about Africa in the last two centuries has been heavily influenced by external sources, which are found mainly in written form. Asian sources, as previously mentioned, form one group, including sources in Arabic and reflecting Islamic values and preferences. These can be very Asia-centered, since the reference point of Islam is in Southwest Asia. Two arguments are usually made to contest the Asia-centered nature of Islam. First, there is the claim that the roots of the principles of Islam are to be found in "Misraim," or "ancient Kemet." According to this argument, the Islamic religion is an Asian manifestation of an African orientation toward God. Yosef Ben-Jochannan makes this argument in *The African Origins of Major "Western Religions"* (1991). The second argument is based on Mazrui's thesis that the Arabian Peninsula was always part of cultural Africa. In that case a religion that originated in the Arabian Peninsula is ipso facto an African religion. The position one takes toward Islam will obviously affect how one judges the significance of the West African centers of learning, such as the university of Sankore. I am not completely persuaded that Islam is not an Asia-centered religion and therefore an external agent that in many places adapted itself to African culture more successfully than did Western Christianity. More research and debate are needed in this area.

There are many historical sources in the external genre from North, West, and East Africa. The following are examples:

— the writings of Ibn Abd Al-Hakam (863–70), which describe the conquest of North Africa and Spain;
— Al-Khwarazui's descriptions (ca. 883) of Ghana and Gao;
— Ibn Hawqal's *Roads and Kingdoms* (988), which describes a trip to Awdaghast, in the Sahara;
— Ibn Battutah's visit to Mali in 1352 and his description of West African societies and how they differed from Asian societies in gender relations; and
— Leo Africanus's (1492–   ) *Description of Africa* (1526), which discusses a visit to Timbuktu at some length.

A wider set of external sources should also be noted. Sources in Turkish include official documents on North Africa produced during the period of the Ottoman Empire. Sources in Chinese report expeditions such as those of Cheng-Ho, a Muslim sent by the third Ming emperor on three journeys to Africa (1417–19, 1421–22, 1431–33), whereas other reports describe a people called the "Ta' Sha'" (Arabic-speaking traders) and a place called "Tso'pa" (Zanzibar). The study of Japanese sources of information has barely begun; we are still trying to decipher the emphasis of their Asia-centered paradigm and how it has been influenced by the Europe-centered paradigm through the transfer of knowledge about Africa via Europe and America.

Asia-centered sources obviously affected Africans who are Muslims differently. As late as the 1990s Somali and Sudanese scholars still identified themselves as Arab. The total dominance of the Asia-centered paradigm affects contemporary policy in the Sudan, Egypt, Eritrea, and most of North Africa on issues of identity and center location. Nonwritten sources may also be affected by this crisis of location. Petrodollar wealth, in favoring this part of the world, may also have blinded some Africans to the issue of center and location in knowledge creation, causing a dislocation crisis in the formation of knowledge about Africa in this region of the continent.

One particular body of sources, based on the Europe-centered paradigm, has come to dominate knowledge about Africa in the twentieth century. By its essence the Europe-centered paradigm centers its information-building enterprise on Europe. By implication it renders Africa and other parts of the world that do not have a special relation to the European world or its economic system "peripheral," making them "Third World" or "Fourth World." As noted, sources of knowledge that reflect a Europe-centered paradigm are not necessarily invalid or anti-African. A Europe-centered paradigm on its own terms is as valid as an Africa-centered or an Asia-centered paradigm. The troubling aspect of the Europe-centered paradigm is its historical and symbolic connection to political imperialism, economic exploitation, and arrogant cultural hegemony. This combination has resulted in devastating intellectual consequences because it has advanced the notion that knowledge created through the Europe-centered paradigm is equivalent to knowledge created through an all-embracing universal paradigm. Through the instrumentality of political imperialism, knowledge generated from the Europe-centered paradigm has been shoved down the throats of Africans, Asians, and Native Americans. Some of the people from these different regions have so internalized this framework that they defend it as their very own.

Indeed, attempts to escape intellectually from the hegemony of a Europe-centered paradigm have often led to shifts from one aspect of the paradigm to another. For example, many African scholars shifted from the "capitalist" aspect of this paradigm to the "Marxist" aspect and prematurely celebrated their escape from the Europe-centered intellectual plantation. Yet the Marxist school, which provides an insightful critique of capitalism, is still essentially a Europe-centered knowledge system.

Sources of knowledge are many and varied in the Europe-centered paradigm and sometimes encompass whole disciplines, such as imperial anthropology and dependency "developmental studies." The creation of knowledge in economic theory has been particularly damaging to African initiatives. Economic knowledge about Africa was particularly misleading, as James Hooker indicated in the case of Malawi, where he noted people who were very much alive although economic analysis placed them at zero income. Culture-based assumptions, as opposed to simple measurements of trends, probably explain many botched development plans on the African continent and elsewhere.

These Europe-centered sources of knowledge have been criticized by Edward Said in his book on "orientalism" and by Molefi Asante in *The Afrocentric Idea* (1987) and *Kemet, Afrocentricity, and Knowledge* (1990). Europe-centered sources, to be sure, are not monolithic. There have been attempts to be sensitive to the "African point of view" within a Europe-centered construct. On the whole, however, Europe-centered sources—such as travelers' accounts, missionary reports, and official papers of European imperial governments—tend to have deeply embedded biases against Africans.

Balance of Paradigms

The knowledge about Africa created by accessing Asia-centered and Europe-centered sources does have a positive side. It enables Africans to view themselves through the eyes of others, thereby expanding their perspective of themselves to a multicentric level. This in itself develops the necessary habit of employing multiple perspectives in analyzing social phenomena, or at least being sensitive to the need for a multicentered knowledge system. Nonetheless, this development cannot meet the Africans' need to view themselves through their own eyes. The essence of Africa-centeredness is to make the African the subject in history and the maker of her or his destiny. Chinweizu has noted the common implication that Africans are regarded as the modern puppets of others (1987). Perhaps the African crisis is first and foremost a crisis of "knowledge identity" in that the knowledge Africans have is based on constructs that are incongruent with the reality that Africans know and experience.

What the Africa-Centered Paradigm Is Not

The emphasis and focus of the Africa-centered paradigm is to create knowledge on the basis of historical, social, and cultural factors, rather than through biology, in contrast to the Melanin school. Although there may be a significant correlation between biological and cultural factors, it is the historical and cultural forces that we regard as crucial and therefore worthy of in-depth study. It is only after we exhaust explanatory models based on this premise that we can proceed to seek biology-based explanations from scholars competent in human physiology and anatomy.

In the case of ancient Kemet, the central issue is the historical assertion that Kemetic culture was African. Reliance on an Africa-centered view of the

Nile Valley views the region and its developments from the south to the north rather than the other way around.

The Africa-centered paradigm should not be confused with attempts to justify errors of fact. This is different from arguments over choice of interpretation, where often a Europe-centered paradigm yields a picture different from that provided by an Africa-centered paradigm. The Africa-centered paradigm therefore provides a framework for knowledge creation that is ongoing, analytical, and critical. An Africa-centered scholar, like any critical scholar, should not accept statements simply because a speaker or author declares them to be Africa-centered but rather should evaluate the accuracy of the information and the consistency of the implied worldview. The Africa-centered paradigm therefore provides a disciplined and focused process of knowledge creation for the twenty-first century.

The Africa-centered paradigm, unlike the Afrocentrism proclaimed by some scholars, is not a political ideology. I should add, however, that there are scholars and leaders who may take the theoretical formulations that emerge from the Africa-centered paradigm to build guidelines for social existence that can become an ideological formulation called "Afrocentrism."

The articulation of the Africa-centered paradigm is not a finished project; it is an ongoing process of separation from the hegemonic aspects of the Europe-centered paradigm as a guide to information about Africa and Africans. It is a loud warning to those who use terms such as *cosmopolitan* to mask a hegemonic Europe-centered paradigm that the ruse will not work. An honest admission of each "center location" needs to be made so that a global multicentered knowledge creation process can be vigorously pursued for the intellectual benefit of all.

What Is Africa-Centered Scholarship?

Asante describes an Africa-centered scholar as one who

> sees knowledge of this "place" perspective as a fundamental rule of intellectual inquiry because its content is a self-conscious obliteration of the subject/object duality and the enthronement of an African wholism. . . . The Afrocentrist seeks to uncover and use codes, paradigms, symbols, motifs, myths, and circles of discussion that reinforce the centrality of African ideals and values as a valid frame of reference for acquiring and examining data. Such method appears to go beyond Western history in order to re-valorize the African place in the interpretation of Africans, continental and diasporan. (Asante 1990:5–6)

An Africa-centered scholar, in sum, is one who employs a paradigm that places Africans at the center of the knowledge creation process. In *An Introduction to the Africa-centered Perspective of History* (1994:128), I indicated that training can provide any scholar the skills and orientation of an Africa-centered perspective. I have always insisted that the whole enterprise of Africa-centered scholarship should be about the reconstruction of the African's place in world history and the acceptance of all the world's people as actors in their own right and on their own terms, subject only to the recognition of the rights of others. This academic charity should begin in the institutions of learning, for without respect for all centers and cultures in the creation of knowledge, there will be no intellectual peace in the global village of the twenty-first century.

References Cited

Asante, Molefi Kete. 1987. *The Afrocentric Idea.* Philadelphia: Temple University Press.
———. 1990. *Kemet, Afrocentricity, and Knowledge.* Trenton, N.J.: Africa World Press.
Bates, Robert H., V. Y. Mudimbe, and Jean O'Barr. 1993. *Africa and the Disciplines: The Contributions of Research in Africa to the Social Sciences and Humanities.* Chicago: University of Chicago Press.
Ben-Jochannan, Yosef. 1991. *The African Origins of Major "Western Religions."* Baltimore, Md.: Black Classic.
Bernal, Martin. 1987. *Black Athena: The Afroasiatic Roots of Classical Civilization.* Vol. 1, *The Fabrication of Ancient Greece, 1785–1985.* New Brunswick, N.J.: Rutgers University Press.
Childe, V. Gordon. 1956. *Society and Knowledge.* London: Allen and Unwin.
Chinweizu. 1987. *Decolonising the African Mind.* Lagos: Pero.
Feierman, Steven. 1993. "African Histories and the Dissolution of World History." In *Africa and the Disciplines,* ed. Bates, Mudimbe, and O'Barr, 167–212.
Keto, C. Tsehloane. 1994. *An Introduction to the Africa-centered Perspective of History.* Rev. ed. Chicago: Research Associated/Karnak House.
Mangoaela, Z. D. 1971. *Lithoko Tsa Marena a Basotho.* Tse bokeletsoeng ke Z. D. Mangoaela. Morija, Lesotho: Morija Sesuto Book Depot.
Masolo, D. A. 1994. *African Philosophy in Search of Identity.* Bloomington: Indiana University Press, in association with the International African Institute.
Mudimbe, V. Y., and Kwame Anthony Appiah. 1993. "The Impact of African Studies in Philosophy." In *Africa and the Disciplines,* ed. Bates, Mudimbe, and O'Barr, 113–38.
Niane, D. T. 1965. *Sundiata: An Epic of Old Mali.* Trans. G. D. Picket. Essex, U.K.: Longmans.
Pankhurst, Richard P. 1967. *The Ethiopian Royal Chronicles.* Addis Ababa: Oxford University Press.
Vansina, Jan. 1965. *Oral Tradition: A Study in Historical Methodology.* Trans. H. M. Wright. Chicago: Aldine.

9   Indirect Rule, Civil Society, and Ethnicity: The African Dilemma

Mahmood Mamdani

This chapter seeks to present an interpretation of postindependence African politics. My central argument is that sub-Saharan African countries faced a threefold challenge in the postindependence period: first, democratizing the state; second, deracializing civil society; and third, restructuring unequal external relations of dependency. Of these, the central and critical task was that of democratization, which was also the objective that met with the least success. That fact goes a long way toward explaining why progress on the other two fronts, deracializing civil society and restructuring international relations, was not only incomplete but also reversible.

The Colonial State and Indirect Rule

The colonial state was in every instance a historical formation, yet its structure everywhere came to exhibit certain fundamental features. I will argue that this was so because the organization and reorganization of the colonial state was in all cases a response to a central and overriding question, generally referred to as the "native question." Briefly put, it is this: how can a tiny and foreign minority rule over an indigenous majority?

There were two broad answers to this question: direct and indirect rule.[1] The main features of these two approaches, and the contrast between them, are best illustrated by the South African experience. Direct rule was the main mode of controlling "natives" attempted in the eighteenth and early nineteenth centuries. It is best exemplified by the Cape experience. The basic features of indirect rule, by contrast, emerged in Natal during the second half of the nineteenth century.

Direct rule was based on the presumption of a single legal order, an order formulated in terms of received colonial ("modern") law. Its other side was the nonrecognition of "native" institutions. The vision of direct rule was based on equality of rights in a multiracial society. But the equality of civil rights did not mean a similar political equality, for political rights were grounded in the ownership of property. A propertied franchise separated the "civilized" from the "uncivilized." The resulting vision was best summed up in Cecil Rhodes's famous phrase "equal rights for all civilized men."

The social prerequisite of direct rule was rather drastic. It involved a comprehensive sway of market institutions: the appropriation of land, the destruction of communal autonomy, and the defeat and dispersal of tribal populations. Given that background, direct rule meant the reintegration and domination of "natives" in the institutional context of semiservile and semicapitalist agrarian relations.

In contrast to this, indirect rule came to be the mode of domination over a "free" peasantry. Here, land remained a communal, or "customary," possession. The market was restricted to the products of labor, only marginally incorporating land or labor itself. Peasant communities were reproduced within the context of a spatial and institutional autonomy. The tribal leadership was either reconstituted as the hierarchy of the local state or freshly imposed where none had existed, as in the "stateless societies." Here political inequality went alongside civil inequality, with both grounded in a legal dualism. Alongside the received law was implemented a customary law that regulated nonmarket relations in land, personal (family) relationships, and community affairs. In South Africa the dominance of mining over agrarian capital in the late nineteenth century posed afresh the question of reproducing autonomous peasant communities that would regularly supply single adult male migrant laborers to the mines.

My larger point is twofold. First, indirect rule came to be the principal form of colonial rule. Although its basic features were sketched in the colony of Natal over five decades in the second half of the nineteenth century, it was elaborated by the British in equatorial Africa in the early part of the twentieth century—by Lugard in Nigeria and Uganda (1965) and Cameron in Tanganyika (see Illife 1979)—and then emulated by the French after World War I, the Belgians in the 1930s, and finally the Portuguese in the 1950s. Second, indirect rule was mediated rule. Its use meant that the vast majority of the colonized never experienced colonial rule as rule directly by others. Rather, the colonial experience for most "natives" was one of rule mediated through one's own. As Jan Smuts, the South African prime minister, emphasized in his Rhodes lecture at Oxford in 1929, "territorial segregation" would not solve the "native problem"; "institutional segregation" was needed (Smuts 1929:xx). A stable colonial order required that the "native" be ruled not just by his own but through "native institutions." Indirect rule was grounded less in racial than in ethnic structures. As its pioneers, the British theorized the colonial state as less of a territorial than a cultural construct.

The Colonial State: A Bifurcated Apparatus

The legal dualism characteristic of indirect rule juxtaposed received ("modern") law with customary law. "Modern" law regulated relations among "nonnatives," and between "nonnatives" and "natives." Customary law, on the other hand, governed relations among "natives."

Customary law was supposed to be tribal law. A tribe or an ethnic group was defined by colonial authorities as a group with its own distinctive law. Referred to as "custom," this law was usually unwritten. Its source was the "native authority," those in charge of managing the local state apparatus. And this native authority was supposedly the "traditional" tribal authority. In this arrangement, the source of the law was the very authority that administered the law. This system meant the absence of a rule-bound authority. Despite the persistent fantasy of colonial powers, particularly Britain and France, that their major contribution to the colonized was to bring them the benefits of the rule of law, there could be no rule of law in such an arrangement, for customary justice was really administrative justice. It could be no other in a situation where judicial authority and administrative authority were fused in the same person.

The functionary of the local state apparatus was everywhere called the "chief." One should not be misled by the nomenclature to think of this as a holdover from the precolonial era. The chief not only had the right to pass rules ("bylaws") governing persons living under his domain; he also executed all laws and was the administrator in "his" area, in which he settled all disputes. The authority of the chief thus fused in a single person all moments of power: judicial, legislative, executive, and administrative. This authority was like a clenched fist, necessary because the chief stood at the intersection of the market and the nonmarket economy. The administrative justice and the administrative coercion that were the sum and substance of his authority lay behind a regime of extra-economic coercion, a regime that breathed life into a whole range of compulsions: forced crops, forced sales, forced contributions, forced removals.

My general point is this: the legal integration characteristic of direct rule defined a form of state based on the rule of law. It was a state form that framed civil society. In contrast, indirect rule was grounded in a legal dualism central to which was the colonial construction of administrative justice, called "customary law." It was the antithesis of a rule of law. It was, rather, legal arbitrariness. Indirect rule was the form of the state that framed the social life of the "free" peasantry.

The Anticolonial Revolt

It is my basic contention that the form of rule shaped the form of revolt against it. This meant that ethnicity (tribalism) was simultaneously the form of colonial control over "natives" and the form of revolt against it. Ethnicity defined the parameters of both the native authority in charge of the local state apparatus and the revolt against it. Indirect rule at once reinforced ethnically bound institutions of control and exploded them from within. Ethnicity, in other words, was never just about identity. Its two contradictory moments involved both social control and social emancipation. This is why it makes sense neither to embrace ethnicity uncritically nor to reject it one-sidedly.

Everywhere the local apparatus of the colonial state was organized either ethnically or on a religious basis. On the other hand, it is difficult to identify a single major peasant uprising over the colonial period that was not either ethnic or religious in inspiration. This situation has a simple but basic explanation: the anticolonial struggle was first and foremost a struggle against the hierarchy of the local state, the tribally organized native authority. Thus, although the cadres of all these nationalist movements were recruited mainly from urban areas, the movements gained depth the more they were anchored in the struggles of the peasants against the array of native authorities that shackled them.

After independence, however, there was a dramatic shift in the political focus of the nationalist leaderships, from the local to the central state apparatus, from democratizing local state apparatuses to a dual preoccupation: deracializing civil society in the towns and restructuring unequal international relations.

The History of Actually Existing Civil Society

I want to understand civil society analytically, in its historical formation, and not programmatically, as an agenda for change—hence the focus on actually existing civil society.

The history of civil society in colonial Africa is laced with racism, for civil society was first and foremost the society of the colons. It was also primarily a creation of the colonial state. The rights of free association and free expression, and eventually of political representation, were rights of citizens under direct rule, not of subjects under indirect rule.

This dichotomy explains why the colonial state was a Janus-type affair. Its one side, the state that governed citizens, was bounded by the rule of law and an associated regime of rights. Its other side, the state that ruled over subjects, was a regime of extra-economic coercion and administrative justice. It is thus no wonder that the struggle of subjects was both against the "tribal" authorities in the local state and against civil society. The struggle against the latter was particularly acute in the settler colonies, where it often took the form of an armed revolt whose best-known theoretician was Frantz Fanon. This, then, was the first historical moment in the development of civil society: the colonial state as the protector of the society of the colons.

The second moment in that development saw a marked shift in the relation between civil society and the state. This was the moment of the anticolonial struggle, for the anticolonial struggle was also the embryonic middle and working classes' struggle for entry into civil society. That entry, that expansion of civil society, was the result of an antistate struggle. Its consequence was the creation of an indigenous civil society, a process set into motion with the postwar colonial reform. But this was a development of limited significance. It could not be otherwise, for any significant progress in the creation of an indigenous civil society required a change in the form of the state. It required a deracialized state.

Independence, the birth of a deracialized state, was the context of the third moment in this history. Independence deracialized the state but not civil society. In fact, as I will show, the independent state played a key role in the struggle to deracialize civil society.

The key policy instrument in the struggle for deracialization was what is today called "affirmative action" but what was then called "Africanization." The politics of Africanization were simultaneously unifying and fragmenting. Its first moment involved the dismantling of racially inherited privilege. The effect was to unify the victims of colonial racism. Its second moment, however, divided that same majority along lines that reflected the redistribution: regional, religious, ethnic, or even just family lines. The tendency of the literature on corruption in postindependence Africa has been to detach the two moments and thereby to isolate and decontextualize the moment of redistribution through ahistorical analogies that describe it as the politics of patrimonialism, prebendalism, or some other such notion. The effect has been to caricature the practices under investigation and to make them unintelligible.

The second interesting aspect of the politics of affirmative action was its ideological side, which was reflected in the language of contest. The ideological shift is explained by the fact that, with independence, the defense of racial privilege could no longer be made in the language of racism. Confronted by a deracialized state, racism not only receded into civil society but defended itself in the language of individual rights and institutional autonomy. To indigenous ears, the vocabulary of rights rang hollow, a lullaby for perpetuating racial privilege. Indigenous demands were formulated in the language of nationalism and social justice. The result was a breach between the discourse on rights and that on power, with the language of rights appearing as a figleaf over privilege and power cast as the guarantor of social justice and redress.

This is the context of the fourth moment in the history of civil society, that of indigenous civil society's collapse into political society. It is the moment of the marriage between technicism and nationalism; it is the time when social movements became demobilized and political movements were statized.

Part of this overall development was the failure to democratize the state. To put it differently, the postindependence struggle tended toward deracialization but not democratization. In the case of the "conservative" African states, this is self-evident. The hierarchy of the local state apparatus, from chiefs to native authorities administering "customary law," continued after independence as before it. In the "radical" African states there seemed to be a marked change. In some instances a constellation of tribally defined customary laws was abolished as a single customary law transcending tribal boundaries was codified. The result, however, was to develop a single countrywide customary law, applicable to all peasants regardless of ethnic affiliation, functioning alongside a "modern" law for urban dwellers. On the other hand, inasmuch as these "radical" regimes shared with colonial powers the conviction to effect a "revolution from above," they ended up intensifying the administrative nature of customary justice. What happened was a change in the title of the functionaries of that justice, from chiefs to cadres. But it was a change in nomenclature without a change in the organization of power. Although the bifurcated state that was created with colonialism was deracialized, it was not democratized.

Conclusion: The Present

The context in which civil society was absorbed into political society during the postindependence period was twofold. On the one hand, civil society experienced a deep division along racial lines, with the state standing at the cutting edge of the struggle to deracialize civil society. But the state was not confined to being the executor of the affirmative action program. For the colonized, state policy in the immediate postindependence period was also the harbinger of a degree of social progress—particularly in the fields of education and health—progress that was remarkable by colonial standards. This was a direct outcome of the deracialization of the state.

The trajectory of social progress came to a close with adverse international economic trends in the late 1970s. The failure to democratize local state apparatuses meant a failure to mobilize a truly national effort to reform international relations of dependency. On the contrary, adverse trends in the changing international context were more or less mechanically translated into a deepening fiscal crisis of the state. Eventually this crisis led to a widespread surrender to an international regime of financial discipline in the form of structural adjustment programs.

It is in this context that the middle and working classes rediscovered the language of rights. That rediscovery is central to the development of what are today referred to as "prodemocracy movements." A key feature of these movements is that they tend to be confined to urban civil society, with little base in rural areas. Except in South Africa, this means that these movements are anchored principally in the salaried middle classes and even weaker unionized wage workers. Their weakness is reflected in their tendency to look at international powers for that final push to effect a reform of the state. They lack the necessary social base or perspective to forge an agenda for change that could address the concrete circumstances of the "free" peasantry. Needless to say, such an agenda would have to go beyond a civil society–bound demand for rights to a demand for a change in the very form of the "indirect rule" state that confronts the peasantry.

Rural protest continues to be framed in the language of ethnicity. Faced with a fused "indirect rule" authority and legal arbitrariness, the peasant movements make demands that are often more participatory than representational. At the same time, these demands are often more localized, concerned with a reform in the organization of local state power, than those of civil society movements, whose demands for political representation have a direct bearing on power in the central state. Thus, it should not be surprising that, when faced with movements both urban and rural, "radical" regimes have found it easier to introduce reforms in the local state so as to checkmate civil society–based movements. Such has been the nature of reforms introduced by Thomas Sankara (Burkina Faso), the early Jerry Rawlings (Ghana), and Yoweri Museveni (Uganda). The thrust of each has been toward localized reform that seeks to incorporate rural constituencies in a state strategy designed to checkmate the demands of civil society for political representation in the central state. The structure of protest continues to be shaped by that of the state: fractured, fragmented, localized, and decentralized.

Note

1. There is an extensive literature on indirect (and direct) rule, ranging from works by colonial administrators (e.g., Lugard 1965; Hailey 1936) to later academic studies (e.g., Berman 1984; Channock 1985; Delavignette 1950; Huessler 1968; Welsh 1973). For further references see Mamdani 1996, especially chapters 3 (62–108) and 4 (109–37).

References Cited

Berman, Bruce. 1984. "Structure and Process in the Bureaucratic States of Colonial Africa." *Development and Change* 15:161–202.

Channock, Martin. 1985. *Law, Custom, and Social Order: The Colonial Experience in Malawi and Zambia.* London: Cambridge University Press.

Delavignette, Robert. 1950. *Freedom and Authority in French West Africa.* London: Oxford University Press.

Hailey, Lord. 1936. *An African Survey.* London: Oxford University Press.

Huessler, Robert. 1968. *The British in Northern Nigeria.* London: Oxford University Press.

Illife, John. 1979. *A History of Modern Tanganyika.* Cambridge: Cambridge University Press.

Lugard, D. F. 1965. *The Dual Mandate in British Tropical Africa.* London: Frank Cass.

Mamdani, Mahmood. 1996. *Citizen and Subject: Contemporary Africa and the Legacy of Late Colonialism.* Princeton, N.J.: Princeton University Press.

Smuts, Jan Christian. 1929. *Africa and Some World Problems.* Oxford: Clarendon.

Welsh, David. 1973. *The Roots of Segregation: Native Colonial Policy in Natal, 1845–1910.* Cape Town: Oxford University Press.

10 Popular Paradigms and Conceptions: Orature-Based Community Theater

Micere Githae Mugo

Any serious project on the reconstruction of the study and meaning of Africa must place cultural discourse at the center of its dialogue, for cultural studies bring us face to face with the history of a people, their self-definition, and an understanding of the dialectics that shape their destiny—together with all these processes' inherent contradictions. It is with this understanding that this chapter posits orature-based community theater as an important option in the quest for alternative paradigms that will take African studies in the arts beyond colonial and neocolonial formulations. In its attempt to depart from traditional Western bourgeois and liberal theater traditions, orature-based community theater may be regarded as an example of what Carol Boyce Davies terms an "uprising discourse" (Davies 1994:80–112). It is, among other things, a response to colonial and neocolonial cultural expressions of domination. Drawing as it does on African orature forms, genres, and aesthetics that inform and shape the artistic production process, community theater is created with the broad masses of the people as the primary intended audience. I will return to this point later, but first I must elaborate on the reasons for the focus on orature and community theater.

The key argument here is that African orature and the performing arts constitute the core of the authentic art forms that bring us closest to the heart of African people's self-expression and practice. They expose us to the type of indigenous knowledge that we should be scrutinizing as seriously as possible. This is especially critical given the crisis in what I call *invasion* by dominating paradigms, which are often veiled under the guise of status quo–controlled and status quo–programmed multicultural study packages. As several chapters in this book demonstrate, even those who claim to be the best friends of Africa and Africans exhibit a consuming appetite for control when it comes to the question of intellectual output and authority on Africa. As I have personally experienced, some non-African African studies enthusiasts are prepared to go to great lengths to silence African perspectives and paradigms that contradict their own.[1] In this intellectual wrestling match, there is particular resistance to ideas centered on mass-based foundations of knowledge, a variation of colonialism's violent refusal to accept Africans as coproducers of intellectual knowledge, a case made eloquently long ago by Aimé Césaire (1955).

It has thus become all the more urgent that African scholars unearth people's paradigms that have the capacity to withstand conceptions imposed from outside by those who control the production of knowledge. The more successfully this is done, the better positioned African scholars will be in bringing to conference rooms their peoples' contribution to knowledge rather than recycled versions of Western scholarship. The focus on home-grown theories and practices will also contribute to the task of weeding out armchair-cum-tourist African studies specialists who have appropriated the study of Africa, analyzed it from a calculated distance, and taken advantage of the current gloomy status of African academic conditions—a process well portrayed in Zenebeworke Tadesse's chapter.

This is not, of course, an argument for fencing off non-African scholars from the study of Africa. Rather, it is an attempt to expose the arrogance and spirit of invasion with which some of them have approached their areas of specialization—a point well made by William Martin and Michael West in their opening statement to the conference on which this volume is based (Martin and West 1995).

To conclusively posit orature-based community theater as a model, it is necessary to reinforce a number of observations. One can convincingly argue that in dealing with any social heritage, when direct personal contact with human resources and their physical reality is not possible, the next most meaningful point of contact is through cultural expression. Within the African setting, it is the performed art forms (and particularly those that are orature based) that put us in direct dialogue with the masses who are the major producers. This in turn exposes us to a long history of cultural resistance that has played a key role in interrogating the impositions of dominating, imperialist transplantations. To explain this fully, I will need briefly to review the history of drama and theater in Africa to show how dominating paradigms were imposed under colonialism and neocolonialism while analyzing these impositions within the context of enslaving education and the propagation of false consciousness. I will then examine emerging trends in African community theater, pointing out ways in which these efforts provide liberating paradigms in dialectical opposition to dominating paradigms. To allow for focus, the chapter will draw most of its illustrations from the East African scene, which I know best.

"Theater" and "Drama"

I begin with a statement from Ruth Finnegan, a specialist in African "oral literature" who argued that drama as a distinct and developed art form is unknown in indigenous African societies: "Though some writers have very positively affirmed the existence of native African drama, it would perhaps be truer to say that in Africa, in contrast to Western Europe and Asia, drama is not typically a wide-spread or a developed form" (Finnegan 1970:500). In making this statement, Finnegan is not referring to the nonexistence of written texts, the essential ingredient in drama, according to Western definitions; rather, she is dismissing altogether the notion that drama is "a *developed* form" within the orature tradition. She describes what exist as "phenomena" and consequently proceeds to argue, rather paternalistically: "There are, however, certain dramatic and quasi-dramatic *phenomena* to be found, particularly in parts of West Africa" (Finnegan 1970:500; emphasis added), identifying "the celebrated masquerades of Southern Nigeria" as examples of these half-baked dramas. Although devoting 300 pages to poetry and another 165 to prose, Finnegan disposes of drama, a very prominent art form in African orature, in a mere 17 pages. Preconceptions and transplantations of concepts dictating what constitutes drama explain this block, at least in part.

Coming from a scholar whose work, *Oral Literature in Africa,* is a standard reference in many universities, including African ones, Finnegan's claim should cause concern. It is a clear case of an imposed paradigm based on a definition that is external to many of the African cultures under discussion. Finnegan falls just short of calling the orature genre "primitive drama," in line with Melville Herskovits, the famous Africanist and anthropologist (Herskovits 1944). Judging from commentaries and assertions on ancient African drama, it is obvious that drama, as an art form, has been practiced widely in African societies since ancient times (see, among others, Equiano 1987; Snowden 1978; Traore 1972; de Graft 1976; Graham-White 1974; Soyinka 1976).

Furthermore, Finnegan does not even define what she terms "quasi-dramatic phenomena." Presumably, since in Western reckoning drama becomes theater only when a written text is enacted, the alleged nonexistence of a dramatic text rules out the question of theater. Compartmentalization of knowledge becomes an additional issue of concern here, reflecting an imposed paradigm on the orature world, which is characterized by "connectedness," as demonstrated by the onion structure theory (see Mugo 1991a) and reinforced by such writers as Kenyatta (1938), Jahn (1961), and Mbiti (1970). In orature the division between drama and theater is illusory rather than clear-cut, if not totally immaterial.

On this matter Zakes Mda, a well-known and respected colleague in African community theater, disagrees. He perceives theater and drama as distinct art forms, though he does not discuss the implications of this for orature:

> "Theatre" and "drama" are often treated inter-changeably, although they are two distinct types of dramatic expression. Drama is a *literary* composition, while theatre is actual performance that may or may not emanate from *literary* composition. Theatre involves live performance that has action planned to create a coherent and significant dramatic impression. Although a *literary* composition may constitute the basic element of a theatrical performance, theatre is not primarily a *literary* art but uses elements of other arts such as song, dance, and mime, in addition to dialogue and spectacle. (Mda 1993:45; emphasis added)

A close examination of this definition reveals an inherent insistence on linking and relating the two concepts even as Mda is straining to do otherwise. The line between the two genres is so tissue thin that it defies division. Whereas it is true that theater need not emanate from literary composition, it does not follow that a nonwritten dramatic composition is not drama.

The use of textuality to distinguish between drama and theater becomes truly problematic when we consider that in the spoken tradition a composition is conceived as a "text" even though it is not written. In other words, an orature composition may not exist in the form of a physical object, but this does not mean that the enacted nonwritten piece is not a text. "The saga of Ozidi," for example, was an oral dramatized creation among the Ijaw of Nigeria long before J. P. Clark captured it in book form (Clark 1966). It was both drama and theater. The notion of text as that which is written thus becomes external and problematic when defining African orature compositions. The following point must be emphasized: no linguistic composition can exist without a text, which can be either in people's memories or on a piece of paper. Nonetheless, many African theater practitioners have come to accept external definitions of drama and theater as binding when discussing African community theater. This points once again to the urgent need for paradigms that unravel our own reality, independent of Western concepts.

African Orature as Historical and Artistic Expression

With this background in mind, I move to the development of drama and theater. I begin with an essential quotation from Amilcar Cabral that helps to situate these artistic expressions as part of the production process in general and more specifically as fruits of culture. Cabral's words also explain why colonial and neocolonial educational paradigms are actively bent on destroying dominated people's artistic and other cultural expressions while enforcing their own impositions. This is his argument:

Whatever may be ideological or idealistic characteristics of cultural expression, culture is an essential element of the history of a people. Culture is, perhaps, the product of this history just as the flower is the product of a plant. Like history, or because it is history, culture has as its material base the level of the productive forces and the mode of production. Culture plunges its roots into the physical reality of the environmental humus in which it develops, and it reflects the organic nature of the society, which may be more or less influenced by external factors. History allows us to know the nature and extent of the imbalances and conflicts (economic, political and social) which characterize the evolution of a society; culture allows us to know the dynamic syntheses which have developed and established by social conscience to resolve these conflicts at each stage of its evolution, in the search for survival and progress. (Cabral 1973:42)

In African orature, drama and theater are more than artistic expressions: they are carriers of history, reflectors of the positive and negative forces inherent in the evolution of society. They are as well vehicles of conscientization that shape people's vision, even as they explore avenues for resolving the conflicts that characterize human development.

From antiquity right up to the slave trade and the colonial invasions of Africa, these are the terms on which drama and theater existed in various African communities. Theater took place at different kinds of sociocultural forums such as commemorations of historical events, cultural festivals, ceremonial occasions, ritual enactments, and ordinary social events. Theater was therefore used for entertainment as well as artistic commentary and critique of social reality. Generally speaking, theater was produced and consumed communally, but like all other forms of artistic and cultural production, it reflected the socioeconomic-political arrangement of the specific society from which it originated. Thus, in "vertical" societies[2] theater performances tended to reflect a feudalistic worldview and were often used to highlight themes featuring the chief, the queen, or the king. Examples of this kind of theater can be found in a number of countries that had feudal structures, such as ancient Egypt, the kingdoms of West Africa, Lesotho, Swaziland, and Uganda. Under such social formations, theater tended to be a tool for the deification and glorification of the ruling class. It was not unknown in such situations to witness performances dramatizing praise poetry that described the ruler as the "great," the "omnipotent," and the "lion that roars," whereas the masses were portrayed through images such as "ants," "rubble," "dust," and "grass" that tremble at the voice of the almighty.

It is also important to point out, however, that popular artists—even when in the minority—spoke loudly and clearly on behalf of the people, creating opposing images and symbols in an attempt to assert the humanity of the majority. This was so more often in "horizontal" social formations, where popular artists dominated the scene, taking their cue from the majority whose aspirations for self-assertion and human development they championed.[3] In their dramatizations, the heroes and heroines become what Wanjiku Mukabi Kabira describes as "the little people" of society (Kabira 1983:1). At the end of the day, it was the small ones—the hare, the deer, the oppressed and powerless small antagonists—who emerged victorious, outdoing bullies such as the greedy hyena, the trampling elephant, and the gulping ogre, who were the antitheses of all that is just and humane.

This dialectical cultural scene was invaded by the Arab and European slave traders, followed closely by Western colonial invaders. The enslavers and colonizers were not unaware that culture plays the role that Cabral has attributed to it. They knew that to effectively disinherit their victims and dominate their economy, they had to "conquer" them culturally. Frantz Fanon convincingly demonstrated this thesis in his two monumental works *The Wretched of the Earth* (1963) and *Black Skin White Masks* (1967). Even more demonstrative at the educational level, however, is the work of Paulo Freire, the celebrated Brazilian emancipatory educationist, theoretician, and community activist. He offers an especially rich analysis of the effects of conquest paradigms that invaders impose on colonized people. He defines cultural invasion thus:

> The theory of antidialogical action has one last fundamental characteristic: cultural invasion, which like divisive tactics and manipulation also serves the ends of conquest. In this phenomenon, the invaders penetrate the cultural context of another group, in disrespect of the latter's potentialities; they impose their own view of the world upon those they invade and inhibit the creativity of the invaded by curbing their expression. . . . In cultural invasion . . . the invaders are the authors of, and actors in, the process; those they invade are objects. The invaders mold; those they invade follow that choice—or are expected to follow it. The invaders act; those they invade have only the illusion of acting, through the action of the invaders. (Freire 1983:150)

Freire further argues that "all domination involves invasion—at times physical and overt, at times camouflaged, with the invader assuming the role of a helping friend" (1983:150).

This final point is particularly important as we examine the plight of African theater under the paradigms of colonial and neocolonial education, whose practitioners claim to be agents of development. In this regard, Jacques Depelchin's argument (see chap. 7 of this volume) that one of the most powerful sources of silencing various aspects of African history comes from within the scholarly discourses of the "major" (read *dominating* or *invading*) histories becomes pertinent. The silencing took all kinds of vicious forms. Indeed, when the enslavers and colonial invaders ambushed African peoples' history, their abuse of human rights went beyond the robbery of African lands: they also sought to capture their victims' souls. Assertive forms of cultural expression were either captured, forbidden, or at best censored.

On the whole, the invaders targeted popular forms such as drama and theater. They repressed those artistic expressions that asserted the people's collective well-being and either condoned or actively encouraged whatever reinforced the power of the ruling classes. In their toleration and promotion of *court* orature, as it might be called, the invaders used divide-and-rule tactics to woo the ruling class into collaboration while silencing the dominated majority. In this way they sought to silence the voices that sang the epic songs of the resisting masses and to chain the bodies that dramatized the theater of the oppressed. Theater performed around festivities, ceremonies, and rituals that celebrated the people's milestones of production, development, and social interaction was gagged. Theater that stagnated in religious swamps and caused trembling before tyrannical court enclosures was applauded. More significantly, the invaders schooled court theater artists and prospective artists in the invaders' own performing arts paradigms. Thus they manufactured robots who became mere imitators of the invaders' values and aesthetics. The players dressed like Greeks, Romans, and Anglo-Saxon gentlemen and ladies, either brandishing swords or playing pianos in upper-middle-class drawing rooms. Passing a vote of no confidence in their heritage and authenticity, this class of theater artists provided the tabula rasa on which—under neocolonialism, for instance—the artistic paradigms of Hollywood have kept soaps such as *Dallas* and *Dynasty* on African television screens long after they went out of circulation in the United States.

Paulo Freire has this to say about the dehumanizing psychological effects of cultural invasion:

> In cultural invasion it is essential that those who are invaded come to see their reality with the outlook of the invaders rather than their own; for the more they mimic the invaders, the more stable the position of the latter becomes.
>
> For cultural invasion to succeed, it is essential that those invaded become convinced of their intrinsic inferiority. Since everything has its opposite, if those who are invaded consider themselves inferior, they must necessarily recognize the superiority of the invaders. The values of the latter thereby become the pattern of the former. The more invasion is accentuated and those invaded are alienated from the spirit of their own culture and from themselves, the more the latter want to be like the invaders: to walk like them, dress like them, talk like them. (Freire 1983:151)

The Kenyan Colonial Invasion

Armed with the previously articulated understanding and determined to cement cultural domination among the colonized, invading educators set out to cultivate this kind of mimicry among their theater students. In Kenya, for instance, expatriate theater houses such as the Kenya National Theatre and

the Donovan Maul Theatre in Nairobi were so heavily subsidized by the colonial government that they could sponsor plays from Britain. In this way
audiences in the colony could be treated to unpolluted, direct importations
from the metropolis—cast, directors, stage props, and all. To complement
these efforts, certain colonial schools were identified as factories for the production of a collaborating local theater elite. These schools specialized in
staging Shakespearean plays such as *King Lear, Julius Caesar, Othello, Macbeth,*
and even the notorious conquest drama *King Henry V.*

The Alliance high schools in Kenya featured Shakespearean plays as an
annual event. The players "patriotically" chanted: "Once more unto the
breach, dear friends, once more / Or close the wall up with *our English dead*"
(*Henry V,* act 3, sc. 1; emphasis added). The colonial African school armies
thus fought the imaginary French and even ridiculed Queen Catherine's
broken English. In the meantime, thousands of Kenyan masses were also
"closing up the walls" of colonial enslavement with their living and their dead,
as they perished under forced labor on commercial plantations and in the
imperialist World Wars I and II.

Insisting on alternative paradigms, however, the African masses were all
along dialectically creating alternative platforms of resistance and self-
affirmation. When colonial agents organized what was sometimes referred
to as "extramural theater" for them, they resisted it. Some of the dramatic
skits, then referred to as "concerts," that constituted this so-called extramural theater were downright insulting. In one of them, the plot depicts an
African village so ridden with filth and rats that a plague eventually breaks
out. Unable to help themselves or resolve the crisis, the villagers die in stag-
gering numbers. Miraculously, a white government official appears just as the
crisis gets out of hand. With the aid of his African understudies, he teaches
the villagers how to clean up their surroundings and manages to get rid of
the rats for them. The villagers are thus rescued, and in sheer awe they there-
after venerate their messianic hero.

In this drama the audience meets, probably for the first time, grown African men and women who are not only so lazy that they helplessly sit wal-
lowing in filth but also so stupid that they are incapable of figuring out how
to kill the rats that are gnawing their children's fingers, toes, ears, and eyes.
As I intimated, the masses boycotted these denigrating invasion theater shows
in which they were made to sit on the fringes of existence, watching history
pass them by, while they were depicted as dumb, lazy, unintelligent, and utterly dependent on their oppressors. To replace these insults, they created
their own conceptions of history, of themselves, and of the world around
them. They made use of the limited space under their control, such as religious venues, converting the ground into platforms on which they enacted
their own versions of reality. They spread political messages camouflaged in

religious symbolism and flowering with militant aesthetics, creating what Carolyn Cooper would call "resistance science" (1994), in the fashion of African American sorrow songs and in the spirit of "Maroon ideology," to borrow again from Cooper. Through these efforts the masses sought to conscientize each other, to decry colonial acts of dehumanization, and to assert their human dignity.

These acts of cultural resistance through theater and other means took place in Kenya under the umbrella of "independent schools" and "independent churches," which Fred Welbourne documented from a historical perspective in *East African Rebels* (1961). These alternative institutions were started as far back as the 1930s, and they mushroomed all over Kenya in the 1940s and 1950s, defying violent censorship by the colonial government right up to the advent of independence in the 1960s. A satirical resistance theater emerged to counteract colonial paradigms, with dramatized skits, concerts, song, and dance thriving. No amount of repression, efforts at prohibitive legislation, bans, or arrests could stop the people.

Amandina Lihamba observes that "as colonial violence intensified theatre forms became more militant in protest and resistance against colonial aggression and exploitation" (Lihamba 1990:26). Further, there was a deliberate insistence on using indigenous Kenyan tongues, another clear message of defiance to colonial educators who had privileged English as the medium of linguistic expression.

The Tanzanian Colonial Invasion

The picture in Tanzania was no different. As Lihamba (1990) has shown, the invaders, unable to repress mass-based theater, decided to employ sinister methods to divert its mission and pervert its artistic goals. Community theater groups were forced to promote colonial business, especially during agricultural shows where the products of commercial farmers were prominently displayed. What Lihamba does not dwell on is the extent to which these Tanzanian performers themselves may have been on exhibition as specimens of "exotic" African cultures. The tradition of exhibiting human beings is not foreign to invading cultures. Though extreme, the exhibition of Ota Benga in a cage with monkeys at the New York Zoological Park in the Bronx (Bradford and Blume 1992) by American Africanist anthropologists at the turn of the century testifies to the inhumanity of the conquering powers' cultural fossilization of dominated people—another common characteristic of invading paradigms in the humanities and social sciences.

Lihamba notes that prior to 1948, the colonial administration not only actively discouraged African traditional performances but in some cases actually prohibited them. They were permitted only for "officially sanctioned events such as agricultural shows where the performances were used as crowd pullers for the potential buyers and consumers" (Lihamba 1990:26). Lihamba quotes a revealing passage from a document entitled, "Report of Group V, Cambridge Summer Conference, 1948" in the Tanzania National Archives/ 38813, which reads as follows: "We attach particular importance to the exhibition or show as a technique. . . . Plays, dances, concert parties, and the like, can be intimately connected with the exhibition technique especially if traditional festivals and celebrations are utilized as a setting for the exhibitions" (in Lihamba 1990:26).

Although awkwardly expressed, the point is made. African artistic performances were faced with yet another danger—commercialization—which would affect them most adversely at the levels of form and content. Distortion and adulteration would accompany imposed paradigms on when, why, how, and for what the performances would be produced. The "directors" and controllers would ensure that invasion was pushed to its limit: the objectification of those invaded and their self-image.

Neocolonial Invasions and Mass-Based Theater

This abuse and commercialization of popular mass theatrical performances has assumed deplorable dimensions under neocolonialism. Ministries of tourism and culture in many African countries have at times used theater artists in the same way as they use animals in the game parks: as a means of raising foreign currency by entertaining tourists still in search of the African wild. Since he who pays the piper calls the tune, to use a hackneyed expression, commercial performing artists will often go out of their way to give the tourists what they wish to see. Needless to say, such compromises negatively affect the paradigms governing the production of the performed pieces, distorting indigenous African art forms and turning them into comical exhibitions for the entertainment of tourists. Authenticity is thus sacrificed as the performers dance themselves lame in near-naked painted bodies that match the profiles of jestering acrobatic buffoons, evoking the "noble savage" image of television's Discovery Channel. The Bomas of Kenya, a tourist center, used to feature an acrobat who specialized in distorting his facial muscles with such success that he would momentarily look like a monster. Here, indeed, was living, visible evidence of the cost of tourist entertainment: lost beauty and human dignity.

With these taunting insults on African masses in view, the progressive theater artist has had no option but to join the masses in their efforts to rescue their art forms from invasion under neocolonialism. More that this, the alliance has recognized the power of the performed word in the process of mass conscientization. This power had been demonstrated throughout the history of anticolonial cultural struggles. Under neocolonial states and dictatorships, the abuse of human rights has acquired forms just as grotesque as those experienced during colonization. Creators of mass-oriented theater are therefore committed to the revolutionization of this most immediate, communicative art form, with a view to turning it into a lethal artistic weapon that the invaded can use against the systems that oppress them.

At this point it becomes necessary to define *mass-based theater,* relating it to orature and identifying the paradigms that distinguish it from the theater of invasion examined previously. In its ideological conception, mass-based theater also borrows paradigms from revolutionary theater practitioners such as Paulo Freire and Bertolt Brecht. In his well-known essay entitled "The Popular and the Realistic" (Brecht 1964), Brecht places popular theater within the realist tradition. Redefining "realism" outside the paradigms of the so-called great tradition, Brecht contextualizes a shift within twentieth-century capitalist Europe in which "the people has clearly separated from its top layer" and in which "its oppressors have parted company with it," becoming "involved in a bloody war against it which can no longer be overlooked" (Brecht 1964:107). He thus contends that from the point of view of the progressive theater artist: "It has become easier to take sides. Open warfare has, as it were, broken out among the 'audience.' . . . The ruling strata are using lies more openly than before and the lies are bigger. Telling the truth seems increasingly urgent. The sufferings are greater and the number of sufferers has grown. Compared with the vast sufferings of the masses it seems trivial and even despicable to worry about petty difficulties and the difficulties of the petty groups" (1964:107).

In addition to making other points, Brecht is arguing that in an oppressive situation, theater cannot evade the burden of functional art, a paradigm that is antithetical to the bourgeois notion of art for art's sake. More than this, he is advocating that theater align itself with the struggles of the oppressed and avoid a preoccupation with elitist trivialities. In making these observations, Brecht might as well be addressing the neocolonial African reality. From Cape to Cairo, from eastern coast to western coast, workers and peasants bend double under the weight of economic oppression, political repression, and sociocultural degradation. More than 80 percent of the continent's population lead a subhuman material existence. Denial of basic human rights—food, clothing, shelter, and the wherewithal for self-determination—leaves the majority of the people in a perpetual begging posture. In particular, children have become ready victims of hunger, famine, disease, and war. Africa is faced with imminent child genocide that will affect the development of generations to come. Given this situation, the theater artist faces a moral choice: whether or not to continue with the paradigms of bourgeois theater, which depict the masses as nothing more than asides or invisible incidentals, when not ridiculing them or wiping them out of history altogether. According to Brecht, to propagate bourgeois theater paradigms is to abet the distortion of reality, if by reality we mean the overwhelming evidence of the wretchedness of the majority in our midst.

Having dealt with the issue of whose side popular art should take, Brecht proceeds to explain what he means by *popular* from the point of view of aesthetics and vision. This definition is pertinent because it is related to the question of why we should promote mass-based orature theater. As he says: "'Popular' means intelligible to the broad masses, taking over their own forms of expression and enriching them/adopting and consolidating their standpoint/representing the most progressive section of the people in such a way that it can take over leadership: thus intelligible to other sections too/linking with tradition and carrying it further/handing on the achievements of the section now leading to the section of the people that is struggling for the lead" (Brecht 1964:108).

This model, greatly elaborated by revolutionary culturalists and educational practitioners such as Paulo Freire, Augusto Boal, Crow and Etherton, and others, is the theater paradigm with which progressive theater artists in Africa have been experimenting during the last two decades or so. This movement follows efforts in the 1960s and 1970s that sought to democratize the stage through such paradigms as the free traveling theater, the open air theater, street theater, and school and college drama festivals. Despite their best efforts, however, these projects still left the masses on the periphery. While recognizing the free traveling theater as an alternative paradigm to colonial theater, I have nonetheless indicated elsewhere its shortcomings:

> Free traveling theatres from western-patterned university campuses could never become the people's theatre. The latter were spectators and not active participants. The themes explored by the theatres were liberal and at best nationalistic. The language used was still predominantly English, even though now and again there were attempts to use African languages. The expressions, mannerisms and aesthetics applied did not draw from the "progressive section of the people." The elite were the stars, the articulators of conflicts, the leaders. In short, the experiment was limited and limiting to the masses: it fell short of the definition of "popular" given by Brecht. (Mugo 1991b)

The same comments could be made about the other experiments mentioned previously.

In East African drama festivals, however, some of the productions made an effort to "return to the source," in Cabral's sense of the concept. On this particular paradigm, I have observed:

> The best thing that resulted from this was the turning to what Cabral has called "the source" in drawing inspiration from the popular, progressive aspects of

African orature. The youth treated their audiences to dramatized symbols of greed, oppression and tyranny—the hyenas and ogres of East Africa's neo-colonial ruling classes. They depicted the masses as the intelligent hares and heroic "little women"/"little men" of orature creations who ultimately struggled against their oppressors to final victory. (Mugo 1991b)

An Orature-Based Paradigm

These efforts created the seeds for orature-based community theater in which the participation of the masses and their artistic forms, cultural paradigms, and languages are employed to shape the form and content of the pieces, as well as the overall visionary perception of the productions. However, the extent to which the various forms of orature-based community theater succeed in doing this varies from experiment to experiment, a subject that has been extensively treated by, among others, Boal (1979), Kidd and Byram (1981), Kidd and Colletta (1980), Crow and Etherton (1980), Mlama (1991), Kamlongera (1989), and Mda (1993). There is thus no need to describe individual community theater projects here. It will suffice to close with a brief, generalized sketch of the process involved in creating a desired orature-based model, with a view to reinforcing its place in the definition of liberating paradigms. The model used is that practiced by the Zambuko/Izibuko community theater group in Zimbabwe, of which I am a participating member. This group has staged performances in English, Chishona, and Sindebele, the three official languages of Zimbabwe, including works such as *Mavambo, Samora Continua!, Mandela—Spirit of No Surrender!* and a current one, *Simukai Zimbabwe! (Rise up Zimbabwe!)*, criticizing "invasions" by the IMF and the World Bank.

As I have repeatedly suggested such undertakings ought to do, the project goes back to the people for its themes and inspiration, deliberately drawing on the most positive aspects of self-expression that grassroots communities have evolved over time. The people are not relegated to the role of spectators but are involved as resources and participants in the creative process as well as in performance. The entire group of theater artists thus begins with brainstorming issues that are of concern to the community in which they are based, discussing them thoroughly before identifying the predominant theme on which the dramatization will eventually focus. The brainstorming exercise is normally conducted in the language shared by the creators of the artistic piece, ensuring that each member has freedom to use the tongue with which she or he feels most comfortable. This means that if Chishona, for instance, is the most common and bonding language, it becomes the main medium of communication. Other languages can be brought in where and when necessary. Members contribute orature songs, dances, stories, and other creations from their communities. Where necessary, these are researched for the specific production. Every rehearsal opens with dance and song warm-up exercises. Liberation songs are the most popular. Indeed, one of them has become Zambuko/Izibuko's signature tune. The song tells how Zimbabwe was liberated through armed struggle, and the artists hold toy guns high as they dance into the theater and onto the stage in celebration of the people's victory.

As the theme is developed and the spoken text shaped, the group begins identifying, from among the available human resources, individuals best suited for specific roles. Each case is discussed openly and critically, with the decision based purely on merit. Workshops in dramatization then begin. As the "script" is developed, each stage of the process is informed by intensive discussion and debate. The group experiments with criticism, alternative suggestions, and viable solutions. Once the oral text is more or less consolidated, scripting and recording finally come into play, but never for the purpose of producing a permanent text above amendment. During the rehearsals improvisation and continuous "writing" supersede the authority of a fixed script. When the rehearsals are mature, early performances are presented to other theater artists and members of the general community of artists for criticism. From the comments received, the group then works on perfecting the performance for the general public. Following some public performances, the audience is invited to participate in a session of criticism and self-criticism. Thus the piece and the artists continue to grow with each performance.

The foregoing discourse posits community theater, and specifically orature-based projects, as a paradigm that creates space for democratic participation, involvement, and collective work. The creative process becomes an embracing act; the final product, a shared experience. This contradicts the paradigm of "art for art's sake" and interrogates the perception of creative artistic productivity as the monopoly of intellectual elites. Furthermore, the paradigm provides a possible meeting place between orature and the written tradition. Complementarity and collective engagement replace the divisiveness and alienation of individualistic approaches. This explains why oppressed classes and groups such as workers and peasants, as well as women and youth, have responded so readily to the community theater project, which they use as a means of exploring the oppressive economic-political realities that have long suppressed their creativity. African studies specialists should pay serious attention to this aspect of creative and intellectual productivity as a paradigm worthy of further investigation.

Notes

1. In 1993 I was invited, along with two other African colleagues, to participate on a panel of "distinguished African scholars" at a conference on African studies and the undergraduate curriculum organized by a predominantly white university. The members of the panel

made critical comments that were not kindly received. Later, when the conference proceedings were under preparation for publication, one of the conference organizers tele-
phoned me, insisting on having my contribution but gently suggesting that I omit aspects
of my original critical remarks. I wrote the paper, ignoring the instructions in the name
of academic integrity. It was, of course, rejected. My probing elicited a long letter of explanation claiming that my contribution did not fit in with the rest of the papers. The
ensuing publication has only one or two contributions by African scholars.

    2. Amilcar Cabral uses this term to describe societies ruled by kings, queens, and chiefs.
Feudal systems, for instance, would be considered vertical in their organization.

    3. Horizontal social formations had ruling councils as the governing bodies. Represen-
tatives on the councils were appointed by the people they represented, usually across age
groups, clans, and villages.

References Cited

Boal, Augusto. 1979. *Theatre of the Oppressed.* London: Pluto.
Bradford, P. V., and Harvey Blume. 1992. *Ota Benga: The Pygmy in the Zoo.* New York: St.
    Martin's.
Brecht, Bertolt. 1964. "The Popular and the Realistic." *Brecht on Theatre,* ed. J. Willet, 107–
    15. New York: Hill and Wang.
Cabral, Amilcar. 1973. "National Liberation and Culture." In *Return to the Source: Selected
    Speeches of Amilcar Cabral,* ed. African Information Service, 39–56. New York: Monthly
    Review Press.
Césaire, Aimé. 1955. *Discourse on Colonialism.* Paris: Présence Africaine.
Clark, J. P. 1966. *Ozidi.* London: Oxford University Press.
Cooper, Carolyn. 1994. "'Resistance Science': Afrocentric Ideology in Vic Reid's *Nanny
    Town.*" In *Maroon Heritage,* ed. Kofi Agorsah, 109–18. Kingston: Canoe.
Crow, B., and M. Etherton. 1980. "Popular Drama and Popular Analysis in Africa." In
    Tradition for Development, ed. Ross Kidd and Nat J. Colletta, 57—94.
Davies, Carol Boyce. 1994. *Black Women: Writing, and Identity.* London: Routledge.
de Graft, J. C. 1976. "Roots in African Dance and Theatre." In *African Literature To-Day,*
    no. 8, ed. E. D. Jones, 1–25. London: Heinemann.
Equiano, Olaudah. 1987 [1814]. "The Life of Gustavus Vassa" (Olaudah Equiano). In *The
    Classic Slave Narratives,* ed. H. L. Gates Jr., 1–182. New York: Mentos/Penguin.
Fanon, Frantz. 1963. *The Wretched of the Earth.* New York: Grove.
———. 1967. *Black Skin White Masks.* New York: Grove.
Finnegan, Ruth. 1970. *Oral Literature in Africa.* Oxford: Oxford University Press.
Freire, Paulo. 1983. *Pedagogy of the Oppressed.* New York: Continuum.
Graham-White, Anthony. 1974. *The Drama of Black Africa.* New York: Samuel French.
Herskovits, Melville. 1944. "Dramatic Expressions among Primitive Peoples." *Yale Review*
    33:687.
Jahn, Janheinz. 1961. *Muntu: An Outline of Neo African Culture.* New York: Grove.
Kabira, Wanjiku Mukabi. 1983. *The Oral Artist.* Nairobi: Heineman.
Kamlongera, Christopher. 1989. *Theatre for Development in Africa with Case Studies from
    Malawi and Zambia.* Bonn: German Foundation for International Development.
Kenyatta, Jomo. 1938. *Facing Mount Kenya.* London: Secker and Warburg.
Kidd, Ross, and M. Byram. 1981. "Demystifying Pseudo-Freirian Non-Formal Education:
    A Case Description and Analysis of Laedza Batanani." Mimeo.

Kidd, Ross, and Nat J. Colletta, eds. 1980. *Tradition for Development: Indigenous Structures and Folk Media in Non-formal Education.* Bonn: German Foundation for International Education and International Council for Adult Education.

Lihamba, Amandina. 1990. "Theatre and Political Struggles in Africa." Paper presented at a Rockefeller Foundation conference, Reflections on Development, August, Bellagio, Italy.

Martin, William, and Michael West. 1995. "The Decline of the Africanists' Africa and the Rise of New Africas." *ISSUE* 23, no. 1:24–27.

Mbiti, John. 1970. *African Religions and Philosophy.* New York: Doubleday.

Mda, Zakes. 1993. *When People Play People.* Johannesburg: Oxford University Press.

Mlama, Penina Muhando. 1991. *Culture and Development: The Popular Theatre Approach in Africa.* Uppsala: Nordiska Afrikainstitutet.

Mugo, Micere Githae. 1991a. *Orature and Human Rights.* Roma: Institute of Southern African Studies, National University of Lesotho.

———. 1991b. "Popular Theatre and Human Rights." Paper delivered at conference, The Defense and Promotion of Human and Popular Democratic Rights in Africa, Feb. 26–Mar. 1, Maputo, Mozambique.

Snowden, Wenig Steffen. 1978. *Africa in Antiquity: The Arts of Ancient Nubia and the Sudan.* New York: Brooklyn Museum.

Soyinka, Wole. 1976. *Myth, Literature and the African World.* London: Cambridge University Press.

Traore, Bakary. 1972. *The Black African Theatre and Its Social Functions.* Trans. Dapo Adelugba. Ibadan: Ibadan University Press.

Welbourne, Frederick B. 1961. *East African Rebels: A Study of Some Independent Churches.* London: SCM.

Afterword

Immanuel Wallerstein

Africa was first studied during the colonial period. It was then studied in the immediate postindependence period. It is being studied today in a third period that as yet has no name. At each moment in time it has been studied rather differently by non-Africans and by Africans (including in this latter category so-called diaspora Africans). At each moment in time the African view of Africa has tended to be critical of the non-African view of Africa. This criticism is even stronger today than it has been in the past. The chapters in this book reflect this state of the discussion among those who study Africa.

There is no useful purpose in my seeking to summarize the arguments. In any case, the introduction by Michael O. West and William G. Martin undertakes that task. What can I add, a non-African who wrote about Africa primarily in the second period, the immediate postindependence period? I will restrict myself to some comments about the larger picture of discussions within the social sciences as a whole that, I hope, may contribute to the specific debate about the study of Africa.

The social sciences were institutionalized in the late nineteenth century as a European form of knowledge that claimed universal validity. (*Europe* here is a cultural term that includes North America and some other areas.) At first non-African scholars who wrote about Africa tended to work within a framework of analysis called "anthropology." Since 1945, however, non-African scholars coming from all the other so-called disciplines in the social sciences have also been writing about Africa. Whereas Africa was categorized as "other" than Europe within the framework of anthropology, other disciplines (say, economics) usually categorized it as the "same" as Europe, that is, as functioning in terms of the same presumably universal rules.

African critics of non-African writings about Africa have assailed both stances. They have tended to suggest that where Europeans saw "otherness," they were being deprecatory or at least paternalist and failing to appreciate the alternative routes to rationality and achievement that existed in human potentiality and had been realized as much in Africa as elsewhere. They argued that Africa's paths were as valid as, if not more valid than, Europe's paths. Such critics thus reasserted the worth and legitimacy of African values and structures. On the other hand, where Europeans saw "sameness," the African critics tended to suggest that they were myopically failing to see that the reality of African life, especially contemporary life, has differed significantly from that of European life because Europe and Africa have occupied different power positions in the world-system. These critics argued that, in insisting on "sameness," the non-Africans were imposing an analytic image and thus a political conformism on African states and other institutions in order to maintain their submission to a world order dominated by Europe.

The basic criticisms have not changed in this third period. What has changed is the world situation, and that in two regards. In terms of the political economy of the world-system, the period of facile optimism is definitively over. In the 1960s the world-economy was still expanding at a remarkable pace, with some economic benefits accruing to everyone, even if these benefits were unequally distributed. In the 1960s Africans also seemed to be regaining some greater political control over their own destinies with the triumph of the anticolonial movements and the equivalent upsurge of liberation movements among diaspora Africans. Thirty years later, however, the world-economy has resumed its acute polarization, and its long contraction has resulted in acute difficulties in many parts of the world, not least of all in Africa. Furthermore, the antisystemic movements, so glorious in the 1960s, have largely faded away, many of them rather ignominiously.

On the other hand, we have seen important new developments. In the world of knowledge, the well-established structures have come under severe questioning. Among the reasons for this severe questioning has been the rise in number and importance of non-European scholars who have challenged the universality of European paradigms. In the political realm, moreover, Africa seems to be in the throes of a second breath with the achievement of a democratic government in South Africa and the emergence, in central Africa and elsewhere, of new movements that target corrupt and dictatorial regimes. This combination accounts for the heightened degree of assertiveness of African scholars, and this increased assertiveness has led to a heightened defensiveness among non-African scholars writing about Africa.

Is there some way to turn this discussion, which is frequently harsh and unproductive, into a dialogue? There are two things to be said about dialogues. First, they assume the existence of two different *logoi,* or there would be no need for dialogue. Second, they assume the possibility and desirability of arriving at a single *logos,* or there would be no point to the dialogue. Dialogues are therefore possible only on the basis of mutual respect. And mutual respect, in a situation of deep social conflict, is not easily obtained.

At this point, of course, we should deconstruct our two actors, African scholars of Africa and non-African scholars of Africa. Neither is a unified whole. There are many varieties of each, and there are some in each category who are not serious or are not prepared to engage in dialogue because they are not prepared to consider that a single *logos* could possibly exist or could possibly be attained in the near future.

If we wish to dialogue, we shall therefore have to start with those who are ready now to enter into such a dialogue. And, of course, the prerequisite for each of these is the readiness to take seriously the validity, at least the partial validity, of the other's *logos.* This dialogue among those concerned with the study of Africa today furthermore cannot be conducted in a vacuum, separate from the wider contemporary dialogue about the very structures of knowledge themselves—the debate about overcoming the two cultures, the search for an appropriate balance between the universal and the particular, and the effort to define more adequately the scholar's relationship to the inclusive politico-ideological arena of debate.

Let us start by recognizing that everyone in the world of knowledge, whether she or he admits it, is interested in being both universalist and particularist. On the one hand, all knowledge assertions are in some way claims about universality. The most solipsistic viewpoint involves a claim that the viewpoint is correct, or the only possible one, and implicitly seeks to persuade all others of this truth. On the other hand, we are all irremediably embedded in our social biographies, which are complex and detailed and inevitably differentiate us from others. Hence our universalistic claims always bear the mark of our interests, our power positions, our sophistication (linked to our experience), and our anticipations of the future (the result of our social biographies as well). Exposés of the self-interest and dubious motivation of others are always possible, often correct, and sometimes revelatory, but this is a double-edged sword and is best used selectively and prudently and with a certain amount of self-criticism.

In an unequal world—and we surely live in an unequal world—the strong or privileged by definition have an edge, and this edge is reflected in, and reinforced by, their efforts in the world of knowledge. Those who struggle against the distortions that are a consequence of unequal power as refracted in scholarship find themselves in a dilemma, for they must fight on all fronts simultaneously, with fewer resources than their opponents, and they find it difficult to locate themselves in impregnable strongholds of either epistemology or substantive theorizing. Nonetheless, their very struggle in this unequal situation is our principal hope that collectively we can surmount the limitations of our social constraints and move in the direction of a synthetic *logos*.

Let us be concrete. Today's African scholarship about Africa is lively, but it also has a weak institutional base precisely because of the weak position of Africa in the world-system. Nor is it self-evident how this institutional base can be made stronger, since outside assistance, if given, is given grudgingly, inadequately, and often in ways that reinforce the dependency. Internal resources for the world of knowledge are also in sharp competition with other urgent social expenditures. Institutions such as CODESRIA and SAPES are remarkable and constructive but have grossly insufficient resources for the task. Furthermore, they find they need to expend a good part of their meager resources on scholarly polemics that, although justified, detract from what needs to be expended on consolidating research and theorizing on the substantive epistemological and analytic issues of social science in general and African studies in particular.

Meanwhile, non-African scholars of Africa are not in a much better position. Those who wish to engage in the necessary dialogue find that they are hampered by powerful colleagues who do not find such a dialogue necessary. So the former too spend much of their time in polemics to the detriment of other work. Some abandon the field. Others retreat into their corners. And the few who remain find themselves under assault.

There is no easy way out of this imbroglio. What one can counsel sounds platitudinous. Continue the discussion, listen to the partner, and lower the decibels of the debate among those who enter into the dialogue. What might be less obvious is another counsel. Go beyond Africa to discuss the underlying issues of reconstructing the social sciences as a knowledge activity. Do not leave these issues to the "generalists," and surely not to the non-African "generalists." We must all be in the center of this overall debate while at the same time not neglecting the study of our particular corners of the social arena. Above all, let us try to keep our antennae open and not closed to our colleagues. We can start by reading this book closely.

Contributors

Horace Campbell, who has taught at the University of Dar es Salaam, Makerere University, Northwestern University, and the University of the West Indies, now teaches at Syracuse University. His publications related to pan-Africanism and Africa include *Rasta and Resistance: From Marcus Garvey to Walter Rodney* and the edited volume *The IMF and Tanzania: The Dynamics of Liberalisation,* in addition to many articles and essays.

Catherine Coquery-Vidrovitch is a professor of history at the University of Paris–7–Denis Diderot, with special interests in urbanization and social change. Her many works include the award-winning *Afrique noire: permanences et ruptures* (1987 Prix d'Aumale; English-language version: *Africa: Endurance and Change South of the Sahara*), *Les Africaines* (*African Women: A Modern History*), and *Histoire des villes africaines des origines à la colonisation.* She is finishing work on a history of Africans in the nineteenth century.

Jacques Depelchin has taught and worked at the University of Zaire (Bukavo), the University of Dar es Salaam, the Centre for African Studies of the University Eduardo Mondlane (Maputo), El Colegio de México, and the University of California at Berkeley. In addition to numerous articles, particularly on historiographical methods, his major works include *From the Congo Free State to Zaire: How Belgium Privatized the Economy—A History of Belgian Stock Companies in Congo-Zaire from 1885 to 1974* and a forthcoming volume entitled *Silences in African History.* He is conducting research in Zaire.

Christopher Fyfe taught African history at the Centre of African Studies, University of Edinburgh, from 1963 to 1991. His published works include *A History of Sierra Leone, Africanus Horton,* and *"Our Children Free and Happy": Letters from Black Africans in the 1790s.*

C. Tsehloane Keto is a deputy vice-chancellor of Vista University (South Africa) and previously was the director of the Institute of African and African-American Affairs at Temple University. His many publications include *The Africa Centered Perspective of History, American–South African Relations, 1784–1980,* and *Vision, Identity, and Time: The Afrocentric Paradigm and the Study of the Past.*

Mahmood Mamdani is the director of the Centre for African Studies, University of Cape Town; previously he served as the executive director of the Centre for Basic Research, Kampala, and was an associate professor in the Department of Political Science at Makerere University. He is the author of *Politics and Class Formation in Uganda, Imperialism and Fascism in Uganda,* and *The Myth of Population Control* and a coeditor of *Academic Freedom in Africa* and *African Studies in Social Movements and Democracy.* His most recent book is *Citizen and Subject: Contemporary Africa and the Legacy of Late Colonialism.*

William G. Martin is a professor of sociology and deputy director for research of the Fernand Braudel Center at Binghamton University. His publications include the coauthored *How Fast the Wind: Southern Africa and the World-Economy, 1975–2000,* the edited volume *Semiperipheral States in the World-Economy,* and essays on the sociology of world-historical and African studies.

Micere Githae Mugo is a professor at Syracuse University and has taught at the University of Nairobi, the University of Zimbabwe, St. Lawrence University, and Cornell University. Her publications include *Visions of Africa in the Fiction of Chinua Achebe, Margaret Laurence, Elspeth Huxley, and Ngugi wa Thiong'o; Daughter of My People, Sing; The Long Illness of Ex-Chief Kiti; African Orature and Human Rights; Zamami and Sifiso; My Mother's Poem and Other Songs;* and the introduction to *Songs from the Temple,* as well as eight supplementary readers for Zimbabwe schools (coedited with Shimmer Chinodya) and, with Ngugi wa Thiong'o, *The Trial of Dedan Kimathi.*

Elliott P. Skinner is the Franz Boas Professor of Anthropology at Columbia University. Between 1966 and 1969 he served as U.S. ambassador to Upper Volta. His many publications include *African Urban Life: The Transformation* *of Ouagadougou, The Mossi of Upper Volta, African Americans and U.S. Policy toward Africa, 1850–1924,* and the edited volumes *Beyond Constructive Engagement: The United States Foreign Policy toward Africa, Peoples and Cultures of Africa, Strangers in African Societies,* and *Transformation and Resiliency in Africa.* In 1995 he was awarded the African Studies Association Distinguished Africanist Award.

Zenebeworke Tadesse served as deputy executive secretary of CODESRIA for seven years and was a founding member of the Association of African Women for Research and Development (AAWORD). The editor of publications for the Forum for Social Studies, Addis Ababa, she has written and lectured widely on knowledge production and gender in Africa.

Immanuel Wallerstein is the director of the Fernand Braudel Center, Binghamton University, past president of the African Studies Association, president of the International Sociological Association, and chair of the Gulbenkian Commission on the Restructuring of the Social Sciences, which produced *Open the Social Sciences.* Among his many books are *The Modern World System* (3 vols.) and *Unthinking Social Science.*

Michael O. West teaches at the University of North Carolina at Chapel Hill. His primary areas of research encompass Zimbabwe, southern Africa, and pan-Africanism, on which he has published numerous articles and book chapters. He is the author of the forthcoming *Rising to a Higher Level: The Making of an African Middle Class in Colonial Zimbabwe.*

Index

IRS (Internal Revenue Service), ASA investi-
gated by, 105–6
Islam: Asian influence on, 178; role of, 183–
84; slavery and, 168
ISSUE (periodical), 11–12
Italy, colonial past of, 161
Ivory Coast: repression in, 137; scholars
from, 48

Jackson, Henry, 91
Jackson, Michael (singer), 8
Jahn, Janheinz, 182, 199
Jamaica: Braudel on, 171–72; scholars' meet-
ing in, 102–3
James, C. L. R., 125–26
Janken, Kenneth Robert, 88
Japan: funding from, 18; sources from, 183–
84
Jefferson, Thomas, 64
Jeffries, Leonard, 116nn16–18, 20
Johnson, Thomas A., 100
Johnson, Willard, 104–6
Joint Low Intensity Project (U.S.), 129
Jones, Quincy, 9
Joseph, Richard, 32n6
Journal of African History (periodical): boy-
cott of, 116n15; editors for, 59; establish-
ment of, 56, 98; influences on, 57; subven-
tion for, 115n13
Journal of Blacks in Higher Education (peri-
odical), 32n9
Journal of Black Studies (periodical), 24, 138
Journal of Modern African Studies (periodi-
cal), 57, 98
Journal of Negro Education (periodical), 21,
87
Journal of Negro History (periodical), 21, 87
Journal of Southern African Studies (periodi-
cal), 57
Journal of the Historical Society of Nigeria
(periodical), 98
Joyce, Joyce Ann, 32n9
Judaism, Asian influence on, 178
Julien, Charles-André, 41

Kabira, Wanjiku Mukabi, 202
Kabou, Axel, 43
Kagame, Alexis, 69
Kagombe, Maina, 116n18
Kamlongera, Christopher, 209
Kampala Declaration on Academic Free-
dom, 125, 134, 141–42

Karenga, Maulana, 80
Keller, Edmond J., 32n6
Kemet: African creation of, 181–82, 185–86;
Islam and, 183; origins of African knowl-
edge in, 24
Kenya: Europe-centered paradigm in, 179;
independence struggle in, 127; Pentagon
studies of, 131; scholars' emigration to,
148; scholars from, 68; theater in, 203–5;
universities in, 151; U.S. exchanges with,
117n25
Kenya National Theatre, 203–4
Kenyatta, Jomo, 68, 199
Keppel-Jones, Arthur, 101
Keto, C. Tsehloane, 22, 23, 24, 25
Khwarazui, Al-, 183
Kidd, Ross, 209
Kikuyu people, 68
Kilson, Martin, 101, 105, 106, 116n20
Kimble, David, 57
King, Martin Luther, 135, 137
Kingsley, Mary, 54
kinship, concept of, 43
Kitson, Frank, 127
Ki-Zerbo, Joseph, 46
knowledge: Afrocentrism on, 138; compart-
mentalization of, 199; critical framework
for, 185–86; definitions of, 175–76; democ-
ratization of production of, 133–34, 140–
42; division of, 49–50; evaluative criteria
on, 180–81; general vs. specific, 110, 215–
16; mass-based foundations of, 197–98;
multiple perspectives in, 185, 214; power
relations and, 159; reconceptualization of,
145; scientific type of, 19, 165–66; sources
of, 181–85. *See also* paradigms
Kofa, Joseph O., 116n18
Kopytoff, Igor, 74–75
Kwanzaa, origin of, 79–80
Kwayana, Eusi, 140

Lambert, Richard D.: on African studies faculty, 95, 114–15n10; on area studies, 108;
funding for, 116n24; on programs'
growth, 89
Land and Freedom Army (Mau Mau), 127
languages: centrality of, 69, 108;
deracialization and, 193–94; paradigms
and, 177, 179, 180–81; theater's use of, 205,
209–10; training in, 54, 89, 91, 108–9,
114nn7–8, 117n26, 132
Las Casas, Bartolomé, 173n1

Typeset in 10.5/12.5 Minion
with Gill Sans display
Composed by Jim Proefrock
at the University of Illinois Press